D0847510

Additional Praise for
What Makes Business Rock

"Bill has the discipline of a sergeant major, the energy of a rugby player, and the heart of a lion . . . a formidable man with a soft charm and the hard facts to sign anyone up to the fight against HIV/AIDS, from kids watching MTV in their bedrooms to CEOs meeting in their boardrooms. He showed that when corporations find the right way to connect with their audience/consumers on these issues, it goes beyond a 'charity' endeavour to become a defining part of the brand."

—Bono

"When he took the job, Bill Roedy made an immediate and profound executive decision: He would take MTV and its core proposition that pop music was the universal lingua franca of youth, internationalize it, and create a powerful vehicle for change, understanding, and good—whilst also building a great business in the process. MTV has changed since then, and so has the world, and Bill is one of those people responsible for that change. He is a remarkable man!"

—Sir Bob Geldof

"It has been said many times that with great power comes great responsibility. Bill Roedy lived by that rule all 23 of his years at MTV Networks. He helped to build a global entertainment superpower, but along the way Bill educated the MTV generation and made them realize they had the power to change the world."

—Jon Bon Jovi

"Bill Roedy has been a tireless fighter in the battle against HIV/AIDS. As he relates in this book, and as his life's story reflects, one can make a profound difference in the greater community by bringing together their individual abilities and corporate resources. When this happens, the community, the corporation, and the individual all win."

—Kenneth Cole

"My friend Bill Roedy is a statesman, an adventurer, a wise man, a humanitarian, and much more all rolled into one. His personal life and career have been exciting, productive, and beneficial to mankind. He continues to lead an incredible life and has always been a remarkable storyteller. Fasten your seat belt and read on. You're in for a great experience."

—Seymour Stein, Co-founder/Chairman, Sire Records;
inducted into Rock & Roll Hall of Fame, 2005

"Few things are more difficult than building a new business. From helping to sell HBO to mom-and-pop cable systems in the 1970s and 1980s to establishing the MTV brand around the world, Bill Roedy has more experience in that art than anyone I know. Those people intending to do business internationally can learn a great deal by reading this book."

—Frank Biondi, Former President and CEO, Viacom

"Bill Roedy expanded the MTV brand across the globe. But for me, he was a key mentor and a great inspiration. His knowledge of the international market is immense, and this entertaining and enlightening book is a must read for anyone, in any industry, doing business internationally."

—Harry Hui, CMO, PepsiCo

WHAT MAKES BUSINESS ROCK

WHAT MAKES BUSINESS ROCK

Building the World's Largest Global Networks

BILL ROEDY

WITH DAVID FISHER

John Wiley & Sons, Inc.

Published by John Wiley & Sons, Inc., Hoboken, New Jersey.
Published simultaneously in Canada.

Library of Congress Cataloging-in-Publication Data

Roedy, Bill.
What makes business rock : building the world's largest global networks/Bill Roedy with David Fisher.
p. cm.
Includes index.
ISBN 978-1-118-00476-0 (hardback); 978-1-118-08290-4 (ebk.); 978-1-118-08293-5 (ebk.); 978-1-118-08294-2 (ebk.)
1. Roedy, Bill. 2. MTV Networks. 3. Mass media—United States—Biography. 4. Rock videos—United States. I. Fisher, David, 1946- II. Title.
PN1992.8.M87R64 2011
384.5506′5—dc22

2011008894

Printed in the United States of America

10 9 8 7 6 5 4 3 2 1

I am privileged to dedicate this book to my wife and partner, Alex, and our four children, Noa, Liam, Rocky, and Tiger, who for so long have been the music in my life. Without their love and support and understanding, my relentless travel would have been impossible.

But in addition, I am grateful to my other "family," the men and women with whom I've worked at HBO and MTV, the most extraordinary group of talented, creative, and devoted people imaginable. I am so proud of the global industry we built together. I would also like to express my deep appreciation to the men and women I served with in this country's military, from whom I learned so much. Finally, I convey my deep admiration and gratitude to the many people I work with at the UN and other nonprofits, who have devoted their lives to solving problems and meeting challenges.

Contents

Foreword

I think the most accurate way to describe Bill Roedy is to say that he is in tune with the universe.

In my childhood in Haiti I didn't have television. We had no electricity. But at night I would look up and see the sky filled with stars. During the day I would watch the birds flying until they disappeared in the distance. I would watch the sun rise in the morning and the moon set at night. I knew that people around the world were seeing that same sun and that same moon; they were looking at the same stars, and the birds were flying into their lives wherever they were. And I understood that I was put in my place temporarily and in time I would be part of the sun and moon.

I have always felt that I was part of a greater humanity. I know that I have always shared those feelings with Bill Roedy. And it is why I have enjoyed describing him with humor as my brother from another mother!

I met Bill Roedy for the first time when I was hosting the European Music Awards in Sweden in 2000. Being invited to host was important for me. I had seen MTV for the first time when I was living in the ghetto, in the Brooklyn projects. My thought was: I'm going to be on that TV channel soon. To me, being on MTV meant that you reached the world.

Until you were on MTV it was local, but once you were on MTV you were global. Only a few years later I was in Stockholm, Sweden, reaching a large part of that world, and there I met Bill Roedy. I didn't know anything about him except that obviously he was an important man. He was the man in charge. But from that first meeting I realized I had never met anyone like him. That day, with the big smile that always seems to be on his face, he told me, "Just go out there and do what you do best. Make people feel good."

Make people feel good. That probably was the first goal Bill Roedy and I had in common, but since then we have become close friends and have moved in harmony toward other goals. As we spent time together, it became obvious to me that Bill and I both understood and appreciated the power of music to change lives. It was music that allowed me to rise from the slums of Haiti, and it was music that has allowed Bill and MTV to reach young people throughout the world.

Among the many things I admire about Bill Roedy is the way he has used that power of music. I believe the lessons that can be learned from the way Bill Roedy has built his business and conducted his professional and private life are vitally important to anyone intending to do business internationally. It is no longer enough for a corporation to simply open the door in a new country and expect its customers or audience to find it. It now has to become a contributing member of that local society. It can't just bring in its product to sell; it has to show an understanding and appreciation of that country and find a way to participate in the local life. No one I know of has done that better than my friend Bill Roedy.

The reason for this, I believe, is that Bill Roedy is both a businessman and a humanitarian. As a businessman he successfully expanded MTV throughout the entire world. There is no place I have been where young people do not know about MTV. But much more than that, in each country MTV has become part of their own national lyric. It is amazing that in each country the young people have embraced MTV as their own. One important reason for this is Bill Roedy's humanitarian work. In each country MTV has become actively involved in the concerns of its people. It has gained respect because it listens to the people. When Bill was serving in Vietnam, he told me, he learned about the importance of winning the hearts of the people. This was something he has never forgotten. By winning the hearts of young people throughout the world,

MTV has also won their loyalty. Young people trust the brand MTV and that has translated into a very successful business.

I have never met anyone who has done more business in more countries than Bill Roedy. I have been with him in the slums of Haiti and at the United Nations, and I have seen the respect with which he is greeted in both places. He has earned that by understanding local cultures and giving them the respect that is due. Anyone who is doing business around the world would do well to pay good attention to the words of my friend Bill Roedy.

Wyclef Jean
March 5, 2011

Preface

On September 22, 2010, Viacom Chairman and CEO Philippe Dauman sent a memo to our colleagues informing them that after 22 years at MTV Networks, I had decided to step down from my "nonstop globetrotting and audience building," adding that I have "crisscrossed the planet, planting our flag on nearly every continent and spreading the gospel of quality, audience-first programming from Beijing to Bangalore . . . [and] established the most well-respected and most popular stable of international television channels in the universe. . . ."

Almost immediately, my BlackBerry began vibrating. Among the first callers was the designer, Kenneth Cole, chairman of amfAR (American Foundation for AIDS Research), informing me that he was recommending that I join that organization's board of directors. Within a week I received invitations from four other international nonprofits to become more involved in their efforts.

Several weeks later, I was in Madrid for MTV's annual *European Music Awards*. As is their tradition, Bon Jovi scheduled a gig at a local club. This is a band I've known for 22 years and over that time we had become good friends. But this year the band broke with tradition and announced that the concert was in my honor, and as I sat there with my wife, Alex, and our four children, they graciously gave me several callouts.

In that way, the three legs of my career—business, public service, and music—were represented. Beginning with a single, struggling channel we built the largest media network in the world, consisting of 200 channels and 400 digital properties in 165 countries. We used our global footprint to educate tens of millions of young people about the threats to their future—from AIDS to human trafficking—and hopefully we saved lives. And we did it by speaking the global language of rock and roll with the local accent of every country in the world.

When I joined MTV in 1989 it was possible for American businessmen and women to focus solely on the U.S. domestic market. Revenue from the international market was seen almost as a bonus. That's no longer true. It's virtually impossible for anyone to have a career in business or industry without being involved in the global market. *What Makes Business Rock* is the story of how we pioneered many of the strategies now considered essential for successfully operating beyond our borders—among them our mantra, "Think global, act local," our emphasis on reflecting and respecting local cultures, and our belief that we were guests in every country and had an obligation to give back to our hosts. We made mistakes (*boy*, did we ever), we experimented, and we tried things no other company had done before. Some of our methods were very successful, some of them not as successful. But we paid attention and we learned. We used to joke that time spent working at any major corporation should be measured in dog years, seven years to every human year. Assuming that's accurate, this book is the sum total of my almost 150 years' experience building a global company in a constantly evolving technological world.

Those lessons are invaluable for any entrepreneur or business person looking beyond our borders—which should be almost everyone. I've learned how to build a local business in 165 different countries. I've probably negotiated in at least 50 languages, in every political system, and through an unbelievable array of government regulations. I've built business that relied on underground cables as well as the most advanced satellite transmission.

Perhaps the biggest difference between building the MTVNI business and most other vocations is that my career had the most incredible theme music imaginable playing in the foreground. I truly know *What Makes Business Rock*—and this is the whole story, from wrestling on the floor with my Russian partners, to dancing on the tables with my colleagues, to spreading our brands through the use of satellites.

So how do you make business rock? Welcome to my life.

Bill Roedy
London, January 2011

WHAT MAKES BUSINESS ROCK

Chapter One

Born in the U.S.A.

Ladies and gentlemen, rock and roll.

—John Lack, August 1, 1981

Television was the miracle of my childhood. The reality of moving images being sent through the air into your home was brand-new when I was growing up in Miami, and for me our 12″ black-and-white TV set was my escape capsule. My family was struggling; my father was long gone and money was a problem. I can remember being in a grocery store and wondering if we could afford a 17-cent jar of mustard or a loaf of bread for 22 cents. But every night at 7 o'clock, my grandmother, my great-aunt, my mother, my sister, and I would gather in front of our set and be transported to places where people were happy and having adventures and living exciting lives. Those people on television didn't struggle to pay the mortgage, or scream at each other, or have to meet an endless series of potential stepfathers. Television was our only respite, and one of the few times I remember hearing laughter in our home.

At 10 o'clock, much too late, my mother and I would sit together and do my homework—with the TV on in the background. The TV was always on; it brought the whole world into my life. Even as a child I realized that television was magical. As I got older, to please my mother, each week I would memorize the entire *TV Guide*, and my mother would proudly have me recite the primetime schedule for her friends. Maybe other kids could recite the preamble to the Constitution of the United States, but I could tell you what time and on what channel *Have Gun—Will Travel* was on.

I loved television. I loved everything about it, and my dream was to work in that industry one day. Even at that age I understood the power of television. It was the ultimate shared experience. Everyone I knew watched TV, and most of us watched the same programs. In school, whatever show was on the night before was almost always a subject of conversation. I listened to the way the people I knew talked about television and I saw how it affected their thinking. It made an impact on me. Television was important to everyone I knew. I figured that if I was watching, so was everyone else—and television could be my way to connect with those people. If I could work in television, I believed, I would have the ability to influence huge numbers of people. And I might even get to meet the star of *Have Gun—Will Travel*, Richard Boone!

It did not occur to me that working in television would allow me to watch as communications history was made. I was there at the beginning of the cable-TV industry, the digital television industry, and the miracle of TV everywhere. I watched as television was transformed from my small black-and-white picture to a 60″ 3-D television or a 4″ screen on my mobile device with extraordinary clarity. In so many ways television has shaped and changed all of our lives, but in my own life, it has made all the difference.

And I certainly never dreamed that one day I would be the person responsible for bringing *Beavis and Butt-Head* to Russia, or *Pimp My Vespa* to Italy. Or that I would support dressing the animated children's character Dora the Explorer in a burka. Or that I would drink moutai with its 53-percent alcohol content with Mongolian cable operators, negotiate contracts with the mayor of Leningrad, rap with rappers in Saudi Arabia, sing "I want my MTV" with 3,000 Pakistanis in Karachi, and visit Mecca to get permission to launch MTV Arabia. Or that television would allow me to be in Berlin when the Wall came down or in Russia at the birth of capitalism. Or that I would have the privilege and the resources to save many lives by educating young people around the world about the dangers of—and the truth about—AIDS. Or that I would be cited in gossip columns as being engaged to Naomi Campbell, the best-known supermodel in the world. I certainly never dreamed I would find myself dressed as a police officer in a Japanese karaoke bar at 5 A.M. and singing a duet with U2's Bono—who was dressed as a nurse. But more than anything else, I never expected that together with an extraordinarily young and diverse organization we would build the largest and most successful media network in the world.

With all the attention television gets, with all the glamour surrounding television and the stars it creates, and the immense pleasure it brings to billions of people in every country in the world, the most important thing to remember about the television business is that it is a business and it has to be run as a business. Like any other business, the bottom line is still the bottom line. The problems that I faced in building MTV Networks International were in many ways similar to the problems any business trying to expand throughout the world will encounter and has to overcome. The lessons that I learned can be applied to almost any effort to expand any company into the international market. My business just happens to be more visible than most.

There was a time when an executive at an American company could basically ignore the rest of the world. Many people spent their entire career at one company focusing only on the domestic market. More and more that has become a rarity. It's now estimated that the average person will have at least 10 different jobs in his or her lifetime. To become a successful manager in an increasingly global business community it's absolutely imperative that an executive understand the way the rest of the world does business. More than ever, as the economic growth shifts from America and Europe to China, India, and the emerging nations, having an international perspective is an absolute necessity.

When I joined MTV Europe in 1989 it was a startup operation. At least once, they had to use a car battery to provide the power to keep the channel on the air. Just before I arrived in London a ferocious windstorm had knocked out all the power in our building, preventing us from transmitting. Much of London had lost power; even the BBC was off the air. Then our security guard, affectionately known as "The Amazing Tony," had a great idea. He drove his Ford Cortina up to the front window, got a long extension cord, and used alligator clips to attach it to his car battery. We managed to get back on the air before the BBC. But in the more than two decades I spent there, MTV Networks International grew from a single channel broadcasting to a few hundred thousand European households, mostly in Holland and Greece, into a giant media network operating 175 locally programmed cable, satellite, and terrestrial television channels and about 400 digital media properties stretching across 163 countries with a potential audience of more than two billion people.

But let me backtrack. I began working in the industry at HBO in 1979, when television consisted almost exclusively of the three national networks as well as several local channels in each city transmitted through the terrestrial signal, frequencies that were picked up by a rooftop antenna. Cable television was in its infancy. For the most part it consisted largely of mom-and-pop operations strung out across the nation. No one possibly could imagine that it would eventually overwhelm the networks and become a $140-billion-a-year industry. In fact at that time there was considerable doubt it would survive. The business model made little sense: Television was free and it had always been free, so why would anyone pay for it? In those early days the most exciting technological advances were color television and the remote control, which allowed viewers to change channels without getting up, therefore creating the couch potato.

The television business was pretty straightforward in those days. The three major networks essentially had a monopoly and advertisers had limited options if they wanted to reach a mass audience. That wasn't true only in television; at that time most industries offered consumers only limited choices, from the products manufactured by the Big Three automakers and a few foreign manufacturers to the three popular flavors of ice cream. America was the largest market in the world, and an industry could remain very profitable without offering multiple choices and certainly without expanding beyond our borders.

Since that time waves of new technology have revolutionized the world. The United States is now merely part of the growing global market. Those companies that were slow to recognize and adapt to these changes exist today in a far different form, if they are fortunate enough to still be in business. Remember U.S. Steel, or Polaroid? In the media world, technology has now made it possible for viewers to choose when and where and how they want to watch the programs of their choice. From the rigid weekly *TV Guide* schedule I memorized as a kid, the business has progressed to the delivery of programming on demand to any of several devices most convenient for the consumer. Technology is forcing the industry to change more rapidly than at any time in the past.

MTV Networks International (MTVNI) has ridden all of those waves and, while at times it has been a very bumpy ride, we've emerged to become, according to the respected *BusinessWeek* and Interbrand annual study, one of the most recognizable brands of any type and the most valuable media brand in the world. We took the original American MTV concept of delivering music with a creative cutting edge and adapted it to the customs and desires of almost every culture on every continent—with the exception of Antarctica (so far). We've adapted our programming to meet the technological changes and the generational shifts. We built our brand country by country; sometimes it seemed like we were doing it house by house. I've watched MTVNI in the tallest building in the world and in a hut in Africa; I've watched it in fevalas and I've watched it in the desert. We've done what few companies in any industry have been able to do: We've successfully maintained our global identity while responding to local cultures. The term we've used to describe it is "glocal," meaning *think local, act global.* That concept has become so common in business it literally is a cliché, but no one can dispute that we were the first company to do it successfully. Ted Turner used to say about Turner Broadcasting, "We were cable before cable was cool," which I amended and said about MTV around the world, "We were local before local was cool."

It has not been easy. As with the growth of any business, we have had some tremendous successes as well as some discouraging failures. While building our brand we helped bring down the Berlin Wall, hosted concerts for more than 500,000 people, introduced extraordinary performers to the world—please don't blame me for the Spice Girls—and made a significant impact in reducing the spread of AIDS and human trafficking. But I've also had to make my share of "apology tours." We have been thrown off the air for a period of time in several different countries and we have made attempts to plant our corporate flag that just didn't work. For two decades I awoke to a new challenge every day.

MTVNI grew up with the satellite and cable industry. In some countries we helped it grow. There was no business model to follow because no media company had successfully created a worldwide brand. Each day brought a new challenge, a new problem, and usually in a foreign language. But we did something no media company had done before and we did it more successfully than any company has done it since. At MTVNI we wrote the rulebook, and we did it by following one basic principle: Break the rules. The foundation of my business philosophy is that in business there are so many rules and so much authority that if you're going to get things done you've got to break those rules.

■ ■ ■

Break the rules; that was my rule and it was the one rule that I insisted everybody follow. It made complete sense to me. I think it is accurate to say I had one of the most unusual backgrounds in the entire industry. I certainly was the only executive I knew who, as a 25-year-old, commanded three missile bases with 36 nuclear missiles aimed at Eastern Europe and the Soviet military.

I'd planned on attending Vanderbilt University after graduating from North Miami High School, where the number-one challenge I faced was winning the fights after school. I was accepted by Vanderbilt; my picture was even published in the freshman yearbook. Unfortunately, we couldn't afford the tuition and instead at the last minute I applied and was accepted to West Point. It was completely a financial decision. In fact, West Point was probably my last choice. My father was a West Point graduate, a career military officer. My parents had been at Pearl Harbor on December 7, 1941. My mother used to tell me that as the Japanese planes flew overhead he stood in front of the bathroom mirror, calmly shaving. She asked him why he continued shaving when the base was under attack and he told her, "Because I know I'm going to be gone for a long time." My sister Peggy was born in a makeshift clinic a month later, and within days she and my mother were evacuated.

He and my mother had divorced when I was four years old, so essentially she raised me as a single parent. She worked many different jobs and because she couldn't afford a babysitter I would go to work with her. For a time she worked in a curbside rental car booth at the Miami International Airport, and I'd spend a lot of time there, which might be why I have always been so comfortable at airports. West Point had been a bad fit for me. I came from an undisciplined environment and intended to keep it that way. I didn't like the highly structured environment there and I certainly didn't like the social life. I'd grown up in a household with my mother and sisters. I had an active social life in high school. And too late I discovered that West Point might be the only college in the country from which you leave with fewer social skills than you had when you entered.

When I enrolled in West Point my high school girlfriend, Nancy, went to Florida State. We agreed that we would be allowed to date someone else once a week. We made that agreement before I knew how little opportunity I would have to meet women. In fact, in my four years there I had one blind date. It was on my birthday and she stood me up. The summer before your fourth or first-class year, every cadet travels to different forts around the country to experience the different branches. For example, I was sent to Ft. Knox, Kentucky, for artillery training. During many of these visits, dances were held for young women to meet West Pointers. I was given a blind date with someone whose name I'll never forget: Willy Wingo. She didn't show up. I waited and slowly everybody else met their date and left, leaving only me and this gorgeous woman, who basically picked me up. I thought, *this is the luckiest day of my life*. Although it was unauthorized, rather than going to the dance she took me to a nightclub off the base. We sat down near the front door and were there for only a few minutes when suddenly the door burst open and a guy about six times my size with a cast on his arm walked in, looked around, and came after me. He swung his cast at me, missing by inches. Within seconds the entire place broke out in an old-fashioned brawl. I crawled underneath the table and as soon as I could, I got out of there. But as I reached the door I looked back and my date was smiling at this monster. I figured it out: She had picked me up to make him jealous. That was my one date at West Point.

At the academy I struggled against authority. I was a member of what was known as the "Century Club," meaning I had accumulated more than a hundred hours of punishment duty. It was there I learned the difference between fighting the system and *finessing* it. I was also overwhelmed by the academic achievements of my classmates. I was convinced that everyone there was smarter than I, and I had to work hard just to keep up with them. I spent a lot of time marching off demerits and graduated toward the bottom of my class. It was at West Point that I learned many of the skills that would enable me to succeed in business, including discipline, time management, the value of teamwork, and the importance of physical endurance. "Duty, honor, country" wasn't just a motto at West Point; it was our way of life. We went to classes six days a week so we never had enough time to do everything that was required of us. To survive we had to learn how to prioritize. In business there are always more things to be done than time allows, and how to best utilize your time often makes the difference between success and failure. Sometimes it's simple: Survival is always the priority. When the enemy is coming out of the Vietnamese jungle or you're about to lose all your distribution in Italy, that is your priority. Otherwise, for me at least, it comes down to intuition, instinct, judgment, and experience—a *lot* of experience.

The reality is that I wasn't even smart enough to understand how much I learned at West Point, and how important what I learned would be throughout my life.

Too often I have seen people focusing on the wrong things—things that are not going to directly or immediately affect their business. Most of us are surrounded by chaff; chaff is the small bits of reflective foil dropped by airplanes for electronic jamming, which my missile base radar had to cut through. Essentially, it's a lot of nothing. Leaders learn how to cut through the chaff to determine priorities and to identify the real target.

I'm an inveterate list maker, which started at West Point. For me, when I just listen I can recall a certain amount, when I recite back what I've learned I can recall a certain amount more, but when I write down something I recall it best. I may not even consult my list, but the action of writing it down seems to inscribe it in my mind. I also have made a point of writing *everything*—my lists, memos, notes, and letters—in green ink. That's one of my few idiosyncrasies. Green has always been my favorite color. It's the color of hope; but more importantly, no one else was writing in green, so when anyone received a document in green ink they instantly knew it came from me. That saved a lot of time.

And people did receive a lot of green handwritten notes—and birthday cards—from me. Taking the time to handwrite a note complimenting someone for doing a good job or remembering to send a person a card on an occasion is an easy and very effective means of giving positive reinforcement. It's a little thing that often makes a big difference.

Teamwork, of course, is essential, whether on the battlefield or in the boardroom. An executive is the sum total of the people he or she works with; I don't believe there is anything more important to success in a large company than putting the right people in the position in which they can be most effective and then allowing them to do their job.

Very few people in business have traveled as extensively as I have, and without the commitment to physical fitness I learned at the Academy that would have been impossible.

The ironic thing about my struggles at West Point is that by the end of my 11-year military career I had accumulated more command experience than any of my classmates. Command time is essential for anyone intending to move up the military ladder. When we graduated in 1970, the Vietnam War was growing increasingly unpopular and people were doing everything possible to stay out of there. I was one of a small percentage who volunteered to go; at West Point we had been taught that the war was the strategically correct response to communism, while every day I was reading in the *New York Times* about the massive antiwar movement sweeping the country. Even among the cadets we debated the wisdom of the war. I decided the only way to reconcile those differences was to get over there and decide for myself. West Point had prepared me for battle; there was a war going on and I felt it was my duty to be there. Instead I discovered that when they drop you in the middle of a combat environment your sole concern is survival. My strategic vision was limited to who was coming out of the jungle to try to kill me.

Many years later I would drive with Tom Freston, the chairman of MTV Networks, for eight hours through the Afghanistani countryside to Bamiyan, where the Taliban had destroyed the ancient statues of Buddha, with only three bodyguards who were in a car far ahead of us. Another night I walked alone through the crime-ridden favela, the slums, of Rio. In a nightclub in Shanghai a group of thugs suddenly surrounded me and tried to rob me. But I was rarely scared. After Vietnam I just never again felt like I was in danger.

I thought I was prepared for combat. After West Point I'd gone the gung-ho route through Airborne school and Army Ranger school. It was at Ranger school that I first encountered the harsh reality of military life. We made a parachute jump one unusually windy night because some brass showed up—and my roommate from Airborne school was killed. We took five minutes to deal with that, then we went right back on patrol. But as I discovered almost immediately after arriving in-country that there is nothing that prepares you for battle—except battle. In Vietnam people used to joke that the life expectancy of a second lieutenant was measured in hours. I was a second lieutenant. As a result I learned "boots on the ground" command management.

In Vietnam I commanded a platoon stationed on the border with the north. We provided perimeter defense along the demilitarized zone for four forward fire bases, we cleared mined roads, we conducted raids into enemy territory, and we spent much of our time dodging Vietcong 122-mm rockets. I still have shell fragments from of one of those rockets that narrowly missed me. We were constantly in danger of being overrun. Every night in command meetings we were told the same thing: The North Vietnamese are massing in preparation for an attack. I spent an entire year without a single restful night.

My platoon was attached to an artillery unit. We had the biggest cannons in the Army, 175-mm long-range guns that could toss a round of ammunition 26 miles and very accurate eight-inch howitzers that fired a 200-pound high explosive about 10 miles. Several of the commanders of the fire bases were real cowboys. When they suspected an incursion, they would level those eight-inchers completely horizontal and fire straight ahead, maybe a thousand meters. That's not a long distance for a weapon capable of firing 10 miles. It leaves a large hole in the jungle. My platoon was armed with 40-mm mechanized dusters, basically small tanks, and mounted quad 50s, which had been designed to provide air support in previous wars, but because we had air superiority we used them for ground coverage. When we sprayed a valley with a quad 50 we made our presence known. My unit was one of only three units in Vietnam equipped with this powerful weapon, which made us very popular with other combat troops.

I spent one year in Vietnam, half of it as a platoon leader and the rest of the time as an aide to a general. The lessons I learned during that time helped shape everything I did after that. I learned the importance of making quick and firm decisions, communicating those decisions clearly to my troops, and then doing anything and everything necessary to implement them. I learned the importance of building morale, camaraderie, and a team spirit. I learned how to deal with the chain of command and how to get around it when necessary. And after living on the frontlines for a year there isn't much that intimidates me. For example, at a concert we produced in Cape Town, South Africa, to increase awareness of the preventative measures that would help reduce the incidence of AIDS, and fight the stigma associated with the disease, we had a problem with P Diddy. He was scheduled to be the closing act that night. Usher had opened the show and his set had run longer than scheduled, so the show was running late. Alicia Keys was onstage. P Diddy told me flatly, "You need to pull Alicia Keys right now or I'm not going to perform." I couldn't believe it. Alicia Keys had poured her heart into this concert, rehearsing practically nonstop with a full choir, and there was absolutely no possible way I could interrupt her performance.

But P Diddy was serious. Admittedly, we shared some of the responsibility. We'd told him he would go on while it was still daylight and the sun had already set. But predictability generally is not a hallmark of a rock concert.

In a situation like that the first thing is reduce the volume, and try to avoid a confrontation. "Why?" I asked.

P Diddy was surrounded by several massive bodyguards wearing their sunglasses. None of them were smiling. " 'Cause I'm so tired," he explained.

I wanted to diffuse the situation, so I put my hand on his arm. It was a friendly gesture, something I often do, but as I touched him one of those bodyguards stepped in and pushed my arm away. His bodyguards formed a tight ring around us. The situation was getting tense. I assume I was supposed to be intimidated. But when you've spent every night for a year in Vietnam waiting for the enemy to come out of the jungle, glaring bodyguards don't have much effect. I explained to P Diddy that the huge audience had come to see him and that he really didn't want to let them down. But rather than simply telling him there was absolutely no chance I would do anything to interfere with Alicia Keys' performance, I told him I understood how tired he was and I would speak with her manager.

It wasn't a lie. I spoke with her manager and told him, "P Diddy is quite anxious about getting on and he wants us to cut Alicia's set. *But* I don't want you to do anything at all." There. When she finished her complete act P Diddy went on to close the show and, as we anticipated, he was tremendous. But the key to solving that particular problem was maintaining a calm, unemotional demeanor.

After completing my tour in Vietnam I returned to the United States and spent 18 months as second in command of a nuclear missile base in Travis, California, right outside San Francisco. The commander of that base was an officer named Jon Thompson, who was also a West Point graduate. The base was austere and one day Jon decided that we needed a pool and he was going to build it. None of these bases ever had a pool. Everyone thought he was crazy, and they continued to think that until they were swimming in Jon Thompson's pool. Watching him reinforced my belief that the first "no" was never a final answer.

By that time I had married my high school sweetheart and we were transferred to Northern Italy, where I spent four years in command of three NATO nuclear missile bases. I employed several hundred people and had responsibility for weapons and materials valued at several hundred million dollars—and the capability to kill millions of people by pressing a button. Each base was equipped with 12 Nike-Hercules missiles; ironically, when my father was an engineer in the Army he had worked with former Nazi scientists at the Redstone Arsenal in Alabama on the program that built the Nike-Ajax, the predecessor to our missiles. The Nike-Hercules was America's last wall of defense. It was a medium-range air defense missile with a range of about 200 miles. Originally, it was a surface-to-air missile, the weapon we would depend on to shoot down the Warsaw Pact's nuclear bombers, as well as any incoming missiles, but later it was converted to a surface-to-surface function. Each of my missiles was 30 kilotons, twice the size of the bomb that devastated Hiroshima.

If I learned how to deal with fear in Vietnam, in Italy I learned how to live with pressure and stress. In Italy, my security clearance was top secret, atomal, cryptographic, which meant that I had access to the nuclear codes and NATO's war plans. There wasn't a minute when I could just relax. When you are commanding nuclear missile bases you learn not to lose your temper, which is a valuable management trait most of the time. *Most* of the time.

When I entered the business world I was used to being calm, cool, and collected no matter how much pressure was being exerted on me. I learned very quickly that in the business world an important element of leadership is showing your staff how much you care. At one point a senior executive at HBO commented to me that I never showed any emotion. I thought about that. I had always been a very emotional person, but I had learned first at West Point and later in the field that a commander doesn't show his emotions; a commander is always cool under pressure. But in the world of business there are people who equate emotion with commitment, and at times my calm demeanor was mistaken for a lack of passion. At HBO I actually found myself acting out emotion to prove to my people that I cared desperately. I don't like to shout, but I learned that sometimes you have to raise your voice in front of your own people to emphasize a point; although never—I have always believed this strongly—never *at* your own people.

In addition to being on the front lines of the Cold War, at that time there were several terrorist groups, including the notorious Red Brigades who had kidnapped and killed a former Italian president, and whose express goal was to penetrate a nuclear missile base, so for years we existed in a state of total preparedness for attacks from both inside and outside the country. We were continually being evaluated and tested. There are few situations more stressful than commanding a nuclear missile site and trying to determine in 30 seconds whether the aircraft approaching the base was a friend or foe. There was no margin for error. We had to be perfect every day. A single failure could mean the end of my military career.

I spent 11 years in the military, almost all of it in command positions. When I resigned my commission I had valuable management experience, but I knew nothing about the business world. I didn't know the terminology, I didn't know how to read a P&L statement, I didn't know about strategic planning, and I did not even know what a *logo* was. I did know how to fire a duster and lead a patrol in the jungle, but I doubted there was much demand for those skills in the business world.

■■■

If I wanted to have a career in business, I realized, I had to go to business school. I believed that would provide the broadest possible base to make the transition from the military to the civilian world. The only business school to which I applied was Harvard, primarily because it was the only business school I'd ever heard of, and miraculously I was accepted. My experience at Harvard was similar to West Point; I was convinced every one of my classmates was smarter than I. I wondered how I'd gotten in, and to do well I had to study six hours or more a day. While I loved the two years I spent in Cambridge, and the exposure I got to a different world was invaluable, beyond learning the fundamentals of the business world I'm not sure the actual education was applicable to real-life situations, at least initially. At Harvard the case studies taught us how to make decisions as CEOs, but in reality those of us whose last name was not on the front door entered the business world at a substantially lower level. In that real world, our initial decision-making opportunities were more often what to order for lunch than how to run the company.

Harvard MBA students spend the summer between their two years interning. Most of my classmates gravitated toward high-paying jobs in banking and consulting in New York, building connections that might result in a lucrative career. I knew I wanted to go into television, so I found a job at the ABC Boston affiliate, WCVB. While my classmates were receiving substantial salaries, I was being paid minimum wage at a local TV station. I didn't care. I was working in the television industry and I absolutely loved it. The first question anyone should ask himself or herself when entering the career market is: What rewards will be the most personally fulfilling? What are those factors that make you happy? Maybe that question seems obvious, but I've found that often people pursue careers for the wrong reasons and end up trapped. I loved the media world, so for me that was the television industry.

At WCVB I learned the dynamics of local television, from the studio to the president's office. My project was to evaluate the existing salary structure to determine whether it accurately reflected the needs of the station. I interviewed every person working at that station and each of them opened up with me, perhaps because we were talking about their salaries. As a result I learned more in that one month than I did in two years at Harvard. I got lessons in management, motivation, and how the television industry worked. I spent much of my time trying to bridge the gap between the creative side and the business side; it was the first time I had to deal with the conflict between programming and sales. Maintaining a wall between the two sides is one of the central conflicts in any media organization, and often it requires mediation and management.

Harvard provided the necessary bridge for me from the military to the business world, without which I never could have been successful. But the truth is that there is nothing that prepares you for business—except business. Students spend much of the second year of the program focusing on getting a job. There is no lack of opportunity for a Harvard MBA. Corporations come to Cambridge to recruit, and there were days on which I interviewed with 10 different companies. I interviewed with every industry—consulting, banking, manufacturing, even insurance companies—and at the end of the process I received several offers, the most substantial coming from the 300-year-old Insurance Company of North America. It was a great proposal from an excellent company, but having spent 11 years of my life in a highly structured environment—West Point and the U.S. Army—I couldn't visualize myself being happy in a traditional corporate environment.

I remember the precise moment I realized what I wanted to do. I'd flown to Chicago to meet with the human resources director of a major manufacturing corporation. Coincidently, it was the evening the Academy Awards was being broadcast. I was sitting with the HR director in the corporate cafeteria, being briefed on our agenda—but as she enthusiastically went over my schedule for the next few days I completely lost interest. A television in the background was tuned to the Oscars and I couldn't take my eyes away from it. I wondered, *what am I doing here?* I decided to pursue my passion. I was going to work in television.

Only two of the several media companies with which I'd interviewed offered me a job. It had been difficult to convince executives that serving in combat and commanding nuclear missile bases had a transfer that would be valuable in the media world. My dream job was working for one of the three networks. When NBC offered me a job as a unit manager, which is basically a financial job overseeing programs, I was very excited. NBC! That was my dream. It was one of the giants of the television industry. I was certain I would take that job. But as I walked the hallowed halls in Rockefeller Center it wasn't nearly as glamorous as I had imagined it. Rather than the exciting, creative environment I'd imagined, it felt very corporate.

The other offer I had was from a startup cable channel, Home Box Office (HBO). My Harvard classmates were accepting those high-paying jobs at the prestigious financial institutions, consulting firms, and on Wall Street. When I told them excitedly, "I got HBO!" they looked at me quizzically and asked, "What's that?" I didn't care; it was television—sort of. Cable television was a new industry, which I believed meant there would be more opportunity for someone like me. Executives with years of experience in broadcast television couldn't afford to take the risk of joining a new and completely unproven business, but I had absolutely nothing to lose by working there.

Contrary to the generally accepted belief, cable television was not founded to bring additional channel choices to viewers. It was simply an alternative means of transmitting a broadcast signal. There were a lot of rural areas that for various reasons could not receive the three networks, which normally were transmitted across the country terrestrially, from tower to tower, so cables had to be laid to connect those areas to the television world. In the beginning no one anticipated it would become an alternative or an addition to those broadcast channels. Initially, people referred to it as *CATV*, meaning *Community Antenna Television*. There also had been several attempts to launch experimental pay-per-view systems. In one of them, for example, when the homeowner wanted to watch a specific program he would literally deposit cash in a box on top of his set. They were also broadcasting pay-per-view events, like championship boxing matches, to movie theaters.

HBO had been launched by Charles Dolan, whose company, Sterling Manhattan Cable, spent a fortune laying underground cables in lower Manhattan to serve those areas that had difficulty receiving clear signals because of the surrounding tall buildings. This was the first underground cable system in America. In addition to transmitting the three networks and some local stations to his customers, Dolan offered them the subscription channel he'd founded called HBO, which broadcast movies and sports events. HBO was cable-TV's first entertainment channel. In the early 1970s, Dolan had begun distributing HBO outside New York through traditional microwave transmission. The magazine publisher, Time Inc., which initially had bought a 20 percent stake in Dolan's channel, bought control of the entire company in 1973.

Several of the offers I received paid substantially more than HBO, but HBO was a ground-floor business and I thought I could grow with it. There was an entrepreneurial spirit there that appealed to me. I was recruited by a legendary figure in the industry named Tony Cox, who was then head of sales and marketing and eventually became president. He was extremely charismatic, a real "people person" who reminded me a bit of a military commander because he had the unique ability to get people to charge up the hill regardless of the chance of success—which reaffirmed one of my definitions of leadership.

Truthfully, my mother wasn't particularly pleased when I told her I'd accepted this offer because she'd never heard of HBO, but she did perk up when I told her it was part of Time Inc., because she'd heard of *Time* and knew I'd be working in the prestigious Time-Life Building.

The opportunity to be part of this industry at this time was incredibly exciting. As decisions being made today will shape the future of the Internet, the decisions being made then would shape the future of cable television and I got to sit in on those meetings and voice my opinion. It seemed like the media version of oil wildcatting. In wildcatting, oil drills are set up in areas not known to be oil fields. It's a risk that can have big rewards. We were building a business, one house, one town, one city at a time—and we weren't sure of the outcome.

This literally was a business being created from under the ground up. Among the many questions to be answered was whether it should continue to be a subscription service, meaning customers paid a monthly fee and received all the programming, or pay-per-view, meaning customers paid only for those programs they wanted to watch. Should programs on HBO and the other new premium channels be sponsored like broadcast television or commercial free? Should programming be broadcast 24 hours a day or only those hours when the bulk of viewers would be watching? There was little data to support any conclusions to these questions. It just came down to somebody making a decision. At HBO, for example, we went back and forth on whether we should sell advertising. Was the announcement "brought to you by . . ." really advertising? Would consumers object to a brief ad at the beginning of a movie? We also debated the wisdom of broadcasting the entire day—who was watching at 4 A.M.? We ended up deciding to broadcast commercial-free television the full 24-hour day more as a marketing tool than because we believed anyone wanted to watch the channel in the middle of the night. The research we did do always concluded that unedited and commercial-free television was our number-one attribute.

■■■

I began working for HBO in 1979. At that time HBO was a subscription channel broadcasting only nine hours a day. Its programming consisted almost entirely of theatrical movies, shown numerous times throughout the day and night "unedited and commercial free" and generally before they were shown on network television, and sports, primarily boxing. The problem was that people would subscribe for a major fight, and then cancel their subscription. What little original programming HBO did was extremely inexpensively produced shows like HBO's first show, the *Pennsylvania Polka Festival*. It wasn't until 1983 that HBO began creating its own original programming, like the comedy-sketch show, *Not Necessarily the News*, and produced its first movie, *The Terry Fox Story*.

In order to understand the business, I began my career at HBO on the front lines—as an installer. After a building was wired for cable, an installer would have to go into an apartment to connect it to the system. That was me; for several weeks I was Bill the Cable Guy. I hooked up cable and made repairs in about 12 apartments a day and it was an extraordinary experience. I remember walking into an apartment and noticing cans of cat food piled high on the kitchen table—but the owner had no cat. Often people would ask me to sit down just to talk because they were desperate for company. And, unfortunately, too often people would yell at me for causing real or imagined problems.

Within several weeks I moved into the job I'd been hired to do. As manager of HBO's National Accounts, my job was to negotiate deals with cable operators and then travel throughout the country to launch HBO on their systems. I negotiated all day, every day with tough, savvy, powerful men who knew how to use that power; and as challenging as it was, I loved it. Ironically, those people yelled at me too.

I learned immediately that in the cable-TV business only one thing mattered: *distribution*. Distribution, distribution, distribution. Later, at MTV, my mantra would become "aggressive, creative, relentless distribution." *Distribution was the whole business*. Cable systems were largely local mom-and-pop operations, many of them struggling to survive. The government had granted these companies *natural monopolies*, recognizing that small companies couldn't justify making the huge investment necessary to build a cable system in a competitive market. In most areas there just weren't enough potential subscribers to support two companies.

Arguably the single most important decision in the history of the cable industry was made by an executive named Jerry Levin. Initially, HBO transmitted its signal to cable operators through a terrestrial-based microwave system, which limited its distribution. But in 1975, Levin made the momentous decision that we would distribute that signal by satellite to cable operators across the country, who would then distribute it by cable to their customers. It was a revolutionary concept and it was extremely controversial. Many people were highly critical of his decision. Unfortunately, the only satellite dishes capable of receiving HBO's signal were huge and expensive. These original dishes looked more like scientific earth stations searching outer space for signals from aliens than a transmission system for the *Pennsylvania Polka Festival*. While Levin's visionary decision was courageous, each dish cost more than $100,000 and few of the smaller cable operators could afford to buy one. Without those dishes in place there was no way we could get the distribution we needed. To help solve that problem HBO initially financed the capital that enabled cable operators to buy the dish and receive our channel. As a result, the cost of those dishes came down. This was one of the first projects I worked on at HBO and it allowed us to transmit our signal across the entire country. It gave us instant access to every cable system in the country.

This was the decision that accelerated Jerry Levin's career. Unfortunately, several years later, he also made the decision to merge Time Warner and AOL, another revolutionary decision that caught the industry by surprise. But unlike his original decision, which led directly to the massive growth of the cable industry, this decision proved disastrous. Sumner Redstone, the brilliant entrepreneur who created Viacom and was my boss for more than two decades, once mused, "One of the smartest people I've ever met made one of the most questionable decisions ever." Unfortunately for Levin this merger was far ahead of its time. In fact, it was later described as "The worst deal of the century." While today the concept of merging a major Internet company with a leader in traditional media may make sense, this took place much too early. It was also very poorly executed. The culture at each company was so strong that rather than combining their strengths and working together, they were at each other's throats. That didn't surprise me. I remember sitting at a large, round table with Quincy Jones and AOL Chairman Steve Case at Davos just after the merger had been announced. I overheard Case say forcefully, "We are going to change their culture." I knew immediately that there was going to be trouble in paradise. Finally, because this took place at the peak of the Internet bubble, AOL essentially acquired the much larger Time Warner. Time Warner had more substantial assets, generated more revenue, and returned greater profits, yet AOL's stock had an inflated value.

As the cable business developed there were two levels of programming, basic cable, which meant subscribers got a package of many channels for their monthly payment, and premium channels, for which they had to pay extra. Time Inc. sold HBO as a premium channel. To see first-run movies "uncensored and uncut" subscribers had to pay an additional fee to the cable operator, of which we got a share. The formula was simple: Cable operators charged subscribers about $10 a month for basic cable, which consisted of about 20 channels, and an extra $7 to subscribe to a premium service like HBO. The fee we charged cable operators varied with the number of subscribers they delivered. Of that $7, for example, the cable operator might pay HBO $3.25. The basic cable channels were much less expensive to the cable operator. Instead of paying $3.25 to HBO, for example, they might pay 10 cents per subscriber for CNN or even MTV. But for those channels distribution was as important as or even more important than the revenue fee, because they also sold advertising, and as with terrestrial networks the price they charged advertisers was based on the number of viewers they delivered. Unlike HBO, which had only one revenue source, those basic cable channels had a dual revenue stream—fees and advertising. It was a beautiful business model: If their advertising went down because of economic conditions or a ratings decline, they still had subscription fees that were consistent and predictable. If advertising went up, you suddenly had rapid growth. Over time, those dual revenue streams made basic cable a more profitable business model than premium channels. It remains a very workable and profitable system.

The biggest threats to the cable industry were the phone companies, because they already were hardwired to just about every home in the nation, and home satellite dishes. The cable industry was spending a fortune wiring the country house-by-house while the phone companies already were connected and satellite companies did not need to lay cable. If the cable signal was not encrypted, meaning put into a code that had to be unscrambled to be seen, viewers at home could intercept our signal, everybody's signal, without paying for it. Fortunately for the cable operators, the phone companies were prohibited by government regulation from carrying programming and the only satellite dishes initially available were very large and very expensive.

I was fortunate to be at HBO at that point. We were in a perfect symbiotic relationship with the cable industry. Our programming helped the cable industry sell subscriptions, while the growth of the cable industry made it possible for us to expand. Consumers wanted HBO but they could get it only by subscribing to a cable service, while we needed the cable systems to reach our customers. There literally was a race to wire the nation. We had a unique product in a rapidly growing industry and the financial support of one of the largest media companies in the world. Cable operators loved HBO because it attracted new subscribers and provided substantial revenue. There was no CNN, no Discovery, and no MTV; there was only HBO. If you wanted movies uncensored and uncut, if you wanted to watch championship fights in the comfort of your own living room, you had to have HBO.

By the time I got into the industry the consolidation that would result in the creation of major corporations like Bob Magness and John Malone's TCI, Charles Dolan's Cablevision, Cox, Newhouse, TelePrompTer, MetroVision, Comcast, and ATC, which later became Time Warner Cable, was just starting. At HBO I worked for the National

Account Group, which basically did deals with these multiple system operators (MSOs). The product I was selling was entertainment, but it could have been almost anything. I was one of the three original employees of that unit, so I grew with it. This was my postgraduate education in deal-making, entrepreneurship, and cable television. I had loved the intellectual stimulation at Harvard, but my education there had little to do with the real world of business. As I had learned to do at Harvard, during my first month at HBO I spent considerable time writing a very sophisticated marketing plan for a small mom-and-pop cable system in Connecticut. I presented this detailed plan to a man named Barry Stigers, who looked at me as if my rocket ship had just landed at the strip mall. It had absolutely nothing to do with his world.

I had the opportunity to work with and learn from a group of impressive, intelligent, creative men who were building an industry. Frank Biondi, a straight-shooter and well-respected executive who later became president and CEO of Viacom, was on the programming side. Michael Fuchs, who eventually became chairman and CEO of HBO, was creating the cutting-edge programming that became a hallmark of the channel. Jeff Bewkes, a charismatic and especially astute executive who eventually became chairman and CEO of Time Warner, started the same week I did. In fact, he looked so young that he told me once he was jealous of my prematurely gray-streaked hair, "because people will take you seriously." Jeff and I actually were involved, at least peripherally, in the creation of Bob Johnson's BET, Black Entertainment Television. Jeff was in finance, and together we negotiated a deal with TCI in which they got a satellite transponder for very little money. In exchange for partial ownership, TCI used that transponder to launch BET, which became a huge success and in 2000 was purchased by Viacom for about $3 billion.

On the business side, I learned from men like Tom Oliver, Peter Frame, Julian Brodsky, and J.C. Sparkman. Cable TV was a new business and we had to invent a whole new vocabulary to describe it: *Penetration* meant what percent of total households potentially reached by cable subscribers and how many of those subscribers bought HBO; *churn* was the constant turnover of customers; there were *new builds* and *old builds*, *head-ins*, and *volume* and *performance discounts*. I grew with our business. Tom Oliver was one of the most creative dealmakers I've ever known. We would sit on an airplane for hours and he would take me through the extremely sophisticated and complicated process step-by-step. From him I learned *performance pricing*, *sliding scales*, *decision trees*, and the thousand other details that make up the art of a deal. Negotiations with the cable systems could be extremely difficult and complicated. We were dealing with monopolies who understood completely the economic value of their distribution capability. There were so many different aspects of each deal to be considered, and it was all new. Much of the time we were fighting over pennies per subscriber, but as I was to learn from the legendary J.C. Sparkman, who ran John Malone's TCI, "A small number times a big number equals a bigger number." *Scale*, as he called it, meant that if you had a large subscriber base, a few pennies eventually became a substantial number of dollars. And those fights sometimes went on for months. Tom Oliver understood it all and was an artist at structuring a deal. He was analytical, especially in crafting a deal, although I suspected he enjoyed the negotiation more than the close.

Closing the deal was a skill I learned from a genius named Peter Frame. While Tom was all about negotiating a deal, Peter was a master at long-range planning—at steadily growing a business. Julian Brodsky was a financial wizard who teamed with the legendary Ralph Roberts and his son, Brian Roberts, to build Comcast into the nation's largest cable system. I learned from all of them, but if there was one person who taught me the art of negotiation, it was J.C. Sparkman.

One weekend during my first year at HBO I'd snuck away to go skiing in Jackson Hole when Stan found me on the slopes and told me with excitement in his voice, "Bill, you got TCI."

I got TCI? That was great, except at that moment I didn't even know what that meant. Eventually, though, TCI became the largest multisystem operator in the industry and HBO's most important client. I practically lived in their office. In fact, I became so close to those people that Sparkman offered me a good job. I was tempted to take it, but I just loved what I was doing and wasn't ready to make a change.

J.C. Sparkman seemed like he had come directly out of Central Casting. He had a very large and dynamic personality. He spoke with the commanding voice of a Hollywood leading man and had the charisma to dominate every room he was in. While John Malone was the financial wizard who devised the strategy that turned TCI into the industry gorilla, Sparkman ran their operation. We were continually doing deals with TCI; we did renewals, product launches, and promotions, so I spent an enormous amount of time with him. Tom Oliver and I would take the 6:50 A.M. flight Monday morning from Newark to Denver and hole up in Sparkman's office all day—and the day usually ended with a parting shot of vodka and a long flight home that landed at midnight.

For J.C. Sparkman, more than anything else business was about relationships. He insisted on dealing face-to-face with people. Business for him was people, not products. I spent countless hours with him over meals and drinks, on trips, and in his office. We'd spend those hours talking about family, politics, sports, the world, but mostly the business of cable television. He taught me about the cable industry; he even taught me about the strengths and weaknesses of HBO. He used to say, "Don't you worry, one day we're going to buy HBO."

J.C. was definitely a hands-on guy. Normally, when you're ready to launch a system you flip a switch and you're on the air. But as we were getting ready to launch in Laramie, Wyoming, there was a massive power outage. The whole system was down. J.C. took the situation in his own hands, drove to the head-in, the location where the earth station receives the satellite signal, and actually fixed the problem literally seconds before we were scheduled to go on the air.

But he also was a very tough negotiator. TCI often demanded that content providers give them partial ownership of the company in exchange for distribution. That's how the Discovery Channel got started; that's how BET got started. J.C. was always searching for a way to increase the rate a penny or two. He was always trying to get us to give him a favored-nations clause, meaning that if we gave another distributor a better deal, TCI would automatically get the same or a better rate, or exclusivity. Occasionally, our negotiations would get really heated. I got used to him getting angry, walking out of the room, and slamming the door behind him as he left. We knew eventually he was coming back. We'd sit there waiting or take a break, although admittedly at times that break would consist of us going home.

But J.C. and I learned to trust each other, and that trust helped us complete a lot of difficult deals. At one point I closed a 10-year deal with TCI that probably was the first billion-dollar programming contract in the cable industry. But as part of that deal, he made me promise that I would be at every premium launch throughout their entire operation to help insure its success. And they were launching an average of three per month. So I crisscrossed the entire country launching HBO. Name a small city in America and I probably have been there. I traveled from Parkersburg, West Virginia, to Cody, Wyoming, to Cedar Falls, Iowa. I often appeared on local television pitching this amazing service: "Movies just like you watch them in the theater, unedited and commercial free, in the comfort of your own living room." Sometimes I would answer phones on the air, as if it were a telethon rather than a new business promotion, taking new subscriptions by hand. At HBO I practically lived on the road for 10 years. I was the cable industry's traveling salesman.

I got to be good at it, probably because I loved what I was doing. In life as well as in business, the ability to sell is the foundation upon which success is built. That is increasingly true as the world evolves. Some people are turned off by the concept of selling, but I think that's because they don't really understand it. Even in Vietnam I had to sell the mission. I had to inspire my troops. In the military, for example, even though I had the formal authority to force troops to obey my orders, I found that if people didn't believe in the mission, I never got a total effort from them.

At HBO I was selling every time I walked out the door. I was selling my product, my company, and perhaps most importantly, myself. That was when I learned to truly appreciate the importance of looking a client in the face when there is an issue to be resolved. As J.C. Sparkman taught me, nothing replaces being there. That became a lot more difficult years later when "there" meant flying thousands of miles to a distant country rather driving a few hundred miles to a neighboring city. But even after technology made it possible to have videoconferences, I continued to get on a plane and make those trips. I am convinced that there is no substitute for face-to-face meetings, especially in the international market where trust and personal relationships mean everything.

I know there are many CEOs who disagree with me. A successful colleague of mine, who runs a major global corporation, never travels. His philosophy is if people want to see him, they should come to his office.

When companies are facing a budget crunch, travel and entertainment are the first things to be cut. Maybe that's the right decision; maybe some trips aren't absolutely necessary. Certainly for inter-corporate communications videoconferencing can be a useful tool, especially in situations like Viacom, where offices are separated by thousands of miles. But relationships can make or break your business, and throughout my career there have been numerous situations in which the personal relationships I'd built during those less-than-essential trips proved absolutely vital in resolving a problem. No one should underestimate the value of forming strong personal relationships, especially when doing business in Asia and the Far East. In the western world, when you meet with an executive from a company with which you want to do business, generally speaking, you'll conduct that business first and then maybe a relationship will develop. But in Asia it's critical to build a personal relationship first and the business relationship will follow. The trust factor that is built through that personal relationship may eventually prove more important than any contract you sign. In my opinion, western executives don't travel enough to that part of the world.

One memorable night, for example, then-MTV Networks Chairman Tom Freston and I had dinner in China's Forbidden City with about 200 cable system operators from across the entire nation. Although I do know there were among our guests several system operators from Mongolia as well as the province of Guangdong, I can't remember every detail because we respected a local tradition—numerous times. The cable operators formed a long line and I had to drink a moutai toast with each one of them. What I failed to appreciate is that each one of them had only one drink, whereas Tom and I had one drink with *each* of them. My plan was to match them toast-for-toast. My plan failed—gloriously. It was impossible to keep up with them. Later that evening we all sang karaoke. The cable operators all sang arias from various opera. It was a scene out of *Indiana Jones*, two somewhat-inebriated Americans in a room filled with Chinese singing operas. When our turn came, Tom sang "The House of the Rising Sun." My original plan was to sing "My Girl." Somehow I ended up singing a duet from *Madame Butterfly* with one of our Chinese guests.

I often quote a man named Vinnie Longobardo, for a time the head of MTV Asia, who once said, "I regret I have but one liver to give to my company!" Getting inebriated hardly sounds like a positive business strategy, but in fact the relationships we built or solidified that night would prove vital in the future. Extending our brand to China was certainly one of our more complicated efforts. For different reasons MTV was pulled off the air by the central government several times. But at those times there were people we could contact who helped us rectify the situation, men and women with whom we had formed personal relationships—oftentimes over alcohol.

Selling HBO had become my life. After 10 years, my marriage had ended; Nancy and I had married too young and had grown apart. Although these many years later Nancy, her sister Annette, and her wonderful father, Baron Capizzi, still remain close friends. In reality, it would have been impossible for me to do all the traveling necessary for this job if we had stayed married. Eventually, I was selling, servicing, and supporting 20 good-sized accounts at HBO. It was absurd; no one person could cover all those accounts. But I had developed a "can-do" attitude at West Point and believed there was almost nothing I couldn't accomplish if I focused on it. Twenty accounts? I'll take some more! A problem? Don't worry about it; I can solve it. As I've learned in my career, at times that can be a flaw. Eventually, you do end up with more than one person can handle.

I had to learn how to *delegate*. But because I had this attitude I objected strenuously when Stan Thomas started taking accounts away from me. When I argued with him he asked, "When was the last time you saw So-and-So?" "A month ago," I said, probably stretching the truth a little, but it still was the wrong answer. "You've got to see them once a week," he said, and then he asked me a question I have never forgotten and have often asked people working for me: "Would you rather do 10 things half-well or five things *really* well?" Decades later, when at first I resisted hiring someone to take over many of my responsibilities, this was the question I asked myself.

While I was helping build HBO, numerous new cable channels were being founded—*boom! boom! boom!* By the early 1980s, they were popping up almost overnight. Cable operators had more channel capacity than they had programming to fill it and they were desperate for channels they could add inexpensively to their basic service. In March 1979, the children's channel Nickelodeon was founded to be, as Warner-Amex President Gustave Hauser explained, "the first children's channel of programming wholly created for cable television audiences." In June 1980, Ted Turner launched the first 24-hour all-news channel in the United States, CNN. And on August 1, 1981, MTV began broadcasting on a single New Jersey cable system.

It's almost impossible to credit any single person as the man who created MTV. I'm not even sure it matters, because what MTV has become is completely different from the channel anyone originally imagined it would be. It's evolved and reinvented itself countless times. I'm also convinced that very rarely is an idea the product of only one person's mind. In fact, in business most ideas are derivative. They grow organically from other ideas. We were broadcasting music videos at HBO before MTV was created. Other stations were experimenting with various music video concepts. As MTV developed, it wasn't simply the idea of a channel consisting of music videos that captured America's attention—it was about the extraordinarily creative execution of every aspect of the channel, from the logo to the content to the marketing. The idea was great, but it was the implementation that made the difference.

Many different veins eventually came together to form this particular goldmine. One of those veins can be traced back to 1977, when Michael Nesmith, the best-known member of the created-for-TV band *The Monkees*, realized that the short music videos rock bands were producing for distant markets would work well on television. Music videos weren't new. As early as 1966, record companies had started filming bands performing their popular songs, primarily to be shown to audiences in places that were either too far away or too small for artists to appear there. For example, videos were particularly popular on Australian and New Zealand television, where they were known as "pop clips." In 1976, a half-hour program consisting solely of music videos went on the air in New Zealand.

Nesmith made a pilot for a half-hour show called *PopClips,* but failed to find a buyer. In 1979, he brought the concept to John Lack, a radio executive who had left CBS to join Qube, Warner's embryonic TV cable operation in Columbus, Ohio. Lack thought it was a great idea and in 1980 began broadcasting Nesmith's *PopClips* on another new Warner channel, Nickelodeon. Its popularity convinced Lack that music videos could form the foundation of an all-music cable channel.

For cable programmers music videos were a wonderful gift; they were creative and entertaining, they attracted the demographically desirable young audience, and most important, they were free. It also was a great deal for the record companies, who were delighted to get this free promotion and practically begged the cable systems to run them. And it turned out they filled a need we had at HBO. Because movies were all different lengths, we were always looking for programming to fill time between the end of a movie and the next natural viewing time, generally on the hour or half-hour. We had been filling these *interstitial blocks*, as we referred to them, with promos and animation. So when these music videos became available, we started running them. In fact, the first music video I ever saw was broadcast on HBO.

What no one at HBO realized was that a sizeable segment of our audience was more interested in the music videos being shown between programs than our programming. With a little imagination we could have created that music channel. Eventually, we did create a half-hour music video show entitled *Video Jukebox*, but by that time it was too late. The fact is we never saw MTV coming.

We weren't the only channel to use these videos this way. At WNBC in New York, for example, a programming genius named Bob Pittman, who had started his career as a radio DJ in Jackson, Mississippi, when he was only 15 years old, began producing the music video program *Album Tracks* in 1978. About a year later, at Warner-Amex Satellite Entertainment Company, which was owned jointly by Warner and American Express, John Lack, John Schneider, former president of CBS and then-president of WASEC, and Bob McGroarty suggested that the cable system create a channel that would show only music videos. While Bob Pittman usually gets the credit for it, at the dinner celebrating MTV's tenth anniversary in 1991, Tom Freston cited Schneider for actually putting the channel on the air. In addition to those three men, the team that was assembled to create TV-M, as it was then called, included Pittman, Tom Freston, and a record promoter named John Sykes, a creative and energetic executive who eventually ran VH1.

Pittman once explained what they envisioned: "The concept I had was to have a clear image, to build on attitude. In other words, to build a brand, a channel that happened to use video clips as a building block, as opposed to being a delivery system for videos. The star wouldn't be the videos; the star would be the channel." Another member of that group, Steve Casey, suggested, "Don't you think *MTV* sounds a little better than *TVM*?" And MTV was born.

■■■

MTV went on the air as a basic cable channel on August 1, 1981. It was pretty unsophisticated at the beginning; at times the screen would go black for several seconds while an engineer hustled to slip a new tape into the VCR. To gain distribution MTV initially was offered to cable operators for free. The plan was that revenue was going to be generated from advertising. As any trivia expert would know, the first video broadcast on MTV was the Buggles' *Video Killed the Radio Star*. Almost immediately, MTV began creating stars; Billy Idol, for example, has credited MTV with providing the exposure he needed after his punk image had scared away radio stations. The audience showed up right away, but not the advertisers. Advertisers were still reluctant to commit too much of their budgets to cable programming, particularly to something as unique as an all-music channel. Nobody really knew who was watching. MTV lost $34 million in its first two years in operation. But among young people the channel was building a buzz, a loud buzz. When record stores began selling music that was being played only on MTV, the music labels finally appreciated its potential and began turning those once straight-ahead videos into unbelievably creative short films.

Music videos became an amazingly creative art form and the best young directors in both advertising and motion pictures wanted to be involved. A great video could make a band an overnight success. But as Bob Pittman and Tom Freston had once predicted, MTV had become much more than a showcase for videos. It had an attitude, a spirit, and a unique style. It broke all the molds of traditionally structured television programming. It had its own instantly recognizable look: It was bright and colorful and brash, accurately reflecting the optimism and enthusiasm of young people in America. In addition to the videos there was news, some gossip, and film reviews, the subjects that specifically interested the targeted demographic—teenagers to young adults. Most of the pieces were short and the programming and advertising was blended almost seamlessly. The logo, a large *M* on top of which *TV* was scripted, was often shown onscreen during programming. It was animated and was continually changing color and shape. The hosts (MTV created the description *VJ* for *video jockey* to differentiate from radio disc jockeys) were all young and trendy, the kind of nonthreatening cool kids you wanted to hang out with. Young people accepted it as their own and began demanding their MTV—and cable operators willingly began paying a fee to carry it.

But MTV failed to generate the revenues that American Express had expected, and some people believed the concept was already running out of steam. In 1985, Warner's partner in its cable company, American Express, decided to get out of the business. Basically, Warner either could buy Amex's share in their partnership or agree to accept an offer for the entire cable division. Warner Chairman Steve Ross agreed to pay Amex $450 million for its stake in the company and immediately began looking for a new partner. Eventually, he sold MTV Networks to Viacom for $525 million. In addition to the music channel, MTV Networks at that time also consisted of Nickelodeon, a struggling children's channel competing unsuccessfully with Disney, and VH1, a music channel for the post-MTV demographic. In 1991, I met Steve Ross at the Midem convention in Cannes. By that time I had left HBO and joined Viacom as Managing Director, MTV Europe. When I introduced myself to him he smiled sadly and admitted, "Selling MTV is the biggest regret of my career." Within five years MTV had become a large and lucrative enterprise.

Viacom had been founded in 1971 when the Federal Communications Commission forced CBS to divest itself of its programming syndication division and its small cable operation. It had grown to become one of the most successful program syndicators in the world. Among the channels it founded was Showtime, which in 1983 had merged with Warner-Amex's Movie Channel to become HBO's primary competition. HBO and Showtime were like Hertz and Avis, the giants of the cable movie business. In 1987, the man who would become my boss for the next two decades, Sumner Redstone, bought a controlling interest in Viacom for $3.4 billion.

Sumner Redstone had built his family's Massachusetts-based drive-in movie theater chain, National Amusements, into one of the largest and most successful movie theater companies in the world. But he also understood the importance of owning programming, and in fact is credited with the oft-quoted statement, "Content is king." I don't know if he actually was the first to say it, but I do know he believed it. It was his belief that cable television, like the multiplexes he built, was an alternative means of delivering programming to a paying audience—with the huge advantage that cable's audience was sitting in the comfort of their own home, often watching the same movies shown only months earlier in his theaters. With his purchase of Viacom, Sumner Redstone joined media giants like Rupert Murdoch, John Malone, and Ted Turner in the early days of cable, and, to a lesser degree, Robert Maxwell.

Through the years I've traveled around the world with Sumner. For example, I was with him in China where he was warmly received by President Jiang Zemin. Sumner is a fascinating, complex man. His basic philosophy of business is direct and uncomplicated: *Win*. He has always emphasized that you just keep fighting, fighting, fighting, until you win. You absolutely *never* give up. He may be the most tenacious man I have ever known, and I loved that about him. In 1979, he was trapped in a fire in the Copley Hotel in Boston. He survived by crawling out a third-floor window, kneeling on a ledge, and holding on by his fingertips. He was terribly burned and was not expected to survive, but after five operations lasting more than 60 hours he made a miraculous recovery.

In addition to Viacom he eventually got control of Paramount Pictures and CBS. Ironically Viacom, which had been formed as a CBS subsidiary, ended up buying its parent. I was at the press conference at which the deal for CBS was announced. I remember Sumner came off the stage, a big smile on his face, and the first thing he whispered to me was, "Roedy, I got control. I got control."

The one thing he did not like was small talk; he wanted to get right to the point. He wasn't impressed by packaging, by ceremony; he wanted to get directly to the heart of the issue. But while Sumner controlled Viacom, the man I actually worked for and reported to, the man who hired me, was Tom Freston.

After working at HBO for a decade I was very comfortable. Maybe that's why I was uneasy. Stan had put me in charge of HBO's West Coast office, replacing the retiring Don Anderson. I had a wonderful life; I had a beautiful apartment on the water in Santa Monica, a job I loved, an unlimited expense account, and all the accoutrements of success. I played beach volleyball every weekend and was engaged to Annie Bloom, the highly talented and vivacious star of HBO's very successful *Not Necessarily the News*. My boss, Stan Thomas, was one of the most decent, charismatic human beings I'd ever met and I loved working for him. I was living the American Dream. I had settled happily into that life and might have remained there for my entire career if MTV had not come along.

I was not looking for a new or different job. HBO was a huge success and I had a significant emotional investment—although unfortunately not a financial stake—in that success. By the late 1980s, the wildcatting days of cable were done. Much of the nation had access to cable programming, either by wire or by satellite. There were no new domestic horizons. All that was left was the rest of the world. It was clear to me that to be truly successful for the long term it was necessary to have a global presence. The day a business stops expanding is the day it begins dying. Doing the same thing today that you did yesterday absolutely will end in failure.

Among other media companies, Ted Turner at CNN and Sumner Redstone, Tom Freston, and President and CEO Frank Biondi at Viacom had begun exploring the possibility of creating a global television network. An estimated 96 percent of TV-owning households are outside the United States, meaning cable TV had barely penetrated the potential market. What was personally disappointing is that HBO mostly missed this opportunity. Fred Cohen, who was running our international operation, lobbied hard to grow that business. The world was there for our taking, but we had a limited international strategy. One reason for that, I have always believed, was that our parent corporation, Time Inc., had gotten so involved in the complicated negotiations to purchase Warner that expanding HBO outside the United States didn't seem to be a priority.

In 1987, Viacom had begun its expansion by launching MTV Europe, a joint venture in which Viacom was the minority partner. In return for supplying the content Viacom had a 24.9 percent stake in the partnership. British Telecom owned 25 percent, and the boisterous, bombastic media billionaire Robert Maxwell, who put up the money for the channel, controlled 50.1 percent. At about the same time, Viacom also began supplying programming blocks to existing television channels in Japan, Australia, and Latin America, but these were insignificant. Europe was where MTV intended to plant its flag.

The original managing director of MTV Europe was a highly respected man named Mark Booth, with whom I eventually became good friends. Mark did such an impressive job setting up the initial MTV structure that Robert Maxwell offered him a higher paying job. That was typical Maxwell. Sumner Redstone was furious when he was informed Booth was leaving, supposedly telling Maxwell, "I don't know about your country, but in ours one partner doesn't go stealing the other's employees." It is not recorded how Maxwell responded. But Booth's departure left MTV Europe without a managing director. It was a chaotic situation. To manage the business they'd set up a rotation system in which the four top executives would be in charge for a month at a time.

I never learned specifically how my name was first brought up for the job. Admittedly, as a former Army Ranger and commander of nuclear missile bases, I was an unlikely choice to head a European rock-and-roll channel. It was my impression that Frank Biondi, whom I knew well from his days as CEO at HBO, suggested to Tom Freston that he consider me, but Tom once told a reporter, "I had already looked at several potential candidates for what I knew would be a difficult job when Bill Roedy was recommend to me by Matt Blank, with whom he'd worked at HBO. At first I thought, what can I do with a West Point graduate who has come from a missile base in Italy. . . ."

The thought of leaving HBO had not occurred to me until I was contacted by Freston. HBO was my home. But Freston described the job as a challenge and guaranteed that I would have almost complete decision-making control. During the next six months we met secretly several times to discuss the scope of the job. Among my concerns was what would happen if Maxwell backed out. What if the business failed? I was giving up a good career at HBO to make this move. We reached an agreement that I insisted include repatriation. Just in case.

I certainly didn't want anyone at HBO knowing that I was considering leaving. Incredibly, when I went to London in September 1988 to see the office, I bumped into a colleague from HBO. I had to make up some sort of silly excuse to explain what I was doing there. Leaving

HBO was an extremely difficult decision for me. It meant completely uprooting my life. I would have to move to England to take charge of a small unit mandated with building the first pan-Europe television channel. It was a completely untested concept. Ted Turner, for example, was focused on distributing his channel, CNN, to hotels, but we had decided to go after households. Nothing of this magnitude had ever been attempted and there was no guarantee it would work.

While I liked popular music and knew quite a bit about it, I certainly wasn't an expert. But I was enthralled by music videos. My friends and I would sit in my apartment on weekends watching hours of videos, and I was mesmerized by the creativity. I remember my friend, dancer Sandra LaValle, deciding, "This is a new art form." In addition to MTV, Turner had a music video service at night. So being involved in that exciting, creative world appealed to me. Living in Europe appealed to me. After spending a year in Vietnam and four years in Italy I felt very comfortable in an international environment, and being in charge of what essentially was a startup operation also appealed to me. Conversely, I loved my job at HBO, I had considerable security, and I had tremendous respect for Time Inc. and Stan Thomas. If I'd had children at that time, I might not have done it. But I was ready to do something different. I had just turned 40 years old and maybe this was the beginning of a midlife crisis. I was ready to take a risk. I decided to go after the adventure.

My job title was Managing Director, MTV Europe. Although it's never used in the States, *MD* is a common title in Europe. And as I liked to tell my friends, "My mother can finally say her son has become an MD!"

HBO did not make my decision easy. Time Inc. President Nick Nicholas called me while I was in Key West, attending my first MTV Domestic meeting, and essentially offered me the job heading a new cable network then called FNN, which eventually became CNBC. Oh, it was tempting. But I'd made my decision. It turned out to be the best decision of my life.

Start the music.

Chapter Two

Survivor

No one can expect to bring together a country which has 265 different kinds of cheese.

—Charles de Gaulle

On my first day in our small office on Mandela Street in London I sat down behind my desk and wondered where to begin. After spending about an hour getting settled I asked the temporary secretary assigned to me to find some paper and pens. That seemed like a practical way to get started. She disappeared and I decided to get a cup of coffee. As I poured myself my first cup of coffee on my first morning as the managing director of MTV Europe, Howard Smith, the head of distribution, came up to me. He frowned as he said bluntly, "We just lost Greece."

We lost Greece? "What does that mean?" I asked. It meant we were in serious trouble, Howard explained. We were using a terrestrial frequency to transmit our signal in that country and, for reasons nobody quite understood, apparently the Greek government had decided to take it away from us. As he informed me, at that point Greece accounted for almost half of our total distribution. Worse, our biggest advertiser, the Inter-American Life Insurance Company, had a Greek affiliate. Without Greece we would lose that business.

I had been there an hour and already half our business was gone. I suspected that had to be some kind of record for failure. I was stunned. I loved Greece, especially Greek food, but why did it account for half our distribution? And our audience was the young people of Europe; why was a life insurance company MTV's largest advertiser? What I could not have known at that moment was that the only truly peaceful hour I would ever enjoy had passed. For more than two decades after that we fought through at least one crisis somewhere in the world every day.

When I officially became managing director in February 1989, MTV Europe was in turmoil. The channel had begun broadcasting in August 1987, and appropriately, the first video broadcast was Dire Straits' anthem to MTV, "Money for Nothing," which boasts, "You play the guitar on the MTV." The office was on the third floor of a converted factory building on a narrow cobblestone street that even London's cab drivers, who knew every street in the city, couldn't find. Five people had shared one desk and one telephone. "Welcome to madness," was their morning greeting, and it fit. When I walked in the door MTV Europe wasn't close to being a business. We had less than a million subscribers, most of them in Greece and Holland, which was the only European country with a viable cable transmission system, and total advertising revenue of only a few hundred thousand dollars. And while MTV was a sensation in America, a survey done in England found that only 6 percent of people in the U.K. had ever heard of it, and that percentage was even lower on the Continent. I quickly discovered there was no cable infrastructure in the rest of Europe, so we had no real distribution. The concept of pan-European advertising didn't exist, so we had no viable ad market, we had no long-range strategy in place, and we had a very small staff. Although our office was in London, we weren't even on the air in the U.K. In fact, the British were quite chipper about the fact we weren't wanted. I remember sitting on a panel with several media experts who explained condescendingly to me, "We have the BBC, one of the greatest institutions in the world, and three other channels. Why would we possibly need more channels, especially one from America?"

I responded optimistically, "I happen to believe in the notion that competition makes everybody better. You're keeping your audience in a cage. If you really believe what you're saying is true, open the door and see what happens. If they really love you, they'll see the rest of the world and then come back to you."

They didn't buy that argument for a minute.

Their attitude didn't bother me; I knew these TV executives weren't my audience. Maybe they didn't want MTV, but I was confident that their kids would. I remembered how the three major networks in the United States had so casually dismissed the cable industry and I strongly believed that in some form we would see a similar response in Europe. This was the only time in my life that I knew I could see the future. Truthfully, though, I did wonder for a long time whether the business model that I had inherited, a single channel that would appeal to all of Europe, was valid. That theory, one-size-fits-Europe, certainly was questionable: There were painfully few pan-European products or businesses, there was no pan-European culture and certainly no pan-European television programming, there wasn't a common language, and, as Mark Schneider, who was then trying to establish America's United Cable in Europe, once said to me, "I've never met a pan-European." Everything was country-centric. In most of those countries U.S. culture was looked upon with disdain, and the last thing the leaders wanted was more of it. In fact, several years later, French President Jacques Chirac warned the world about the spread of our culture, claiming, "All other countries would be stifled to the benefit of American culture."

This European pride reinforced my fundamental belief that we could not simply be an American export. In response, I emphasized that we were a European channel, and that rather than blending or blurring cultures, our mission was to enhance European cultures. "MTV USA is a completely different channel," I emphasized. "MTV Europe is a local channel with a European point-of-view. The packaging might be similar, but the contents are very different. Our programming is put together specifically for the European audience." For the next 23 years, "respect and reflect local cultures" was my constant theme. And over time, even our packaging became very different.

There were a lot of smart business executives and media critics who were certain we wouldn't survive. Earlier attempts to launch music channels in Europe, Music Box and Sky Trax, had both failed. Several other companies trying to establish pan-European general-interest channels were struggling. Rupert Murdoch and the Italian media magnate,

Silvio Berlusconi, had both looked carefully at the European television market and decided that the only possible way to succeed was to create channels targeted specifically at each country or region that spoke a common language. How could we ever expect to create a channel that would appeal to young people in the very different cultures of Europe and find enough advertising to support it? It was becoming clear to me that only thematic channels might work. And even then it was all about implementation, all about execution. I knew we had a great brand, even though it wasn't widely known in Europe, but I believed it would be our execution of the concept that was going to make the difference.

The business plan for MTV Europe was based on the belief that only thematic channels that focused on a single subject with appeal across languages and nations, like music, movies, and sports, could successfully cross all those cultural and language borders. Like Hollywood movies, American and British music was popular all over the world. Music was the common language that kids spoke. The line I often used to emphasize that point was "*A-wop-bop-a-do-bop, a-wop-bam-boo* means the same in every language." Even young people in Western and Eastern Europe, in Asia and North and South America, who couldn't understand a word of the lyrics responded to the Beatles and Rolling Stones and other very popular groups. Music connected kids to their peers everywhere in the world. We used to point out to potential advertisers, "An 18-year-old in Pittsburgh and an 18-year-old in Mumbai, India, have more in common with each other than they do with their own parents." In addition to music, they share an interest in fashion, eating habits, movies, even attitudes. We stopped saying that, though, when we realized we were upsetting their parents. But it was obvious that young people throughout the world had common interests, and that was our demographic.

What did offer a glimmer of hope was the existence of the "one-Europe" movement. European governments had begun to understand the potential economic power of a strongly allied Europe. By 1989, the groundwork was being laid for a more united Europe, a European currency, which would become the euro, a single European army, and eventually a Europe without borders. Politicians in every country were telling their citizens that eventually Europe was going to become one happy family, an economic force capable of countering the United States. There was optimism in the air. Anything was possible, including a pan-European music channel.

It was possible, but as a business proposition not very probable. No matter how I looked at it, there wasn't a particularly good rationale to support the business plan. But as I had learned a long time ago, it is possible to take an average idea and implement it very well and it will succeed; conversely, a good idea implemented poorly will fail. I was committed; I'd moved to London; I'd rented a flat. Rather than wasting time questioning the business plan, I decided to embrace it. For me, the objective was execution. I had to find a way to get our product to the market—distribution, distribution, distribution. I had to create a structure that could deliver music to the masses of young people who I hoped were waiting for it. I had a hundred different pieces that I believed would eventually fit together to form a beautiful picture; I just had to figure out how to put this particular puzzle together. The possibility that within a decade that little channel struggling for survival would become the largest media network in the world would have seemed ludicrous.

There were many times during my first year that I got discouraged. Going from a top-floor office in Century City with a Pacific Ocean view to the grime of Mandela Street was a bit of a culture shock. Instead of playing beach volleyball in the California sunshine, I was slogging to work under the gray skies of London. I was alone in a city I didn't know with few friends and little time for a social life. I'd wonder what I was doing in London chasing after this windmill. I worked long, long hours and it seemed like I was always exhausted. There were many nights that I laid awake thinking, *boy did I make a huge mistake taking this job*. I got so down that one weekend I flew back to Santa Monica just to spend the weekend playing in my regular beach volleyball game in the California sunshine. I'm sure there are many executives who have never had a single doubt about the viability of their business, but I wasn't one of those people. I've never quit anything in my life; I was really unhappy at West Point but it had never occurred to me to quit. I wasn't about to quit this job.

My military experience proved invaluable. As I had been taught by the army, I began by prioritizing. After spending a considerable amount of time analyzing our business I realized I had to focus on three things: creating a product that would appeal to a large cross-section of tastes and interests among young people in Europe; getting distribution across the entire continent; and generating revenues. But the first thing I had to do was get my people in place. No matter how wonderful your product is, no matter how brilliant your business strategy is, unless you have the right people in place to implement it you are going to fail. This is especially true in an international organization, where distance makes it impossible to keep hands on. I had to establish an effective command-and-control structure. Once my team was in place we could begin implementing that strategy.

■■■

I suppose there were many different ways to start building our business, but for me this way of proceeding made sense. There is nothing more important than hiring the right people and building a team. As a manager, you will never be better than the sum total of the capabilities of your team. Success begins by putting the right people in the right position to succeed, giving them the support they need, and then letting them do their job.

There were about 20 people working in the office when I arrived. Their average age was probably 23 or so. As a group, what they lacked in experience they tried to make up in enthusiasm. In the military, commanders are dealt the cards and have to figure out how to make that deck work. In Vietnam, where our lives were at stake every day, I couldn't fire anyone. In that situation, I had to figure out how to use each person's capabilities to the benefit of the team. And truthfully, you don't like to fire people with rifles. In my military career I'd had to manage both elite soldiers as well as some others who were lacking some pretty basic skills. For a long time, I didn't believe in getting rid of people. I prided myself in being able to train, coach, and motivate my people to improve their performance. But I learned quickly that in business sometimes it is necessary to let people go.

In Italy, as commander of nuclear missile bases, generally I was assigned elite troops. We operated under the Nuclear Reliability Surety Program, which meant every individual had to pass several layers of security checks. Toward the end of my career, out of loyalty, I stuck with a warrant officer whose competence was in question and he let me down. One of our regular inspections tested our ability to assemble, activate, and deactivate the actual nuclear function of the missile. There was a long checklist of things that had to be done perfectly. If we missed one step, we failed, although we were given the opportunity to correct that error.

The lieutenant under me who had direct responsibility for one of my bases was a dedicated officer, but he was headstrong and impatient. For some time he had been warning me that the warrant officer who actually did this work was incompetent. I liked this warrant officer. He was considerably older than both of us, he had far more experience than the lieutenant, and his career was on the line if something went wrong, so rather than listening to this lieutenant I remained loyal to the warrant officer. Unfortunately, during an inspection it was discovered that he'd overlooked a blown fuse. The failure to replace it almost caused us to fail that inspection. A nuclear base failing an inspection was a big deal. That was an important management lesson for me. I'd allowed my loyalty to overcome legitimate questions of competence. In the extreme, the blown fuse meant that this weapon probably would not have functioned. In real time, we were able to correct it. That was an important lesson for me. From that time forward I accepted the fact that a leader listens to his people, and then makes the changes that are necessary.

Unfortunately, over the years I've had to let way too many people go. At times this included people with whom I had worked closely for years and who had become close friends. "Fire" is a cold word that does not take into account the impact on lives. It's a word I try not to use. People are let go for a variety of reasons. Sometimes it's for cause; sometimes they're casualties of a restructuring. Firing someone has never been an easy thing for me to do and I've never done it lightly. I strongly believe that if a new hire doesn't work out, it's as much the responsibility of the person who hired that employee and put that person in that position as it is the responsibility of the employee. I'm aware that many people disagree with this, but after more than three decades of managing people this is what I believe.

There are times when people fire themselves. For example, when I took over there was a woman in sales who was slowly, but with great determination, sleeping her way through the entire male staff. While I encouraged socialization, to me she was a bit overzealous about it. I probably would have let her go for that when she got up to six people, but she made the decision particularly easy when she caused us to be 45 minutes late for a meeting with a Swiss client. It is never good business to be even one minute late for a meeting with a Swiss client.

It also was less painful to fire disloyal employees, and unfortunately they exist in every organization. For example, when I found out that one of my department heads had been in New York trying to convince them that he should replace me, I fired him immediately. When I let someone go I always tried to do so with compassion, and in a way that allowed him to retain his dignity. But this was a rare case in which I had absolutely no regrets.

The most difficult personnel decisions involve cutting staff during a downturn, merger, or acquisition. That means letting competent, productive, loyal employees go. There is nothing more difficult for a manager to do than make those decisions. For example, until 1999 MTV and Nickelodeon had operated independently internationally. It was an unnecessarily expensive situation with a lot of overlap. When those brands were finally merged, in many cases I had to choose between equally competent people who had basically been doing the same job. That was brutal, and those decisions were excruciatingly painful. We did the best we could to find a place for everyone, but some people were left out. That's reality; as a manager you do what's necessary.

While generally I accepted the recommendations of my department heads, I also made it a point to be visible when those decisions were made. That was important. I've always believed that a commander has to be the first person on the battlefield in the morning and the last one to leave it at night. For me, it's even more important to be visible during the bad times than when things are going well.

Hiring certainly was more pleasant. The first thing I looked for when hiring was someone who was passionate about working at MTV. We were fortunate; young people literally begged to work there. We would get letters from people throughout Europe offering us their firstborn child—offering anything—in exchange for a job. "Give me a job," they would write, "I'll clean the toilets." They would send gifts and chocolate and CDs. I wanted to hire people who, if they weren't working at MTV, would have been home sitting in front of their television watching it, people who would work all day at the office and then go home at night and watch MTV. One young woman, I remember, practically camped in our lobby. She returned day after day and sat there politely and patiently, but she refused to leave until I agreed to meet her. She even baked me a cake once. Finally, I did agree to meet with her and was so impressed by her perseverance and her passion that I hired her on the spot. Perseverance and passion alone aren't sufficient, but they do help make an impression. I was always looking for competent, intelligent, honest people, able to work as part of a team. What really makes a difference is the passion to charge up the hill, to go that extra mile.

What was essential to me in building my team was diversity of every type—not just geographical but color, sexual preference, and, as I used to joke about myself, age and military background. When I took over, our staff included people from a variety of European countries—and one American. I consciously did not hire any more Americans. In fact, throughout my entire career I hired thousands of people, and, with the exception of people working in New York, I probably hired a total of six Americans. That irritated some of my colleagues, but I felt it was absolutely necessary. The biggest misperception that any American-based company has to fight is that they are bringing another American product to Europe. There remains a strong sentiment throughout Europe against the importation of more American culture, or what is referred to internationally as *cultural imperialism*. So at every opportunity I emphasized that we were a European channel with a European sensibility. To emphasize our diversity I would often bring guests into the office and literally point out the number of people we had working there from each European country, in many cases people from traditional enemies: "Over here, we have a Serb and a Croat working side by side, we have Greeks and Turks, we have Dutch and Germans, we even have the French and English working side by side." And after a pause I would add, "But that's not working as well." Finally, I would mention that we had only one American in the office. When asked if I was counting myself, I would respond, "I'm an internationalist!"

In addition to the obvious symbolism, there was a good business reason for this: As much as possible your employee base should reflect your audience, or in most businesses your customer, which will enable you to understand and address their needs. It's absolutely essential that the diversity of the employee base match the diversity of the audience. I wanted to hire Europeans because our audience was European. While hiring a reflection of your customer base has now become a common business practice, we were far ahead of the curve on this.

The result was that our international organization was one of the most diverse companies in the world. Outside the United States, diversity actually includes a variety of different groups, among them people discriminated against for geographic, economic, and ethnic reasons. While we haven't always succeeded in including everyone, we have always made the effort and continue to do so.

In my quest for diversity I did make some mistakes. For example, when I realized that we didn't have a single manager from France I knew I had do something about it; I also wanted to put more women in leadership positions. After conducting a long search I hired a French woman with an impressive resume to run our communications department. She had been the communications director at Goldman Sachs. The problem was that she came to MTV from the corporate world and never made an effort to fit in. The rest of the staff just didn't respond to her. For example, everybody in the office normally dressed casually, basically in jeans and T-shirts. She wore designer clothes. Personally, I didn't care. But the way she dressed was symbolic of her attitude. She was very aloof; she didn't really try to mesh with the other employees. My staff wanted me to let her go but that was difficult for me. My instinct was that they were rejecting her because she was different: She was French and she was a woman. I kept telling them to accept diversity. I was passionate about that. Different is good, I argued. In fact, I felt so strongly that I failed to see that she just wasn't a good fit for our culture. I tried hard to keep her, perhaps for the wrong reasons, but eventually for the sake of office morale I had to cave in.

What qualities do I look for when hiring someone? There is a cliché in business that when you interview an applicant for a job one way of judging the individual is to decide if you'd like to sit next to him or her on an airplane for three hours. That's not a particularly bad criterion. With all the traveling I've done the range of people I've sat next to stretches from pleasant to *if they come any closer to me I'm going to have to leave the airplane.* But generally it comes down to whether that person is likeable. Does he have those traits you can relate to, is he curious about life, and is he compassionate? Now, I've never bought into that completely because I can think of several people with whom I worked for a long time whom I didn't particularly like, but who were valuable to the organization. Then, of course, there are experience, skills, competence, intelligence, problem solving, creativity, the ability to be part of a team, and finally, just that gut feeling that this is the right person. Instincts matter and you should pay attention to them. Every person on the team doesn't have to be likeable. The great puzzle is fitting together an entire team to make it as strong as possible. I'm a big believer in creating a team that includes people with different strengths. For me, at least, one plus one equals three.

While I was putting my team in place I also set the tone for the office. My objective was simply to make it the best possible place to work in the world, that's all—I wanted MTV to be the least corporate corporation imaginable. I wanted my employees to think of the office as their home; in fact, I wanted them to hate having to leave at night to go home. Our team was young and enthusiastic and they burned the candle at both ends. We had no dress code and no rules about hair length or style, and we had flexible hours; people were welcome to come and go as they pleased—as long as they accomplished our objectives. My basic philosophy was to break all the rules. What I meant by that was that instead of following traditional business techniques, I wanted my people to be innovative and creative when faced with a problem. We were an entrepreneurial organization and it has always been my belief that corporate rules and policies tend to restrict creativity—and creativity is an absolutely essential element for an entrepreneur. The mantra they heard from me every day was, "Never accept 'No' for an answer," especially in an international environment where there is always an objection to be overcome. We were attempting to do something that had never been done before, so if we paid attention to the "no's" we would never get established. "Take chances," I urged them, "take risks, don't be afraid to make mistakes; don't be afraid to go against convention, because if you don't you're going to get caught in the quagmire"—as long as they learned from their mistakes.

I was especially adamant about not taking "No" for an answer. That has been a guiding principle throughout my life. I warned them that we would be dealing with people whose first answer to anything new or different would be "No." If we wanted to survive, we couldn't accept that answer. We had to go for it everyday. The speech I probably have quoted more than any other in my entire career was given by Sir Winston Churchill, who in a speech at his alma mater, Harrow School, said simply, "Never give in. Never, never, never, never, never." I wanted my people to respond to "No" as if it were a challenge. I often reminded them that in many cultures the first answer you always hear is "No," so they couldn't be discouraged by it. At times, when a person came back to the office and told me something couldn't be done or that she had been turned down, I'd sent her right back to try it again. Obviously, sometimes "No" actually means "No," but often "No" is just the beginning of a negotiation. Often barriers can be overcome with the right strategy and nurturing the right relationships. China, for example, has always restricted the importation of foreign cultures, so it was difficult for us to get permission to launch there. But over a period of several years we were able to demonstrate that our channel would reflect their culture rather than introducing another culture. In that situation, Sumner Redstone was particularly important as the Chinese greatly respect wisdom, experience, and seniority and his presence gave them comfort. But China would be a good example of persistence finally turning years of *no*'s into a *yes*.

We broke all the rules. We paid to get on the German cable system, which no company had ever done before. We ran our programming on terrestrial systems, which cable channels didn't do; we transmitted our signal direct-to-home unencrypted so anyone with a dish could get it; we pushed cultural norms; we ran edgy programming, like a demonstration of how to put on a condom; we created public service programming and gave it away to any channel that would run it; and at times I allowed things to get on the air without having the proper rights. Running material without first clearing the rights was controversial, but we did it. For example, there were times when we used music in our long form programming when we didn't have the rights and didn't even know how to get them. At that time content piracy was not the significant issue it has become, but more importantly we already were paying a fortune—for us—for rights to every conceivable music organization in every country, and under the deal we'd made with VPL the record companies were receiving 20 percent of our gross.

My insistence on breaking the rules was controversial. Executives who reported to me often asked me to tone it down a little, telling me that this approach sometimes made it difficult for them to manage their people, who insisted on breaking the rules. Brent Hanson, who was working at MTV as a junior producer when I arrived and eventually became our creative director and finally president of MTV Europe, hated hearing me say this—although creatively Brent broke more rules than anyone.

Among other rules I urged our people to break were those that limited socialization between employees. In fact, I encouraged socialization. I became known for reminding everyone at the beginning of every party, "More than one dance with the same person is a relationship," meaning, "Go ahead and dance with everybody, get to know as many of your colleagues as possible." I wanted our office culture to mirror the spirit of our product. If MTV was the place we wanted our audience to be, the staff certainly should want to be there too. I needed to attract the type of people who could produce a channel with a cutting edge and that meant I had to give them the freedom to be creative. Creative freedom is a huge workplace incentive. I tried to protect it at every opportunity. I was ferocious about this. An entrenched bureaucracy laden with rules prevents creativity.

We needed only the flimsiest excuse to have a party. When we signed a new advertiser, we had a party. We added one household in Belgium, let's have a party. Someone passed her driver's test—party time! Eventually, we even had our own in-house band. If it sounds like sometimes it got a little out of control, well, it did. At times, that was me dancing on a table. And there was a rumor spread around the office that I had been spotted in Regent's Park at 5 o'clock in the morning hanging out with the kids from the mailroom.

I walked the tightrope between being an active participant and a responsible executive. At times, for example, I would pretend I was drinking but instead toss my drink over my shoulder or on a plant. I may have always had a glass in my hand, but it was usually the same glass for hours. Once, however, I did, have a space cake in Amsterdam. A space cake is a muffin laced with marijuana, which is legal there. Our team there dared me to eat it and joke, joke, joke, I thought that as the leader I had the obligation to play along. That one time I did. I wasn't used to the effect, so I barely noticed it. In fact, the next morning I was in a meeting confident that it hadn't affected me at all—until I realized I had absolutely no idea what I was doing in that meeting.

That story is still told with admiration in our Dutch office.

My point was that we couldn't be one thing in the office from 9 to 5, or in our case often from 9 A.M. to 11 P.M., and something completely different on the air. I would always say in my speeches, "You can see the spirit of the people in the office on the channel." As obvious as it seems, if you're happy in your job, you are going to be more productive.

We were trying to do something that basically was impossible, and if we were to have any chance to succeed we needed a total commitment from everyone who worked there. By creating the team atmosphere we had people working extraordinarily long hours without complaint for the good of the channel. We established a lively, friendly, incredibly creative atmosphere. Work was fun, fun was work. For me this was liberating; this is who I was *before* spending 11 years in the military. Our office snowball fights were legendary; three flakes fell and we were down on the street, although generally it would be everyone in the office against me. On a few occasions we even had snowball fights *in* the office. On business trips I would sneak into hotel rooms and short sheet beds. We worked hard, but we laughed a lot, and in the background there was always music playing.

I often told people that internal marriages would be a great accomplishment. And we had our marriages. Our top VJ married a member of our press department. Brent Hansen married another VJ, Pip Dann. Frank Brown, who pioneered the concept of pan-European advertising for us and eventually became head of MTV Asia, married a woman who started with us as an intern. And eventually I married an extraordinary woman, Alex Lindemann, who came from Germany to work in our ad sales department.

Of course, when I began seeing Alex I didn't want anyone in the office to know about it. My attempts at secrecy became a popular office joke. Once, when I wanted to communicate with her I wrote my message on a Post-it and folded it up, and as I walked by her desk I dropped it, believing no one noticed. They say the boss is the last to know. In this case, I was the last one to know that everybody knew Alex and I were seeing each other.

One thing I did that might have been necessary at the beginning but later annoyed my managers was bypassing the chain of command. At some point almost every day I would wander around the office talking to the people on the front lines. This was exactly the same thing I'd done in the military, where I'd seen the benefits of a leader spending time with his troops. There was no better way of learning my business. As our business grew I continued to do that, and eventually it did cause some internal problems. Although it benefited morale, it was making it difficult for managers to run their departments because I was going directly to the people who reported to them, rather than following the structure I'd established. In the end the goal is to find the proper balance.

But in those early days, almost of necessity, we blurred the lines of responsibility. We encouraged everyone to be as creative as possible. During one of those friendly conversations, someone working in the post room laid out his concept for a whole production for me, so I decided to promote him. There was a lot of pushback; some people complained that he had no experience as a producer. I replied, "He's got enthusiasm, he's got a vision, he's very creative, and we should give him the opportunity." James Hyman started in our press office stuffing publicity releases into envelopes and after suggesting we do a show on club culture ended up being a programmer, producer, director, an on-air presenter—and our senior press officer. John Dunton Downer, "John Double-D" as he was known, was a Harvard graduate who had majored in Sanskrit but started with us as an assistant to the executive producer, meaning he was in charge of sending polite rejection letters to people applying for a job. But like almost everyone else, he also sat in on creative meetings to help decide our programming. We put people who had never been in front of an audience in their life on the air. If someone had a creative, cutting-edge idea and wanted to try it, two weeks later he or she might be hosting a program. Brent Hansen's secretary, Vanessa Warwick, had bleached white hair, tattoos, and nose rings long before they were fashion statements, as well as a vast reservoir of knowledge and a passion for heavy metal music. We put her on the air as host of a very successful show called *Headbanger's Ball.* A VJ from France named Sophie Bramly was into rap and wanted to do a rap show. Why not? *Yo MTV Raps* proved so popular that a year later a similar show was successfully introduced in the United States, where it was hosted by Fab Five Freddie. I was amazed and proud that MTV USA would actually pick up programming from our little startup.

While it did not look or feel like a typical office, I had to make certain that our people remembered we were running a business. I believe strongly in symbols. So to lend some formality to the chaos, for most of my first year I wore a suit to the office every day. Although with my suit I also wore sneakers, or trainers, as they're called in England. I *always* wear sneakers. I own sneakers in almost every color. Sneakers have become my trademark, although that certainly was not my intention. I wear them because years ago I injured my back jumping out of airplanes and running marathons and they make my back feel better. It was never meant to be disrespectful, but as an added benefit it helped encourage the creative environment I wanted to instill. Sneakers are symbolic of physical fitness, endurance, comfort, and flexibility. I wear them at home, I wear them in the office, and I wear them when meeting government officials in foreign countries—I even wore them when I met the Queen—or when walking the red carpet at one of our events. When I was privileged to be the first private citizen to address the United Nations General Assembly, as a result of my work fighting AIDS, I wore a dark suit and black sneakers. Only once has it been an issue. We did an extraordinary program in South Africa with Nelson Mandela, and after two days of filming the two of us were to have a private meeting. We were at the Saxon Hotel, and as I waited to be invited into his room his head of security looked me up and down and said, "You're wearing trainers."

I nodded, "I always wear them."

For a moment it threatened to become a problem. But finally he frowned and walked away. If Mandela even noticed, he said nothing.

■■■

From my first day, even while building a staff and establishing our corporate DNA, I focused on building distribution. The ultimate reality faced by any business is that no matter how good your product or service is, unless you can get it to your customer, it doesn't make any difference. The best product in the world sitting in the back of a truck has no value. When I took over, we had limited distribution. We were broadcasting to only a few countries. It was obvious that if we didn't drastically increase distribution, we couldn't survive.

I became the distribution zealot. Just as I had done at HBO, I preached aggressive, creative, relentless distribution. I wanted us to be everywhere. I preached "every household in Europe" to anyone who would listen. I wrote that phrase on memos, I included it in every speech, I even wrote it with magic marker in large letters on the wall of every one of our offices throughout Europe. "Every household in Europe" was a simple premise that I reinforced at every opportunity: We were going to get into as many homes as possible and we were going to do it any way we could. This was the only way we could build a business. I wanted every household in Europe to have access to MTV. I wanted every hotel, every bar, and every public viewing area to have it. My people were constantly on the road and I believed that visibility in hotels was an important marketing tool. In fact, I had a rule that when an employee checked into a hotel the first thing he or she had to do was find out if that hotel offered MTV or Nickelodeon. If it did not, they were to march down to the front desk and explain that if the hotel did not get at least one of our channels, our employees would no longer stay there. I believed strongly that if we were able to build a large enough audience, we could overcome all of our other challenges.

I wanted MTV Europe to be the 500-pound gorilla. Advertisers would not be able to ignore us. In the United States, MTV was broadcast on cable TV, but most of Europe did not yet have a cable infrastructure. The available technology in Europe was borderline antique when I started. While other media companies sat back and waited for the infrastructure to be built, I felt that I didn't have that luxury. If we were going to be Europe's biggest network, I couldn't wait. In countries that did not have a cable system, I wanted to be available by satellite. If there was no direct-to-home satellite capability, I wanted to be broadcast on a terrestrial frequency. If we could have carried the signal on horseback from house to house, I would have done that. We were the only media company to actively seek terrestrial frequencies. Where it was necessary, to get distribution I compromised; I had to start off for partial carriage, meaning we were on the air only a few hours a day. If we couldn't get our own 24-hour channel, I was willing to put several hours of our programming on someone else's channel. MTV Europe became the first MTV Networks channel to be distributed terrestrially. Italy, Greece, Spain, Brazil, Russia, Indonesia, and France did not have a viable cable infrastructure. But unlike other programmers, I didn't want to wait for it to be built. We had to have terrestrial distribution. But in each of those countries there was only a limited number of terrestrial frequencies available and they were all allocated, so to get on the air we had to form some very complicated partnerships with broadcast companies that owned that territory. For example, if you've ever looked behind a busy executive's desk and seen the incredible array of twisted wires, that was sort of what our partnership structure in Italy looked like.

I made two significant decisions during my first six months at MTV Europe that greatly increased distribution, going direct-to-home by satellite and paying for distribution on the largest cable network in Europe. Anyone who has built a business knows that deciding where to invest your resources—particularly when you aren't earning substantial revenues—often makes the difference between success and failure. Most of the time you don't get a second chance. Initially, advertising was our only source of revenue. Without viewers we couldn't sell advertising, and without advertising revenue we didn't have a business. We weren't like most other international companies: We didn't need shelf space like a soft drink; we didn't need a brick-and-mortar facility like a fast-food chain. We needed distribution to millions of households.

While I had been at HBO, our technology guru, Ed Horowitz, who later moved to Viacom, had purchased a number of large satellite transponders that HBO would need when it expanded to Europe. That expansion never happened, which allowed a company named Société Européenne des Satellites to buy them from us cheaply and build a business around them. In 1989, SES launched Astra 1, the first satellite capable of transmitting a signal that homeowners in Western Europe could receive with smaller and more affordable K-band dishes. That opened up a new means of distribution. Rupert Murdoch put his entire Sky-TV network on this satellite. Renting space on Astra was very expensive; the cost was almost $10 million a year. That was substantially more than the cost of satellite distribution in the United States. It was a huge investment for us, but I believed it was absolutely essential. I encountered a lot of resistance from our partner, Robert Maxwell. Finally, though, we got permission to rent transponders on that satellite. This was my first strategic victory.

Astra 1 instantly gave us access to consumers throughout the continent. Anyone in Europe without cable access, and that was most of Europe, could buy a dish and get MTV. Astra 1 also provided access to several Eastern European countries behind the Iron Curtain. Polish television, for example, was government controlled and therefore limited in content. Poland had no cable infrastructure. But suddenly there was this thing called "satellite television" and Polish citizens were asking relatives living in the United States to give them the $1,000 it cost to buy a dish. For the first time since World War II, by pressing a few buttons Polish citizens were connected to the rest of the world. As many others have said, I believe that by giving people behind the Iron Curtain their first look at life in the western world those satellites helped change the world.

I had a glimpse of the future in November 1989. Earlier that year, I had been invited to East Germany to address a seminar entitled *Is Music Television Erasing All Traditional Cultural Barriers?* at the first music and media industry conference ever held in Eastern Europe. Less than two decades earlier, I'd been in charge of nuclear missiles that could have wiped out much of that part of the world; now I had been invited there to discuss the power of music in general, and MTV specifically. I agreed—with one condition. I insisted that MTV be available in the hotels in which the people attending the conference would be staying. After two months of negotiations with East German government officials, they agreed, making MTV available in East Germany even before much of West Germany received it. The hotels bought the required satellite receiving equipment and we handed out door hangers announcing DO NOT DISTURB—I'M WATCHING MTV to all guests.

Going into East Germany, I had to pass through Checkpoint Charlie at the Brandenburg Gate. When I arrived there on November 3rd freedom demonstrations were already being held, as they were throughout the Communist Bloc. Three nights later I attended a government reception, where I was scheduled to meet with members of the Politburo, but none of them showed up. Coincidently, this was one hour after we had hooked up MTV. I didn't know what was wrong—later I learned that the entire East German government had resigned. The Berlin Wall was being ripped down before my eyes. As a Cold War veteran, this was one of the most extraordinary moments of my life. I was witnessing the end of Communism. I was mesmerized; I'd grown up watching the events that changed the world on television, and now television had allowed me to be there in person. It happened so quickly, so unexpectedly. No one had predicted this. Several months earlier, I had met with a group of Russian government officials in Moscow and they'd whispered to me: "The other countries will end Communism, but not East Germany. The government will never give in." I had a camera crew with me filming the conference for MTV News but instead they covered these historic events, so many East Germans actually learned that the Wall was coming down from MTV. As East and West Germans met freely for the first time in more than four decades I had a conversation with several young East Germans in the hotel. "What do we do now?" one of them asked me. "We don't know how to be capitalists. Where do we start?"

At that moment, the best answer I could give them was, "You'll learn. Freedom will eventually outweigh the uncertainty."

As East and West Germans embraced each other freely our director of network development, Michiel Bakker, took what was to become an iconic photograph of East German border guards dancing on top of the wall holding an MTV umbrella. I loved that picture because it visually represented what I wanted to do, and from it I created our slogan, "Breaking Down Barriers." When I returned to West Berlin, Checkpoint Charlie no longer existed. I've often heard it reported that two days after MTV began broadcasting in East Germany the Berlin Wall came down. My point is not that we were responsible for the end of Communism but rather to emphasize the fact that satellite transmission was such a powerful force it had the capability to change the world. Five years later, when we produced the first European Music Awards, we celebrated unity by constructing the largest tent in history in front of the Brandenberg Gate, right where the Wall had once stood.

Rupert Murdoch also understood the potential of satellite television, and unfortunately for his business he said so out loud. When doing business internationally you have to consider the impact of every word you utter in public. One sentence—a few words—even innocently spoken can be devastating for a company. My advertising director, Frank Brown, and I happened to be at a meeting at 20th Century Fox in Los Angeles, which Murdoch owned, when he was making a speech to his employees around the world. It was a morale-booster. Murdoch had made a total commitment to satellite television and was talking about its power to spread ideas anywhere in the world. He went so far as to predict that it could bring down dictatorships. He was right, and he certainly did not intend that remark as an insult, but that one line, that one thought, doomed him forever in China. The Chinese never trusted him again. He tried very hard to regain their trust. His media empire was careful not to criticize China, he published a favorable biography of Chinese leader Deng Xiaoping written by Deng's daughter, and he invested hundreds of millions of dollars in that country, but none of that made a difference; he was never able to build a business there and essentially he's taken himself out of that market.

In many ways I agreed with Murdoch about the power of satellite transmission. If I had to cite the one event that was the key to our success, it would be successfully getting on Astra 1. But almost immediately after we'd bought space on that satellite I had to make another crucial decision.

Sky-TV channels were encrypted, meaning their signals were scrambled and those channels couldn't be seen unless they were decoded. Sky offered programmers like us a monthly fee if we would encrypt our signal, which would have allowed it to set up a lucrative subscription service. Sam Chisholm, the managing director of Sky-TV, leaned on me heavily. And it was difficult to resist him. While it would have instantly generated much-needed revenue from the U.K., it didn't fit my strategic vision for Europe. By making MTV available to anyone with a dish, we instantly gained access to a vast audience who did not have access to cable. My financial projections were based on generating pan-European advertising. As much as I wanted subscribers, at that time I needed viewers. So I turned down his offer. But five years later, after we were established in Europe, we entered into one of our strongest partnerships worldwide with Sky.

The second strategic decision that I made was to pay a fee to get on German cable. Germany had the largest economy and the largest cable infrastructure in Europe. For advertisers, this was the most important market on the Continent. If we could get distribution in Germany, advertisers would have to begin paying attention to us. The problem was that the German cable system was entirely controlled by the government-owned and -regulated Deutsche Bundespost-Telekom, the largest telecommunications company in Europe. If I thought TCI had been difficult to crack while I was at HBO, it didn't begin to compare to the challenge I had negotiating a deal with Deutsche Bundespost-Telekom.

In the United States, cable operators paid fees to channels in return for running their programming, which attracted viewers, but in Germany we would have to pay the cable system for distribution. Once again, there was resistance to this from our partners. It was a different way of doing business and for a long time people weren't comfortable with it.

The negotiations were complex and protracted. Every word had to be painstakingly translated to maintain its contractual implication. Howard Smith, from our domestic distribution system, was very instrumental in getting it done. The German government did not know what MTV was and, frankly, didn't care if we were on their system or not. We had to convince them that a pan-European channel would be of great value to them in the effort to unify Europe. I am very careful never to use the word "desperate" in business because it alerts people that you're out of control—but in this case we *were* desperate. Fortunately, they never realized how badly we needed their distribution. This was the only game in town for us.

We eventually negotiated a very fair deal. We paid a flat annual fee and in return got immediate distribution to more than eight million households. By flipping one switch we got all of Germany. It was a huge win for us. The distribution through Astra 1 and German cable gave us the foundation for a viable business upon which we began building.

For the first time, I could see that MTV Europe was going to succeed.

The German deal also led to the most emotional negotiation I've ever had. In every executive's career there are going to be moments where there is no good answer. For me, this was that time. Soon after concluding this deal, I was negotiating for distribution in Israel. No country in the world built a cable infrastructure faster than Israel and part of the reason for that is their system is above ground—they just connected the wires. It took them less than three years to connect the entire nation. Israel's five cable operators appointed a man named Tommy LaPid to represent the entire industry in negotiations with programmers. Tommy was a wonderfully charismatic storyteller who became a good friend; he was a Holocaust survivor, who ultimately formed his own political party, the secular-liberal Shinui party, and he was a tough negotiator. We were at an industry conference in Cannes, meeting at the MTV stand in the Palais. I had negotiated what I considered a good deal for us to get distribution in Israel; even though every Israeli with a satellite dish could get MTV for free, the Israeli cable operators were going to pay us. Tommy and I were down to the last few deal points. Suddenly he laid his hand on top of mine, looked me right in the eye and said softly, "Bill, I know what you did for the Germans. You can't give the Germans a better deal than you give us and you know why."

I just sat there looking back at him. How could I respond to that? Obviously, the two deals weren't comparable. We had been desperate for German distribution; truthfully, we didn't *need* distribution in Israel. There was no possible way I could give Tommy anything approximating the German deal and he knew it. But what a negotiating tool! Eventually, I did cave in on the last few points; I don't remember the details but it was probably something like a penny a subscription.

We did whatever was necessary to gain households. In some countries, we had to navigate around government restrictions on non-local entities owning media. In some countries, if you were a member of the

European Union, you were not treated as a foreign company, so for a while we declared ourselves European. There were some countries in which no matter how hard we tried we couldn't get a frequency. There were various reasons for this, so we had to find a partner who either had access to a frequency or owned a frequency. In that sense, it was similar to what I had encountered in the States, when giant cable operators like TCI demanded equity in a company in exchange for distributing a new channel—which is how TCI ended up owning several channels.

Because of the complexity in getting distribution we made several different types of deals throughout Europe. There are three categories of ownership. The first is *owned and operated*, which means sole ownership. Second is a *joint venture*, a partnership in which we would own 50 percent or less. And third, is a *licensing agreement*, in which we would have no ownership position—we would simply license the right to broadcast the channel to an operator. These decisions were strongly debated at Viacom. Sumner Redstone always wanted to own as much real estate as possible—he wanted to retain ownership. I agreed with him, although I'm not sure I was always right. Tom Freston felt that the world was so complex that we needed local expertise that could be provided by partners who would share the expenses and the rewards. In reality, I was a pragmatist; I did what was possible where it was possible. Where distribution was a challenge, for example, we found a local partner able to navigate its own market. Several years later, when we began expanding throughout the entire world, we actually created a grid including every country and how we wanted to operate there.

Sole ownership carries the most financial risk, but it also has the biggest upside. We had to make the investment, but in return we got all the asset value. Where the market was particularly challenging, confusing or government regulated, a local partner could help both strategically and financially. The advantage of a licensing deal was that it required no capital investment but still provided distribution, trademark and management fees, and some advertising revenue, which was particularly attractive in smaller markets with a limited upside. Generally, these were countries in which we wanted to plant our brand, like Romania or Lithuania, but didn't justify the investment that opening an office would require. In both joint ventures and licensing deals our contract included an option for us to take complete control. That protected us. And in some countries we went back and forth, moving from one structure to another as market conditions changed.

No matter what type of arrangement we made, we retained the ultimate creative control. While only rarely did we exercise that power, we couldn't risk allowing local programmers to make decisions that might affect our global brand without some level of oversight. We tried to empower local employees to connect to local audiences, but we had to maintain some boundaries. I remember getting a phone call one morning and being told that MTV Taiwan was broadcasting *nude male wrestling*. Well, that's *one way* to ruin a nice morning! I immediately sent them a cease-and-desist letter. Fortunately, that type of thing did not happen very often.

Somehow, we cobbled together a viable distribution system. In some countries, such as Italy, we had to link together a chain of terrestrial stations from town to town, basically creating our own national network. Our European distribution network certainly wasn't pretty, but it was an extensive patchwork of various platforms

Unfortunately, when MTV Europe was launched our management at that time had been forced to make a very bad deal with the record companies for the use of their videos. They knew that financially it was unsustainable in the long term but in fact there were no options. The channel was totally dependent on these labels for product. Music Television without music videos was going to be a hard sell. Years later we would own an extraordinary collection of music and video segments, but at the beginning all we had to run was what they gave us. When MTV had been founded in the United States the record companies had no idea how successful and powerful it would become. It was a nice little channel that was giving free exposure to their artists. These companies and those artists were so thrilled with the increased sales that resulted from MTV playing their videos that basically they gave them away. But by the time MTV Europe was launched the major labels had learned that lesson—and they weren't going to make *that* mistake again.

■■■

Tom Freston had suggested that the first thing I should do in London was make friends with the record industry. I took that to a new level. When I arrived in London I made a point of meeting the heads of the five major record labels. While the record industry is global, the U.K. often is considered the center of the music world. These were extremely impressive executives; they were legendary characters who had helped create the modern music industry. I had great admiration for each of them and I worked very hard to establish a relationship. My whole life at that time was defined by business, so my most important clients became my closest friends. We had meetings; we had many dinners; I spent a considerable amount of time with each of them. Decades later some of these executives remain close friends, among them giants of the industry like Chris Wright, who founded Chrysalis Records and transformed it into an impressive media conglomerate; Rob Dickens, who was the youngest managing director of Warner Music U.K. and also producer of Cher's huge hit "I Believe"; Paul Russell, who ran Sony Europe; Paul Burger, who ran Sony U.K.; managing director of Polygram U.K., Maurice Oberstein (or "Obie," as he was widely known); and Jorgen Larsen, who ran CBS Records in Europe and eventually became chairman and CEO of Universal Music. Nick Nicholas, who was then running Time Warner, urged me to meet Ramon Lopez, head of Warner-International, the most important record company in the world. Eventually, I would spend long hours over lunch with him in his office talking about the world and the record industry.

These men were also tough, experienced businessmen. They'd spent their entire careers fighting for pennies. And unfortunately for me, as beneficial as exposure on MTV could be for their artists, they knew that without their videos we didn't have a channel. As I learned, borrowing a phrase from John Malone, completing a deal with the record industry was "like tying the tails of two cats together and throwing them over a fence."

Rather than negotiating individually, the five major record labels and a group of independent music companies had formed an organization to negotiate an overall agreement for all of them. It was called Video Performance Limited (VPL). VPL was an oligopoly; it had all the power and exercised it. Before we launched we had to obtain the rights to play music videos through this one entity. I have always believed that at the end of a fair negotiation both sides walk away satisfied; MTV Europe walked away from these negotiations with an untenable deal. VPL was intractable; they wouldn't budge. It had become obvious that if MTV Europe wanted to run their copyrighted videos we would have to accede to their demands. Those demands were, basically, a piece of the business. When I arrived I discovered that we had signed a deal that gave them 20 percent of our revenue. That isn't 20 percent of bottom-line profits; that's 20 percent *off the top of every dollar that came in the door.* The actual business term to describe this deal is *holdup.*

And in addition to VPL, we had to pay an array of other fees for music rights. In every country we had to pay fees for performance rights, fees for mechanical copying rights, and we had to pay fees to the copyright houses. We had to pay fees on the local level and the European level. I had to spend an inordinate amount of time negotiating these rights.

There is an old joke about a businessman who lost a nickel on every thingamajig he sold. When asked how he could make a profit if he lost money on every sale, he replied confidently, "Quantity." That was my situation. I knew when I accepted the job that the contract with VPL was not sustainable. I didn't know how I would break it, but I knew once our revenues started increasing that I couldn't survive if I didn't. Maybe I was hoping that exposure on MTV would become so valuable to the labels that they would modify the deal, but hope was all I had.

From my first day I struggled to find ways to break or modify that contract. I believed VPL was an illegal cartel. The head of VPL was a man named Roger Drage. I spent countless hours with him talking, talking, talking, trying to build a relationship, trying to convince him to modify the deal. Just give us something that would enable us to survive. But he was intransient—he wouldn't budge a penny; in fact, he wouldn't even negotiate. I offered every possible argument and made absolutely no progress.

When that effort failed our attorney and later my COO, Greg Ricca, and I spent two years approaching every single record company to try to convince them to break away from VPL and sign a separate deal with us. We knew that if we could get one major label to leave VPL, the rest would follow. I offered the major labels every incentive we could legally guarantee, including specific commitments to market a number of new acts, heavy rotation on our playlist, promotions, and guest artist appearances. Several times I thought we were very close to a deal, but no one would make that final commitment. It was becoming clear that if MTV Europe was to survive, eventually we would have to take legal action against the cartel. Deciding to take legal action against my most important clients and some of my best friends would be one of the most difficult decisions of my career, and the ramifications of that decision eventually would transform MTV. It would lead to the creation of our strongest competition. But before I took that drastic step, I had to build a viable business. I wanted the record companies to need MTV as much as we needed them.

We struggled throughout the first year. There were days when even I doubted we could make it. Every month I would have to go see our majority partner, Robert Maxwell, to tell him exactly how much money we needed to pay the bills. Our third partner, British Telecom, never interfered. In my years at MTV I have been privileged to meet the most extraordinary human beings; but certainly one of the most complex and unforgettable characters I dealt with was Robert Maxwell.

Robert Maxwell rose from poverty to build a publishing empire, eventually even becoming a Member of Parliament and one of the wealthiest men in the world. But his real name was Jan Hoch, and he was a Czechoslovakian Jew who survived the Holocaust by escaping to Britain. While serving in British Intelligence during World War II he was given several different operational names, finally settling on Robert Maxwell. And essentially that was the problem in dealing with him; it was never possible to know what was real. At one time the media put Maxwell in the same category as Rupert Murdoch and Sumner Redstone, but I never believed that. Maybe I knew him too well. Sumner Redstone was a skillful negotiator, a dealmaker; Maxwell was not a particularly good negotiator. His ego too often got in his way.

The stories told about him were legendary. For example, he enforced a strict no-smoking policy in his building, which was known as "Maxwell House." Supposedly, one afternoon he got into an elevator with one of his executives and discovered a man in there smoking. He was irate—furious about this man's blatant disregard for company policy. "How much do you make, young man?" he demanded.

"About £12,000 a year," the man responded.

Maxwell took out his checkbook and wrote a check for a year's salary. Handing it to him, he said, "I never want to see you in my company again."

"If that's how you feel," the man said, "you'll never see me again." When the elevator reached the bottom floor he walked out and disappeared. Only later did Maxwell discover that he had just paid a year's salary to a deliveryman dropping off a package.

That story may well be apocryphal, but a story I *know* is true took place right before I arrived. This was during that period when we had rotating managing directors. The director of the month had to attend her first board meeting at Maxwell House. Maxwell was notorious for being late for meetings. Finally, about a half hour after the meeting was scheduled, his helicopter landed on the roof of the building. Minutes later, the great oak doors burst open and Maxwell charged into the room. Before he said one word, he slammed his fist on the table, then bellowed, "This channel is a piece of shit and all of the people running it are idiots! I'm pulling my money out right now."

Our executive director was devastated. Maxwell was shutting off our financing. But before she could protest, Maxwell's aide leaned forward and said quietly, "Bob, no, this is *MTV*. These are the *good guys*."

Maxwell paused for a few seconds. "Oh," he said, "I'm sorry. Wrong channel." And with that he walked out of the room.

As our director discovered, Maxwell often ran as many as six meetings simultaneously. He'd pop into one meeting for a few minutes, then leave and go to the next one. In this instance, he went to the next office and pulled the plug on his movie channel, *Premiere*.

The difficulty with him was that he was our principal funder and our funding was never on time. We were operating on a shoestring, completely dependent on Robert Maxwell to cover the difference between our costs and our revenue. At the end of almost every month I would have to meet with him to get that money. It was never easy.

I never looked forward to our meetings. His office reflected his ego; it was huge and very formal, and his logo, which was basically his initials, was everywhere. It was on the wallpaper, it was in his carpet, it was wherever you looked. I'd sit across from his massive desk and tell him how much funding we needed and why we needed it. With me he was always charming—he could be very personable—but other times I saw him snapping rudely at people who worked for him.

Our original business plan called for us to become profitable in five years, but we actually reached the breakeven point in three years. In 1990, Viacom decided to explore the possibility of buying out Maxwell and British Tel. Making a deal with BT was easy; it was a huge company and we were so small they paid little attention to us. We were not a strategic business to BT. We caught them sleeping and purchased BT's 25 percent share in the company for about $10 million. It was an extraordinarily great deal; we couldn't believe they had sold so easily and so inexpensively. But I was certain negotiations with Maxwell were going to be a lot more contentious and expensive, and take a long time to complete. Maxwell was a tough businessman and fought for every penny. What no one knew, however, was that Maxwell had been looting his own pension fund and his crime was about to be discovered. He was desperate; he was walking a financial tightrope and we showed up unexpectedly with a safety net. Years later, the highly respected Tom Dooley, who has long been close to Sumner and eventually became Viacom's COO, told me that Sumner had sensed Maxwell's desperation and pushed hard to close the deal. We were incredibly fortunate; Maxwell needed to sell as much as we wanted to buy.

Sumner Redstone negotiated the deal in less than a month. We completed the deal in August 1991, paying $65 million in cash and stocks for his 50.1 percent. Several months after we completed the buyout, MTV Europe was valued at more than a *billion dollars*.

The mystery surrounding Robert Maxwell did not end with that sale. Three months after the deal was done Robert Maxwell was dead. While cruising on his yacht off the Canary Islands, he supposedly fell overboard. The official ruling was that it was an accidental drowning. But nobody ever determined what actually happened. There are people who believe he was murdered, while others believe he committed suicide. After his death, stories were written claiming Maxwell secretly had been working for Mossad, the Israeli Intelligence Agency, and that connection had led directly to his death. In fact, there may well be some truth to this; he was buried in Israel and given what appeared to be an official state funeral on Mount of Olives in Jerusalem, where Israel buries its leaders and heroes. He died just like he lived, surrounded by mystery. I had spent a considerable amount of time with Robert Maxwell, but reading all those reports I remember thinking that I had not known him at all.

We were building MTV Europe week by week, house by house, country by country. Somehow we managed to cobble together a network. We now had the ability to transmit our programming throughout Europe. We had every available cable system, including Germany; we had Astra, which gave us the direct-to-home universe; and in other places we had terrestrial frequencies. Now we had to build an audience and sell it to advertisers that didn't exist.

We had created a pan-European hill. Now it was time to begin our charge.

Chapter Three

Money for Nothing

Europe had a tightly regulated broadcast spectrum, no cable penetration and satellite dishes were considered a blight on the cultural landscape. There was very little marketing outside the mainstream channels. And then came MTV Europe. It is fair to say that true consumer engagement for youth brands began with MTV.

—Matthew Freud, Chairman, freud communications

MTV Europe was an experiment. No one would know whether the concept of a single channel broadcasting across Europe was viable until we went out and tried to sell advertising. There were people at Viacom in New York who argued that it would be considerably less expensive to simply direct the American feed to Europe rather than funding a new channel. So I was aware that we had an undetermined but limited timeframe in which to prove we could be profitable. The clock was running. I had no choice but to rely on my time management lesson: Prioritize!

My first day on the job had been about securing distribution. My second day was about generating revenue. That second morning, Frank Brown and I made a presentation to Columbia Studios. HBO hadn't run commercials, so I'd had no experience selling advertising. But as always, when making a sales pitch I tried to be enthusiastic, compelling, and convincing—even if I wasn't completely certain what I was trying to convince Columbia to do. On occasion, it's possible to make up in enthusiasm and confidence what you lack in specific knowledge.

Unlike in the United States, where basic-cable channels have at least two revenue streams, at least initially we were going to have to rely mostly on advertising revenue. And we were a tough advertising sell. The idea of a pan-European media business was new. The few media companies that had dipped a toe into that water had failed miserably. Even those few companies that did market a product across Europe generally had nation-specific brands. The same product would have a different name in a different language in each European country. It might even have a different use. As a director at a major London advertising agency told a reporter for a trade publication, "It's no good advertising something on MTV that doesn't sell on a pan-European basis."

What made it even more difficult for us was the reality that we did not have enough households in any single country to justify national advertising, and the advertising industry in Europe was not set up to buy the entire continent. Instead, each nation had its own advertising industry designed specifically to sell products directly to its citizens—and in some eastern European nations, Russia for instance, there was no advertising industry at all. The job title, "European Marketing Director," did not exist in advertising. In fact, I don't remember meeting a single person in the advertising industry who had the authority to make a pan-European buy. Agency budgets were set at a local level, so to convince any client to spend on a centralized level we had to get tremendous cooperation. For some consumer products as many as 50 different marketing managers each would have to agree to contribute a portion of his or her national ad budget before the company would make a pan-European buy. The process of getting a consensus was incredibly labor intensive and time consuming. Generally, these managers resisted having their decision-making power taken away.

Being a pioneer is never an easy trek. As I had often heard John Malone say, "Pioneers often end up with arrows in their back." Over and over I sent out our reps with the slogans by which we lived, "Aggressive, relentless, and creative," and "Don't take 'No' for an answer." We were not a traditional company, so traditional strategies wouldn't work for us. If the advertising agencies wouldn't support us, we bypassed the agencies and went directly to chief executives of fashion, lifestyle, technology, fast-food, and soft-drink companies that marketed directly to our audience. As our director of advertising sales, Bruce Steinberg, explained, "We had to go to the clients and the ad agencies in each of the countries in which they operated and convince them that MTV was an effective buy in comparison to their national TV. . . . Each country's contribution is based on how many homes we have in their country. If 10 percent of our network is in the U.K., then 10 percent of the budget should be from the U.K."

We had identified our weaknesses, but we focused on our strengths. Telling the story you want potential clients to hear is always a good strategy. What we did have was a sexy brand; we were the only youth-positioned channel and we worked hard to create a buzz. The pitch we made to potential advertisers was that we could reach that elusive young consumer they were chasing better than any other media outlet. If you wanted to market to young Europeans you had to be on MTV. We emphasized our belief that music was global, and that while our audience might live in many different countries they all listened to the same music, wore essentially the same type of clothes, went to the same movies, ate the same fast foods, and drank the same beverages. We claimed that even though our audience was spread over many countries it actually was more homogeneous than a mass audience in any specific country. We were the meeting place for the young people of Europe. Our unique selling proposition (our USP) was that we were offering a larger audience than they could reach in any single country, all of whom were potential customers. We made a compelling argument—combined with the fact that we kept our advertising rates low. In some instances we were charging less than half of what commercial stations in the U.K. were charging.

That was our pitch, although initially we couldn't prove the size of our audience. The advertising world now has access to an extraordinary array of statistics. But two decades ago there was no pan-European research being done. Beyond the number of people watching at any time and their age group, not too much was known about an audience. Because we didn't have statistical evidence to support our claims, we emphasized the tremendous popularity of MTV USA, which was perceived by American companies to be this really sexy, exciting brand that you'd better be part of if you wanted to sell your product to kids. Many of those same multinational companies advertising in America took for granted the fact that eventually the same thing would happen with MTV in Europe.

We did, however, come to rely on focus groups for feedback. We brought in a lot of young people and we listened to their responses. They gave us some important directional tones. I made a point of observing as many of these groups as possible and we often used their comments—"Everybody's watching MTV," "MTV is cool"—in our sales pitches.

Eventually, though, advertisers did want to see evidence that we were reaching their audience. I have often quoted the legendary retailer John Wanamaker, who said a century ago, "Half the money I spend on advertising is wasted; the trouble is I don't know which half." What do you do when you don't have a research unit capable of measuring your audience? In our case, we created one. In effect we commissioned our own research. We joined with several other channels to create and fund an entirely independent organization called Pan European Television Audience Research (PETAR). It was basically the European version of America's Nielsen ratings. The advertising side supported it strongly, but the programming side was concerned that our quest for numbers might take away their independence. PETAR conducted two surveys annually. Twice a year it would measure our viewership for one week, and during that week, sweeps week, like every other channel we would do anything to boost our ratings. In media today, the concept of advertisers buying time based on research conducted twice a year is laughable. But that's all we had available to us.

To attract wary advertisers we created a dynamic environment. We actually began running high-quality Coke ads for free—although few people besides me knew we were doing this. Coke was doing a small amount of advertising with us, but I gave them a major amount of commercial time. To this day I don't know if Coke was aware of it. I've worked with a long succession of chief marketing officers at Coke, from Bill Lynn to Joe Tripodi and his deputy Scott McCune, and have never admitted it to one of them. We actually did that with several prestige brands. At one point we probably were broadcasting more unpaid commercials than paid advertisements. That's the kind of strategy you can get away with only in an entrepreneurial situation. It was a gamble but I believed it was absolutely necessary. When developers build a shopping center they begin by attracting one high-quality tenant, believing it will draw similar stores. That's all I was doing. I wanted potential advertisers who marketed to the same demographic as Coke to see that Coke believed we were a sensible buy. We ran Coke commercials that had a high production quality so other brands would want to be associated with them—and MTV.

I also knew that the best strategy in negotiating with a market leader is to get a deal done with its primary competition. That's true in just about every product category. If you have Coke as an advertiser, for example, you're going to get Pepsi. In our case, Coke was the bait and we used it.

To accommodate potential advertisers we broke the traditional rules, creating a unique and flexible advertising environment. When I was at HBO I saw that the once-impregnable wall between ad sales and editorial content was beginning to come down. Time Inc. emphasized editorial integrity, which was referred to as "church and state," but I saw it eroding. At HBO, boxing was an important part of our programming. Mike Tyson was practically a franchise property for us; he brought in ratings—and a week or so before a championship bout *Time* magazine put him on its cover. Everybody at Time was aware of this "coincidence" and all of us at HBO were very happy about it, but nobody said a word out loud about it. Admittedly, when I got to London I knocked down what was left of that wall. Today, there is no hesitancy about cross-promoting different media properties. Nor is there any concern about it from the audience. The word used to describe it is *synergy*—although at that point no one understood what "synergy" really meant. For example, Time Inc. tried to launch a cable version of *TV Guide* called *TV Cable Week* in an attempt to unite its print and video divisions. It lasted less than six months and lost almost $80 million.

We blended our advertising and programming, calling it *integrated marketing*. I didn't think there was anything wrong with it. It has become an important revenue source for broadcasters. MTV Europe wasn't a news channel; we were providing entertainment. We didn't have to be neutral. We attracted clients by creating programming that was relevant to our audience and enhanced their product. *The Pulse with Swatch*, for example, was a monthly program about fashion. *The Coca Cola Report* reported about music and music industry gossip, the arts, concerts, and tour news. My programming people hated sponsor-titled shows like the *Coca Cola Show*. That caused a huge fight inside the company. They felt we were selling out, diluting the brand. I listened sympathetically to their arguments. I understood their point and agreed with much of it, but ultimately I went with the branding. As the CEO responsible for growing the business, "selling out" had a very different meaning. It meant selling out all of our advertising time, and we were a long way from doing that. As I pointed out, if we weren't profitable we wouldn't be around to even have this debate.

■■■

We didn't break down the wall; we walked a tightrope. Unlike most broadcasters, we weren't simply selling ad spots. Instead we integrated entire marketing campaigns into our programming, which included running creative idents at the beginning and end of programs. Nobody in media was doing anything like this. We tried to blend our advertising and programming in clever, creative ways. Rather than making black-and-white decisions, as had been the tradition at Time Inc., instead we tried to find shades of gray that were acceptable to everyone.

Ad sales and programming were always fighting about this. Brent Hansen was a purist; he wanted as little advertising as possible on the channel, while our advertising group wanted to sell the light fixtures. This was a fight that never ended; the creative side always wanted to put the chicken before the egg, while the commercial people wanted to put the egg before the chicken. I came down firmly in the middle. I knew we couldn't sell advertising without a strong creative product and we couldn't afford creative programming unless we sold advertising.

Hansen was adamant that becoming too advertising-oriented would alienate our audience and damage our brand. At times he simply refused to run certain spots. For example, Braun electronics, one of our first substantial advertisers, wanted to convert the title sequence of a show it sponsored into an ad. They wanted to bleed out of their commercial directly into the programming, believing that would strengthen the connection in the viewer's mind between Braun and the program.

It was an interesting idea—but in the title sequence they wanted to include product shots, including a hair dryer. Brent's team refused to run product shots in the opening. Eventually we worked out a compromise; rather than products we ran fashion and cosmetic images that the viewer could relate to. It didn't work well for either us or the sponsor. When our creative team and our advertising staff couldn't resolve a situation, I stepped in to mediate quickly and firmly.

Generally, though, we managed to find ways to blend advertising and our programming. Both at MTV Europe and in the United States we broadcast *Dial MTV*, a video request show sponsored by Pepsi. When viewers called in to request a specific video we allowed Pepsi to conduct its own survey. In 1996, we signed a three-year multimillion-dollar worldwide deal with Pepsi that included program advertising, cross-promotions, marketing tie-ins, and large-scale events featuring our VJs. It made Pepsi the exclusive soft-drink sponsor (meaning no Coke) of our *Video Music Awards*.

Movie studios were extremely important advertisers for us. They had large advertising budgets and we shared the same audience. So we created two programs specifically to attract them; *MTV at the Movies* and *The Big Picture*, which were essentially the same show. *MTV at the Movies* was a daily half-hour show that included news, interviews, and reviews, with much of the news supplied to us by the studio's PR departments. We interviewed the stars and showed clips of their new movie, exactly what the late-night talk shows do, although we took it to a new level. *The Big Picture* was also a half hour and featured trailers from new movies—trailers that were supplied to us by the studios. These movie shows achieved two important objectives for us: Our audience was interested in movies and movie stars and accepted these shows as entertainment rather than advertising, and there was no resistance from the creative side on this (probably because we didn't call these shows *The Columbia Pictures Movie Show*). But these shows were really long commercials for the studios, and I thought it was a clever and effective way to solidify deals with clients.

In 1989 it was advertising from the studios that helped us survive. We needed that advertising desperately. I remember making those sales calls on the studios with Frank Brown. Frank is the most articulate, effective salesperson I've ever known, and I have great respect for him, but one day I really came down hard on him. Having lived in Los Angeles I knew how awful the traffic could be, but he didn't listen to me and scheduled two meetings without leaving sufficient travel time. To me, being late for a meeting with a client was the worse thing that could happen, and on the way to that second meeting we got caught in that traffic. As if it wasn't bad enough for Frank to be caught in a massive traffic jam, he had to sit there for an hour listening to me loudly lecturing him.

To increase our visibility in the movie industry we began sending our VJs to the major film festivals, especially Cannes. Cannes, of course, is the most important film market and we started throwing an annual party there. By the mid-1990s the MTV party had earned a reputation as the hottest party at the festival, the one that everybody wanted to attend. *The Hollywood Reporter* used to rate our parties "Three cocktails!" People literally would climb walls to try to crash a party. They would form large groups and try to overwhelm front-door security. We held several parties at Pierre Cardin's villa, which was built on the side of a cliff, and people actually would scale the craggy cliff trying to sneak in. In 1996 a young man named Dave Sibley joined MTV Europe as head of sponsored events and one of his first events was a party in that villa to celebrate the animated film *Beavis and Butt-Head Do America*. We lost control of that party early, and Dave retreated to the VIP room determined to maintain control there. I remember walking by him as he was pushing against the door while a mob was shoving from outside trying desperately to break in. It was like a scene from a movie; hands literally were reaching inside. Later he told me he was terrified when he saw me, believing his first event was a total disaster. Of course, he was new to MTV. In the midst of that chaos, as I walked by, I said the three words that he later told me were the best words he ever heard: "Dave! Great party!"

One year we held the party on the beach across from the Hotel Carlton and it was so crowded, Security wouldn't even let me in. I had to go around back and sneak into my own party.

People tried various strategies to get inside. They would produce elaborately counterfeited invitations or even impersonate stars. If Robin Williams was in Cannes to promote a new film, for example, a limo would pull up and a person who in bad light remotely resembled him would get out and try to bluff his way in. And there were occasional fights; I can remember a security guard leaping out of a second-story window into a melee—and breaking both ankles.

We didn't want to be just another broadcaster covering the festival; we became an integral part of the festival. For a small operation, we had a large presence. We set up shop at the Hotel du Cap, the most glamorous hotel in Cannes, and eventually we became the absolutely essential stop for any producer, director, or actor promoting a movie.

We established a wonderfully symbiotic relationship with the studios, even stronger than we had with the record industry. The studios supplied their stars to us, which enabled us to draw a viewing audience that wanted to see those stars, which in turn made us attractive to other advertisers, and then our audience went to see those movies. In fact, MTV eventually became so important to the studios that they changed their traditional release pattern in Europe. Rather than rolling out a film country by country across the continent as they had always done, they instead coordinated a narrow pan-European release window to take advantage of MTV's promotion. As the European head of publicity for one of the major studios told *The Hollywood Reporter*, "MTV is providing strong editorial support aimed directly at the profile of European moviegoers. Their [programming] has a substantial rating and is targeted directly at our consumers."

We created the art of integrated marketing. We worked with our advertisers to create commercials that looked very similar to the videos we were running, so those ads flowed almost seamlessly into our programming. In some instances we actually behaved like a pan-regional advertising agency, working with clients to produce their commercials. This was another service that no channel had ever offered before. For example, in 1989, Nike signed a three-year deal with us. Rather than create their own advertising, David Flack, one of our top creative people, designed a billboard opening for them that showed the Nike Swoosh while audio from one of Nike's priority sports—tennis, football, golf—played in the background. It was brilliant in its simplicity and Nike loved it.

Rather than offering only strict 15- or 30-second spots for commercials, we encouraged advertisers to sponsor specific programming, allowing them to attach their brand to segments: "This video is brought to you by Swatch"; "This tour report is brought to you by Wrangler." We tried to be as flexible as possible, offering to create tailor-made campaigns to meet their needs. Advertisers loved it; it gave them a chance to directly associate their product with artists they otherwise could never afford. "We offer a broad range of promotional opportunities for potential advertisers. Our programming format is very friendly to advertisers," I pointed out, "because it tends to be in short spurts and if you have a commercial in an MTV style, it blends very well with the programming format."

Out of necessity, we changed the way television advertising traditionally had been sold in Europe, working with companies to create platforms that went far beyond commercials. For example, when Pepsi signed on to sponsor M.C. Hammer's European tour, we collaborated on a promotional program. In addition to covering the tour on our shows, we ran specially produced commercials that featured M.C. Hammer and we even conducted an on-air competition in which the prize was an opportunity to dance with Hammer. We were always conducting some kind of competition to draw viewers. In addition to giving away substantial prize money, other contests offered an opportunity to cruise down the Nile with Tom Petty or spend several days on tour with Sting in Scandinavia.

At times we succeeded so well that critics complained, "The entire MTV network is an advertising program."

It worked—even better than we had anticipated. In 1989, there were no pan-European advertisers; within a year we had signed 45 regular advertisers. A year later we had more than 130 clients, among them Coke and Pepsi, Levi's and Wrangler, Nike and Reebok, Swatch, LA Gear, Kodak and Pentax, Mastercard and Visa, Phillips and Braun, and IBM and Apple. As much as 90 percent of our revenue was derived from advertising. While we had successfully created a new advertising model, selling it involved good old-fashioned hard work.

In fact, our formula worked so well that we were able to move faster than our projections. Noting our success throughout Europe, other broadcasters began copying our music video format. In fact, many of the same videos we were showing were also being shown on other channels. While the programming quality of most of MTV's competitors was low, they did create confusion among the audience. When a video was playing there was no way for the viewer to know which channel he or she was watching. To combat that, I focused on building very strong brand recognition. MTV was a very well-recognized brand in the United States, but initially much less so in Europe.

■■■

There is nothing more important to a product than building brand recognition. In the United States, I'd noticed, when I zapped through the channels each of them seemed to be distinct. That was less true in Europe. Often our channel was at the end of the spectrum and there was nothing that instantly distinguished us from our competition. That became a problem during the twice-annual PETAR surveys when it was essential that our viewers knew they were watching MTV. We ran contests to draw viewers and flooded the channel with promotional images; but if viewers were channel surfing, they might miss those promos, so we needed a means of providing instant recognition. To ensure that our viewers always knew they were watching MTV, we broke another rule. We decided to put our logo in the corner of the screen and leave it there. No one had ever done that before. Now, of course, imposing a channel logo over programming is pretty much standard. But we started it. This logo is not to be confused with the creatively brilliant interstitial logos that MTV had started running in the States. Those were animated, wild, colorful morphing images that helped establish the creative brand for the channel. Our on-screen logo was small and very crude, just a block-letter *M* with *TV* written in script over it. Initially we even kept it on the screen during commercials. It wasn't particularly visual or colorful. But we did it first so viewers would know instantly they were watching MTV.

In my quest to bring some business structure to our creative chaos we held a weekly management meeting at which we discussed strategy and made decisions. That way everyone knew what was going on and had an opportunity to voice their opinion. It was one way of getting everyone to buy into our objectives. Leaving the logo on the screen was a controversial decision and we debated it. And as we often did in those days, we debated it loudly. A lot of our creative and programming people were adamantly opposed to putting our brand on content. They believed it was too obvious, definitely uncool, and an unnecessary distraction. They were passionate about keeping the channel pure and viewer-friendly, pointing out correctly that at times it would obscure information about the video being played. To satisfy their concerns I agreed to an experiment. We would leave it up only during the PETAR survey, and at the end of the month we'd take a look at the result. As it turned out, we received few viewer complaints, and it appeared to increase brand recognition. Among other evidence, when we posted our logo on the screen the number of entries we received in our contests increased measurably. It was clear that keeping the logo on the screen was actually working; viewers found us and stayed there, so I decided to keep it there. I had become a very strong advocate of this.

As a consolation to the creative side I provided the additional funding needed to create a more visually exciting logo. "The bug," as we called it, eventually progressed from a simple white logo to a three-dimensional, full-color animated logo designed to continually morph into an infinite number of shapes and colors. We left it on the screen all day, every day. It was revolutionary. At times, though, it led to a small infestation of bugs: For example, some stations that carried a block of MTV programming, particularly in eastern Europe, had their own bugs, so often there were two of them on the screen at the same time. In one instance I remember three bugs on the screen and even I thought it might be too much.

I don't think I'd like my legacy in the television industry to be that I was the man who stuck the logo on the screen and kept it there, but I know it has been effective. It helped us establish our brand in Europe and later throughout the entire world. Viewers knew instantly they were watching MTV, rather than one of our competitors.

MTV's station identifications also were revolutionary. Traditionally station idents, which MTV was running between videos, had always been static and unimaginative. A station ident is the visual representation of a product, and it should convey in one glance the emotional message the company is trying to communicate: We're reliable. We're whimsical. We're futuristic. We're fun. Probably the most recognizable ident in America was the CBS eye, while the most creative was NBC's peacock opening its colorful feathers. We took the concept several steps further. Our idents were works of art. While in the beginning MTV Europe primarily used idents from MTV domestic, eventually we hired the best graphic artists in Europe to create pieces with a European flavor and gave them the freedom to do it. The results were the most visually exciting pieces running on television anywhere in the world and they set a tone and creative standard that has endured. American MTV had set a creative standard—and I believe we met that hurdle and adapted it for Europe. Brent Hansen, described them accurately as "optical attacks" that "made your eyes bleed."

These on-air idents could be flowing mercury or neon or colors so bright they almost blasted people out of their chairs. They were elaborate, whimsical, startlingly innovative 10- or 15-second computer-generated animated pieces always ending with the creation of a colorful MTV logo. In one of them, for example, a baby in his highchair threw gobs of colorful food directly at the viewer, and the food formed the letters.

Another took place in Hell where prehistoric creatures flew into the form of the logo. "King Kong" featured a film-clip from a 1950s black-and-white horror film in which people are fleeing the approaching monster—which in this case was a giant letter *M*, the legs of which stomped through the city until it hit electrical wires and bolts of electricity formed the *TV*. These idents were unlike anything that ever had been done on European TV. We became an instant trendsetter.

Our logo and station idents became a visual expression of our creativity. We referred to the idents as "the on-air programming look" and we had thousands of them. Brent Hansen correctly pointed out, "Our logo is the biggest star on MTV." But more importantly, as Hansen added, that logo accurately reflected "in visual language . . . all the different colors and vibes of the audience."

Our objective was to be the most visually engaging channel in the history of European television. We tried to project our "break-all-the-rules" attitude in everything we put on the air. We knew our audience self-identified as rebellious, irreverent, creative, and connected and we programmed our channel to reflect that. We wanted them to feel this was their channel. Everything from our camera-shots to the way our presenters dressed was fresh and different. Everything was fast-paced, short-form programming—instantly recognizable as MTV. No image stayed on the screen too long. The graphics were bright. Backgrounds were spare. Not your parents' TV—*yours!* No mistaking it for anything else.

One of the most important decisions about our programming was that it would be in English. I knew we would get pushback on that from countries concerned about being invaded by American culture, but we really didn't have a choice. We were sending the same signal to numerous countries in which a variety of languages were spoken. English was the lowest common denominator. On occasion we would joke that maybe we should do our shows in Esperanto, which was created to be a one-world language but never really caught on. English successfully crossed more borders than any European language. English is the default language of Europe, the language spoken by most people after their native language. That's true even in France. A survey conducted before I got there demonstrated that young Europeans believed that when they understood comments in English about a subject they knew, they felt connected to the rest of the world.

English-language music is popular in most parts of the world, while it's rare for songs recorded in languages other than English to sell beyond the borders where that language is spoken. Our VJs all spoke English, although mostly as their second language. They combined English and their native language in a unique way—just as our audience did. In fact, our German VJ, Kristiane Backer, didn't speak English very well at all. Actually, I liked the fact that she struggled with English because I thought that would match our audience and there was something charming about it. Our VJs were taught to speak slowly and distinctly, and they were instructed to avoid trying to make puns or wordplays because most of our audience wouldn't get them.

The government of China would even use our channels, MTV and Nickelodeon, to teach English. More people speak Chinese Mandarin as their primary language than any other language in the world, but the government wanted to promote English as the universal second language. During one of my many trips to China I learned that high school students substantially increased their chances of being accepted to a university if they mastered four skills, one of them being a proficiency in English. In fact, one of the first programs we ran in China was called *MTV English*, which used music videos to teach English. While the video was running, the lyrics were scrolled in English across the bottom of the screen, and the Chinese VJ regularly would stop the music to translate those words.

Although Fidel Castro's Cuba never got its MTV because of the American government's trade restrictions, when I visited there Castro told me he also wanted to use our channels to teach English to the Cuban population.

Whatever language our VJs spoke, if viewers didn't want to watch our product even the most extensive international distribution network in the world wouldn't make any difference. HBO had become a success because we owned that marketplace; if viewers wanted to see first-run movies in their homes, they had few options. By the time competitors like Showtime appeared, we were an established brand. I didn't have that advantage at MTV Europe. Kids had choices, so we had to create a programming environment that was unique, that connected strongly enough with our target audience to bring them back again and again.

■ ■ ■

Our product was our programming. When I arrived in London, I didn't have the slightest idea about the nuts and bolts of programming a music channel. There was an experienced woman in charge of programming and one of my first decisions was to let her go. She actually was too experienced for our network; if we really intended to break the rules, we needed someone in that position who had not spent her career playing by the rulebook. To succeed, we needed to be different from anything then on the air. I wanted somebody willing to take chances. I settled on a long, curly-haired producer named Brent Hansen, a wildly creative New Zealander with strong opinions and a tremendous knowledge of music. He had even named his daughter, Marley, after Bob Marley. Brent gave the channel its look and feel, I later appointed him to oversee all international programming. But at the beginning we all had to learn the basics. We started with almost an empty slate; we had 24 hours, seven days a week to fill. Programming is a skill and an art, and it can't be learned from memorizing *TV Guide*. A man named Yarl Mohn, who had changed his name to Lee Masters when he was working in radio, was in charge of MTV programming in the United States and at my request he came to England and spent two weeks with me and several of our programming people. We holed up in a little conference room right outside my office for 12 hours a day as Yarl taught us how to program our channel. Yarl looked at the schedule as a pie and taught us how to slice it into a programming grid consisting of commercials, promotions, lead-ins, and all the other segments that fill the day. Eventually we would be programming more than 150 channels 24 hours a day, seven days a week. Obviously some of it was already produced, but undoubtedly it was the most extensive programming output of any media company in history. That started in that conference room with Yarl Mohn, and I was tremendously indebted to him.

While we promoted ourselves as a lifestyle channel, initially we were completely dependent on music videos for our programming. Most of our shows were live, hosted by our diverse group of VJs, and served mostly as the framework that enabled us to put videos into categories. *Club MTV* played dance music. *Headbanger's Ball* played European heavy metal. *Yo!* was our rap show. To break up the blocks of music video programs we ran a music-and-lifestyle news program, and we had a dance music program, movie programs, a quiz show, a magazine show that reported the latest pop-star gossip and tour news, one minute of pop news every hour, and at least some social awareness programming.

For most corporations public service involvement has never been especially important. MTV was no different. It requires employee time, it takes money, and there are legitimate questions about how valuable it is to the bottom line. Initially it wasn't part of my agenda, and it wasn't on the business plan. I needed to build a profitable business. At that time I didn't envision that MTV would become the leader of the corporate world in the fight against HIV/AIDS.

By 1989, the channel already was running occasional public service spots fighting alcohol abuse and smoking and raising AIDS awareness, issues that impacted our audience. Environmental awareness was a major issue in Europe, so we commissioned 28 of the best directors and production houses in Europe to produce a series of irreverent station idents with an environmental theme. We premiered these pieces during a special Green Weekend, intended to create awareness among our viewers of the problems facing the environment. Some of these spots stretched the accepted boundaries. My favorite was an animated talking turd sitting on a beach under an umbrella urged listeners to keep Europe's beaches clean. For several years we dipped into issues without making them an essential part of the brand. Each year at Christmas, for example, we promoted an album presented by the Shriver family that promoted the Special Olympics. For media companies social awareness campaigns are very tricky. MTV was providing entertainment; if we were going to do public service programming we had to do it in a way that was consistent with our brand. If we preached our audience might change the channel, which would have defeated our purpose. We could present public service programming only after we had firmly established a brand connection. There was no chance MTV could educate anybody if we didn't entertain them first and foremost.

Although our mission was to create a European channel, we also were fortunate to be able to include some American programming. By this time some Europeans had seen pirated versions. We wanted to give them a slice of American culture, but much less than a whole meal. Initially we ran only three shows produced in America: a half hour from NBC's *Saturday Night Live*, which included mostly the music performances, MTV's *U.S. Top Twenty Countdown*, and *Club MTV* for dance music fans.

Because of the language barriers we focused on music, not talk. It would be stretching the truth to describe our programming as intellectually challenging. In fact *Newsweek* once reported, "For every eco-spot or factoid, there is a deluge of programming as intellectually nutritious as microwave popcorn."

That was fine. We weren't trying to challenge or teach our audience; we wanted to entertain them. For example, we created a European version of the popular MTV USA quiz-show parody, *Remote Control*, on which contestants answered trivia questions about pop culture, picking from categories like "Dead, Alive, or Indian Food?" *Remote Control* was MTV's first long-form show and cost $17,000 per episode, a large sum at that time. The first show we introduced in Europe, *Buzz*, had a magazine format that included segments like "Fashion," "Lust," and "Sex," and featured fascinating factoids like what Barbie's measurements would be if she were life-sized (39-23-33) and the number of years a Zimbabwean could serve in prison for ridiculing local politicians (not longer than one year and a $20,000 fine).

We used what little market research capability we had to determine what our consumers wanted to see and hear, and then we gave it to them. And what they wanted to see were music videos and more music videos. In 1989, about 95 percent of our programming was music videos. Generally, we played more than 250 videos every day. While music had always been an important part of my life, I lacked the in-depth knowledge that I thought I needed. Tom Freston introduced me to a radio music programmer, Jeff Pollack, who served as my expert music advisor, and stayed with MTV for two decades. Our most popular videos were replayed as often as 8 to 10 times a day in what was called *heavy rotation*. Selecting those videos was a very competitive process. In less than a decade the music video world had exploded. From a trickle of filmed performances it had become a flood of expensively produced, highly creative short films. Careers were invested in those videos. Each week we would receive as many as 70 new videos from the record companies that were desperate to get them played on MTV. In addition to those official submissions from the labels, we also received inexpensively shot videos in the mail. Wherever I went, people handed me videos and CDs. Once I was on a British Air flight and a flight attendant told me that the captain "needed" to speak with me. That was unusual. I was escorted into the cockpit. I wondered what this was all about—until the captain told me that his son was in a band, then handed me a CD and asked for advice. On another occasion, I was in Cuba and someone handed me a video—abd Cuba didn't even have MTV! That experience was common for everyone who worked at MTV. Even the people who cleaned the office at night would submit videos that friends of friends had asked them to submit. At times it seemed like everyone in the world had a son or a nephew whose band had produced a video. From all those submissions we would select as few as seven of them to add to our weekly playlist.

Having their videos selected for our playlist was vital to the record companies. There was a direct relationship between the number of plays and album sales. Statistically, the sales of records played in heavy rotation increased by as much as 20 percent. For a new band, having their video played on MTV could make the difference between success and obscurity. We were well aware of our power so we took that selection process very seriously. Videos were the foundation of our programming. We would have two production meetings each week, the first one to pick the new videos, the second to determine the rotation, meaning how often they would get played. We based our choices on several factors, including the Top charts, record sales, and radio play, but eventually it came down to personal tastes.

The first rule of any business is to listen carefully to your customers and then give them what they tell you they want. But we had only limited feedback and to succeed we needed to attract a large audience with a variety of tastes. Our playlist meetings lasted for hours and they were always combative. The people in our talent and music programming department were knowledgeable and passionate about music, they were out at clubs listening to new bands almost every night, and they had strong opinions about what we should be playing. Those meetings often got very emotional; there was a lot of screaming and yelling and even some tears as people fought for their choices. These meetings got very personal at times. There rarely was a unanimous decision. Getting a video you liked played in a heavy rotation was considered a great victory.

Everybody wanted to discover a band popular in one country and introduce it to the rest of Europe. Brian Diamond, who ran Talent Relations and Programming, told them, "The only way we can get people to pay attention to new music is to give the masses the music they like to hear and then if we sneak in something new they'll give it a test drive. A lot of people in Europe buy five albums a year and go to half a dozen concerts. They'll go to see Roxette or Genesis or Simply Red, so we have to play that music. But if we do play them, we can have some fun with the rest of the playlist and get some new stuff in and maybe those people will pay attention to them."

At the beginning I often attended those meetings. I intended my presence to be the voice of reason, a subtle reminder that we were running a business. While admittedly I probably knew less about music than anyone in the room, I knew what I liked and at times I'd raise my hand and voice my opinion. It did not surprise me that videos I said I liked sometimes ended up in heavy rotation. But after attending half a dozen of these meetings I realized I was making a huge mistake. I was much older than our demographic and my musical tastes were very different. I was skewing the choices older. I was doing precisely what I'd promised myself I wouldn't do: I'd hired people to do a job because I believed they could do that job and I found myself telling them how to do it. So I pulled myself out of those meetings and never went back. As much as I enjoyed being part of that process, I had to remind myself that I was a manager, and I had to delegate decision-making authority to those people I trusted.

But I have never stopped watching new videos and silently picking my personal favorites. The hold that the videos had on me when I first watched them in my Santa Monica apartment never dissipated. I appreciated the effort that went into each one of them. I admired the creativity and I looked forward to seeing the new videos from cutting-edge artists. It's not surprising that I've often been asked to list my favorite videos and I usually avoid doing it. But, after all of these years, after watching thousands of videos, my top 10—in any order—are: A-ha's "Take on Me," R.E.M.'s "Losing My Religion," Fatboy Slim's "Weapon of Choice," Michael Jackson's "Black or White," Madonna's "Like a Prayer," Beyoncé's "Single Ladies," U2's "One," Frankie Goes to Hollywood's "Two Tribes," Lady Gaga's "Bad Romance," and Peter Gabriel's "Sledgehammer." But how could you have a top ten without Dire Straits' "Money for Nothing" and Aqua's "Barbie Girl"? But this list is subject to change, as I still watch and enjoy the videos.

A problem I had to deal with were requests from the friends I'd made in the music industry to intervene for their artists. Some of these executives were quite upset that 24-year-old "kids" with little experience were making decisions that affected careers. These executives didn't think it was fair that they would put time and money into breaking an artist and have someone that young determine whether they succeeded. I didn't pay too much attention to them. When I was 24 years old I was commanding a nuclear missile base, so I had no doubt a 24-year-old could select music, plan an event, or sell advertising. On occasion these executives put me in a difficult position by asking me to promote a particular artist or song. On rare occasions, for the sake of our business and artist relationships, I would very carefully add a video to our playlist.

One of the issues that MTV domestic had faced in the mid-1980s was the accusation that it would not play true black music, the music being played in the streets. Lionel Ritchie's music got played, Michael Jackson got played, but they were considered mainstream musicians singing pop and ballads rather than black music. Rap was rarely played. The implication was that this was a racial decision. But by the time I got to London MTV domestic was playing all types of music.

Internationally that issue was never raised. One of the questions asked often, both before and after I got there, was how did MTV Europe intend to show that it was not simply the European extension of American MTV? So Europe was compelled to think of ways we could differentiate our channel from MTV domestic. At one of the early meetings of our playlist group the suggestion was made that we do an entire program about rap, which was considered the real black music. By then rap videos were being played domestically and internationally, but no one had done an entire program featuring rap. We created the show *Yo! MTV Raps* in 1989. The problem we had to solve was that few rap videos were being produced. The labels wouldn't spend the money to make them. *Yo!* changed the climate for rap, introducing it to a lot of Europeans who hadn't previously been exposed to it. Certainly MTV Europe wasn't solely responsible for the explosion of hardcore rap, but it did play a significant role in making it happen.

After those first few weeks I got involved in playlist selections only when there was a question about the content. We had guidelines that we fought to uphold. Artists were always trying to push the envelope; some bands were willing to do almost anything to attract attention. We walked a tightrope. Our head of Standards and Practices was a woman named

Rosemary Stocks. She looked more like a conservative librarian than the typical MTV employee, which is what I wanted. Rosemary would review every video. There were disagreements about what was appropriate, but fewer than most people would anticipate.

We didn't want to censor creativity, but we were very sensitive to portrayals of violence, sexism, and racism. Violence was simple; we wouldn't show any videos with guns or knives. But setting guidelines about sex was more complicated. We had to be realistic: Sex sold music. Sex was the subject of countless songs and the undertone of a lot of videos. A lot of rap was very sexually oriented. Europe generally has a more sophisticated attitude about sex than the United States, so we permitted sexual suggestion. Although we didn't permit graphic sex, nudity, or overt sexism, many videos included beautiful, sexy, provocatively dressed women and macho men. It was a wavy line. I was very concerned about this and would often discuss it at great length with Judy McGrath, who was heading MTV in the United States, and Judy was equally troubled by it. There was no simple answer to this, but at Judy's suggestion, when it was possible we emphasized female empowerment. We went through several different phases. Sometimes we would compromise by running a sexy video—but only on late-night shows, after 10 P.M. For example, Madonna's *Justify My Love* video was pretty sexually explicit. We debated whether to run it and finally decided to show it only at night. There were times when the decisions made by our programmers made me a little uncomfortable, but I reminded myself that I was not our audience.

The record companies often produced two videos for the same song, one considerably less risqué than the other. If we turned down the first submission for being too violent or sexy, they would submit the second one. Racism was rarely a problem.

Today those standards seem archaic. In 1989, Cher did a memorable video for a song entitled *If I Could Turn Back Time* in which she was dancing on a battleship, wearing a skimpy, revealing black bodysuit—straddling a huge cannon. Although it was about as subtle as a hammer, at that time it was considered borderline acceptable. We ran it only on our late-night programs. In 2010, Cher appeared on our *Video Music Awards* wearing precisely the same outfit—and until she told the story nobody even commented on her see-through costume. Based on current standards, it was practically demure!

The only other aspect of the video selection process I tried to influence was the inclusion of as much European music as possible. At every opportunity we emphasized that we were not an American MTV clone, and that we did not intend to import more American culture to Europe. Unfortunately, the majority of high-quality music videos were being produced in the United States and the U.K. by U.S. and British artists. We tried to encourage video production in Europe. If the music was good, even if the video quality was not, we tried to find a way to play it. The one thing we were looking for were videos that had a strong lyrical or musical hook so that even if people didn't understand the words, they could sing or repeat them. In those early years Anglo-American music dominated our playlist. Our viewers demanded mainstream artists like Madonna, Prince, and M.C. Hammer and we gave it to them.

But at every opportunity we supported European artists. We wanted the 16-year-old in Belgrade to hear the most popular bands in Scandinavia. When we were launched in 1989, our objective was to introduce a diversity of music to young Europeans. Initially, at least, it wasn't possible. Those videos didn't exist. To fill that gap, at times we would film local bands or do a special from a city; in 1990, for example, we did a program from Prague called *Forty Bands Banned for Forty Years*. Outside of the U.K. there wasn't a strong music video industry in much of Europe. Our basic guideline was that we wouldn't run a video unless the record was released in a majority of European countries. It was estimated that only about 10 percent of the records produced in Europe were released in more than one or at most two countries, which meant we had a limited number of videos from which to choose. My rule was that if the music was good we would run an average video, but if the music was bad we wouldn't run it even if the video was great.

I knew our video selection process was fair because we received complaints about it from a wide variety of sources. For example, the French government continually complained that we didn't play enough French music. We played as much as we could; for example, we were playing Algerian Khaled's video "Didi" even before it made France's Top 50, we played Mano Negra, but obviously we didn't play enough French music to satisfy them. Germans complained that we didn't play enough German music. We had a large German audience and I wanted to play German music, but basically there was no German music industry. Because of the long-time American military presence in that country, the German music scene was dominated by American artists. Every radio in Germany played either American or Schlager music, which was essentially pop ballads. We worked very hard to encourage the German music industry, which initially took the form of techno-bands like Kraftwerk pop singers like Falco and the eurodance band Snap! We played as much of it as we could. MTV had the unique capability of introducing music to different cultures and I was very proud of the fact that we successfully brought a diversity of music to the world. We gave European exposure to groups like Sweden's Roxette and the Creeps and Ace of Base, Denmark's Lois Lane, and the electronic band Enigma from Romania. Our Song of the Year in 1994 was "7 Seconds" by Senegalese Youssou N'Dour and Swedish rapper Neneh Cherry. I remember sitting in the largest disco in Seoul, South Korea, listening as German techno blasted through the sound system—and thinking proudly, *we helped make this possible*. When the independent labels complained that we didn't give their artists exposure, we created an entire show, *120 Minutes*, and played two solid hours of independent-label music.

We had the power to create hits, to change lives, and some of the independent record promoters would do just about anything to break an act, to get their video played. We always had to be careful about our selection process and playlist. The long list of scandals that have plagued the music industry dates back at least to the 1950s, when record companies would *pay* popular disc jockeys to play their records. I've seen payola on the fringes of our business; for example, there were Russian music channels that blatantly accepted payment for running videos. I also believe that around the world some of our smaller competitors have accepted a payment for playing videos. It happens. But we've done everything possible to prevent that from happening at our channels. We talked about it; we had strict controls in place; we watched carefully for it. Have we prevented it from happening 100 percent of the time? It's impossible to say that. But, while I wouldn't doubt it has happened, we've never had evidence that someone at one of our channels had accepted something of value in return for adding a video to our playlist. I do know that if it had happened, we would have stopped it instantly.

■ ■ ■

Our on-air representatives, our wallpaper, our image-makers were our VJs. These were our hosts, the public face of our brand. We wanted to create a strong emotional bond between MTV Europe and our viewers, and we selected our VJs with that in mind. I was asked once how we selected them. I explained very seriously that we conducted a wide search for those people who best reflected the diversity of our viewers, who understood music, and who had a pleasant personality. I went on for a while and finally concluded, "And then we hire the most attractive people we can."

Contrary to what was generally believed, that wasn't true at all. Our objective in selecting VJs was to find the type of people our viewers would want to hang out with. For that reason, we selected them carefully to *mirror our audience*. Diversity was extremely important in our staff; they came from different countries, they were different nationalities and religions, they liked different types of music, and they had worked in both high-profile and quite normal jobs; we covered as much territory with our VJs as possible. Whoever our viewer was, we wanted him or her to have at least one VJ with whom to identify. I wanted some VJs to be funny, some VJs to be stunning, some VJs to have an encyclopedic knowledge of music—and all of them to be accessible. We found our VJs by advertising for "presenters" in newspapers all over Europe, holding auditions, listening to recommendations, and even looking at the hundreds of unsolicited tapes that arrived at the office. We even held open competitions for VJs and had literally thousands of entrants show up or submit entries. VJs would come to us by all different routes. We relied on the young members of our team to make the judgments because, in essence, they were our audience.

And while we did want nice-looking on-air talent (who wouldn't want attractive people representing their business?) it was more important that our viewers would feel comfortable with them. The German magazine *Stern* accurately described our VJs: "They have to be one thing, a perfect image of their viewers. Young and fashionable and equipped with a dose of self-consciousness which no one is going to break. They've got to be like a suburban beauty, not a 'Miss World'; a funny clown among friends, not a dream man. They have to move in front of the camera as if they were talking to friends at a party."

Many people thought that being a VJ on MTV was the best job in the world. That wasn't true; the best job in the world was conducting the talent search for the VJs. In addition to looking good on camera, our VJs were bright, alert, aware, actively involved people, almost always with a good sense of humor. We had our choice of presenters and these were the people who emerged.

Our first major star was 30-year-old Ray Cokes. He was instantly likeable, with a ready-smile and a self-deprecating attitude. He began hosting *Ray's Request*, a call-in show, which featured segments like "The Bingo Wall of Death" and "Clean Our Souls." There was nothing physically magnetic to set him apart, but when his girlfriend left him he told the whole story on the air—and then he started crying. That was probably the most heartfelt thing most of our viewers had ever seen on television, and so many of them could relate to him. They had experienced the pain of breaking up with a girlfriend or boyfriend. Ray was deluged with a flood of letters, many of them from women who wanted to comfort him. Almost instantly it turned him into a cult figure throughout Europe.

Ray hosted our first hit show, *MTV's Most Wanted*. It was a nightly live show from 8 to 10 P.M. and our staff would hang out at the office after work to watch it. It was like a party every night, and it would be very difficult to overestimate what it did to build our corporate spirit. In included live performances, music videos, viewer phone calls, and silly contests, but mostly it was just Ray Cokes wandering around the entire building being brilliantly creative. It was impossible to know what to expect, because Ray ad-libbed the show, not just breaking through the fourth wall, but smashing it into pieces. Ray Cokes created some of the most inspired breakthrough television I've ever seen. I feel certain he is the only male host to wear a bra, for example. His regular cast included the technical staff, in particular, "Rob the Cameraman," who would follow him wherever he went. The camera was Ray's prop; when he asked Rob a question the camera would bob up and down if the answer was yes and move horizontally for no. Ray Cokes made MTV Europe "must-see TV." The show became a huge cult hit and helped unite Europe. Like the kids around the water fountain in my school discussing *Have Gun—Will Travel*, Europe was talking about whatever Ray Cokes did the night before.

Ray Cokes eventually married a girl from the media department. I loved him, but after he became famous he started making all kinds of demands from his salary to perks. He wasn't quite as difficult as Russell Brand, though. Russell Brand became a VJ in 2000, and predictably, now, he was as outrageous as anyone we ever put on the air. He was fired when he came to work the day after the attack of September 11 dressed as Osama bin Laden.

When I saw him in late 2010 on the Red Carpet at the VMAs in Madrid with his wife, Katy Perry, I reminded him that he had been an MTV VJ; and in return he reminded me that he had been fired! To which I replied, "And that's the best thing that ever happened to you. Or you'd still be working twelve-hour days in our studio."

Our VJs came from all over Europe. When we got distribution in Germany I knew it was imperative that we have a German VJ on the air, so we advertised in a music magazine which was how we found Kristiane Backer, a radio reporter and producer in Hamburg. Kristiane was a VJ for seven years and became very popular. After dating Pakistan's most famous cricket player for two years, she very publicly converted to Islam. Carolyn Lilipaly was Dutch-Indonesian. Marcel Vanthilt was from Belgium. Pip Dann was a New Zealander. Tim Kash was a Brit who eventually became a very successful VJ on American MTV. Eden was an Israeli who has since become a major star in that country. Davina McCall, who presented on Cokes' *MTV's Most Wanted*, eventually became one of the U.K.'s most popular personalities and has been the host of the highly rated *Big Brother* since its inception. Cat Deeley started in the U.K. and became a popular TV host in the United States. Our first Italian was a singer-rapper named Jovanni who on occasion would play his own music and after leaving MTV became a major star, and another Italian VJ, Enrico Silvestrin, has become a major movie star.

Our VJs had a great variety of backgrounds. Ray Cokes had been trained as a cook before becoming a presenter. Steve Blame, who read the pop news, had earned degrees in math and science. Irishman Paul King, who became known for what was described as his "cockatoo haircut," was a rock star, the lead singer of a band that had two albums go gold. Marijne van der Vlugy was a Dutch model and singer. Carolyn Lilipaly had studied law and worked in media and public relations. Italian presenter Camila Raznovich was a ballerina.

In addition to hosting shows in the studio our VJs reported from all over the world. They were on location constantly. I brought them to launches all over Europe. We tried to broadcast from as many countries as possible; the MTV Europe VJ broadcasting from your city was a big deal. We wanted our viewers to feel like they were part of the home team, which meant broadcasting from places within their experience. We went to the hottest clubs in every major European city; we covered concerts across the continent and music and entertainment news from each nation. During Michael Jackson's second solo tour through Europe, we were given exclusive access and our VJ Sonya Saul reported from the tour on a show we called *Michael Jackson's Dangerous Diaries*—which was sponsored by Pepsi. James Hyman went from a club in Detroit to Iceland, where he recorded a festival at which Bjork performed. As he reported, the entire village spent the winter drunk, because all they could do in the dark and the freezing cold was drink, race around on snowmobiles, and have sex. James also was warned to be wary of the bears and reported that there was a big ax by the public phones just in case a bear wanted to use the phone while someone else was using it.

Initially, we broadcast from a studio we licensed several blocks away from our office on Mandela Street. It was the right space for us when we started because it enabled us to keep our expenses low and accurately reflected our cutting-edge culture. But having the studio blocks away from our office was inconvenient. For example, when the news show needed a photograph of an artist from our files, somebody literally had to run it to the studio. But by 1992, we were firmly established and had outgrown that building. We moved into a beautiful facility bordering Regents Canal in Camden known as the Breakfast Television Centre.

Years earlier, this building had been a brewery, and then a car showroom, but it had been transformed into the headquarters of *TV-am*, which was basically the British version of the *Today Show*. It was a wonderfully modern building that featured several large plastic egg-cups on the roof. *TV-am* had been very successful; among its hosts and stockholders was David Frost, whose office I inherited. But in 1990, during a government review of commercial TV properties, it had lost its broadcasting franchise. Nobody really understood the reasons for that—it was a popular show—but it enabled our CFO Phillip McDaniel to negotiate a terrific deal for us. To close that deal I had a very long dinner one evening with *TV-am*'s managing director, the legendary U.K. TV figure Bruce Gyngell. We negotiated into the early morning hours.

Bruce told me he actually had received a higher offer for the facility from a religious broadcaster, but "I want to sell it to you because you're MTV." We purchased the building and all the broadcasting equipment, including three fully equipped studios, for £3.2 million. A couple of years later it was valued at £20 million. To me, moving into this building was a coming of age. It meant we had hit the big time.

We did all of our taping and live broadcasts in that building, so there were always musicians walking around the halls waiting to perform or promote a record, or simply to be interviewed. There was no way of predicting whom you might meet when the elevator doors opened. Bono, Seal, Green Day, Garth Brooks, Prince, or the Foo Fighters might walk out, or it might just as likely be an unknown new punk band. The Spice Girls used to hang out there, waiting for their break. They appeared on one of our afternoon shows but nobody had any interest in them. Of course, this was before they became *the* Spice Girls. They were five attractive young women of questionable talent who sang bubble-gum music and did a lot of jumping up and down—and eventually became the biggest act in Europe.

Working in that building made everyone feel like they were at the epicenter of the entire music world. Our offices were upstairs, but our technical facilities were downstairs in what we referred to affectionately as "the engine room." I was so proud of our offices that I was constantly giving tours to anyone who came in—even if they didn't want to go. We kept more than 10,000 music videos in our library. When we wanted to broadcast a video, we would put it in what was called a beta cart and transmit it by wire to east London, where it was uplinked to the Astra satellite. The satellite then sent our signal back down to earth stations (those big receiving dishes) around Europe.

By the time we moved into this building we were firmly established. By the end of our third year we were breaking even. This was way ahead of our business plan, an amazing accomplishment. We'd proved that a pan-European channel could work. We were adding distribution every week. At first I met with our staff each Friday afternoon to tell them how many homes we'd added that week, but we were growing too fast to keep up with those weekly meetings. We had just about doubled our advertising revenue each year and advertisers were approaching us with package requests. We had become an influential part of European culture, so much so that a popular magazine wrote, "If it hasn't happened on MTV, forget it." And we certainly had bonded with our audience. Some of the hundreds of letters and phone calls we received each week were amazing. We would receive requests from someone in a country at war, like Serbia, asking, "I love your show. My house is being bombed but if you could play Bon Jovi for me I'd be happy." It was surreal. A girl from Budapest wrote touchingly, "You are the only beautiful thing that I have."

Absolutely anything to do with MTV Europe was incredibly hot. If one of our employees was wearing an MTV-branded baseball cap or T-shirt or carrying an MTV umbrella or a record bag or just about anything with our logo on it, people noticed them and often would initiate a conversation. They just wanted some kind of personal connection with our channel. One of our producers was walking down Camden Street wearing an MTV T-shirt when someone tapped him on the shoulder and said bluntly, "I want that T-shirt."

The producer was a bit shocked. "I'm sorry," he responded, "it's mine."

It wasn't a mugging. The person continued, "No, no, I'll buy it. I'll give you 20 pounds for it." When the producer explained that he wasn't about to walk down the street without a T-shirt the man said, "Okay, I'll give you *my* T-shirt." Right on the street they made that deal.

I realized we had made it one Sunday morning late in 1992. I was reading the *Sunday Times of London*'s annual review of "What's In and What's Out." There has always been a strong backlash against anything American in Europe, so what was *out* was "Anything American." But on the same page, in the opposite column, I saw my dream had come true. What was *in* was "MTV Europe."

I sat there, sipped my coffee, and smiled.

Chapter Four

Mo' Money Mo' Problems

I couldn't go to bed without watching Beavis and Butthead. *They have a certain semantic system that can be grasped very quickly . . . heh, heh!*

—Russian English teacher Vladimir Kurilov

There was a joke I told often in the office: "The definition of a *good boss* is a person with great integrity who pays you well and provides the support you need, offers advice at the proper times and in a positive manner, and protects your back and gives you the credit that you earn. But the best attribute is being 3,000 miles away!" By that definition, I had the perfect boss. CEO Tom Freston was a terrific person to work for—and he was also a great ocean and a five-hour time difference away. MTV Networks management was generally supportive of everything we did, and in most ways, as long as we continued to deliver positive results we were permitted to maintain our independence. Besides, we were moving forward so fast that by the time a situation could be analyzed and a decision made in New York, we were already in the middle of the next crisis.

For me, that management freedom was only one of the many advantages to living in London while our corporate headquarters was in New York. Many U.S. executives can successfully manage an international operation from the States; but I couldn't, especially when we were in the formative stage. To build an international business, I felt I had to be in an international environment. Even though I intended to return to the United States eventually, I believed it was imperative to have a global perspective. I did a monumental amount of traveling—in one month, for example, I visited 20 different countries; in another three-month period I spent fewer than 10 days at home—and living in Europe cut down greatly on that travel time.

Even while I was on a trip I was busy planning the next trip. When asked how I decided which countries to visit, I responded that I went where the most important opportunity existed, but truthfully more often I went where problems had to be solved. I spent a tremendous amount of time in Italy and China. In Italy we almost lost our distribution, which would have been devastating, and China, as it has throughout history, offered tremendous opportunity. I used to joke that there were times I went to China more often than to my office in the U.K.—and that office was only 10 minutes away.

I have always believed it is important to cover as much of the world as possible, especially in a far-flung organization like MTV Networks, because the farther flung an office is, the less attention it will get. Australia, for example, didn't get priority because it was our most remote and one of our smallest operations. But giving attention to distant and sometimes small operations was important in building morale; in addition to demonstrating our commitment to our internal team, these trips gave me an opportunity to forge personal relationships and provided a tremendous reservoir of information that would often prove important later on. These trips enabled me to learn about the market. I was able to experience the culture rather than learning about it through a PowerPoint presentation. I got to meet our audience and see firsthand those things that made a difference to them.

I made many trips whose purpose wasn't immediately apparent. Very early on I visited the Spanish resort island of Ibiza. Dance music was gaining in popularity and Ibiza was the dance capital of Europe. For a time it was *the* place to be in Europe. I went there with Brian Diamond, who was in charge of music programming and artist relations. As a result, we did many shows from Ibiza that tapped into the unique culture of Europe's dance scene.

And finally, whenever possible, I tried to attend important music industry events, for example, the brilliant Claude Nobs' prestigious

Montreaux Jazz Festival. I tried to be at as many channel launches, awards, and honors shows as possible. For many channels, awards and honors shows are arguably the most important programming events of the year, as well as tremendous business opportunities, so years later, when we would broadcast as many as 35 awards and honors shows a year, I would go to as many as I could fit into my schedule.

Choosing where to live when running an international business obviously is both a personal and corporate decision and the reality is that for an executive there is no right or wrong answer. Tom Freston wanted me to stay in London, which proved to be a good fit for me. In 1989, I had signed a three-year contract and I had expected to return to New York at the end of that period to continue building my career. Business textbooks suggest that's about the proper amount of time to spend away from corporate headquarters. I stayed longer, *way*, longer, because MTV's international business continued to expand and being there made managing Europe and Asia much easier for me. With time changes, trying to manage an Asian business from New York can be very difficult. Being five hours ahead of headquarters proved to be an advantage for me. I had worked in LA, which is three hours behind New York, and in London, which is five hours ahead—and I much preferred being hours ahead because it provided a time cushion to work out a solution or think through my approach to a challenge before speaking with people in New York.

But there was a cost to my career. By spending only a limited amount of time at our headquarters, I missed being part of the social and political infrastructure. Overall, it has been a positive experience. I have no regrets. What is unusual is that in addition to building a career in Europe, I also built my whole life there. Going back to the military and my experience at HBO, I've always felt more comfortable in the field-command position. That's where the action is.

And while certainly I love the United States, rather than thinking about what I was missing, I focused completely on what I was doing. In fact, when I was running the NATO missile bases I had spent four years in Italy and without making a single trip back to America. By the time I settled in England I had been married and divorced, and my only meaningful connections to the United States were my beach volleyball games, my mother, and my extended family, especially my sister Peggy, her husband Bart, and their daughter Lauren. As I was single in the early 1990s, my mother would occasionally be my companion on business trips. Who could ever turn down a guy traveling with his mother?

London was my base, but I was constantly in communication with Tom in New York. A command-and-control structure can work efficiently only with frequent communication. From my first days in Europe, Tom and I spoke regularly for extended periods of time. We always had at least a one-hour-long phone conversation per week, during which I would download the world to him in a methodical way. It's easy to get distracted during these conversations, so I always had a firm agenda which I drove through country-by-country. I would prepare for these conversations by making extensive notes and go through business developments country by country. I tried to be concise and I set priorities, but to be certain he knew everything, sometimes these conversations were exhausting.

In addition to my conversations with Tom, I was also in touch with others in New York as well as my managers throughout the world. As communications technology improved, we adapted to it and used it beneficially, but the added bells and whistles didn't change the basic structure of our communications. Eventually, Viacom used videoconferencing for our weekly strategy sessions, in which I would participate with our other division heads unless I was traveling.

A key factor in those conversations was absolute honesty. I had learned in the military that if you exaggerate or sugarcoat facts you may lose lives, and perhaps lose a battle and maybe even the war. In business, if I didn't bring to light small problems, they had the potential of growing into serious challenges.

In fact, it didn't matter that much where I lived; for several years I lived pretty much in the office or on an airplane. I used to tell people that the most expensive apartments in New York boast of having great views and 24-hour service. So I had no complaints about spending so much time on an airplane because I had the greatest view in the world and 24-hour service.

■■■

Building MTV International was more than a full-time job—it was a total commitment. My first year there I was often in the office until midnight. It was fortunate I didn't have a family at that time; that would have made my business life very difficult, if not impossible. I certainly could not have given the time that was needed to both a family and my company. None of this is meant to be a complaint. I knew that I had the best job in the world, even better than searching Europe for VJs, and I loved every minute of it—seven days a week, week after week, month after month.

I did have a reasonable social life. I had sufficient time to have several semi-meaningful relationships, but I didn't have the time that really is necessary to make them work. I was married to my job. Once, I remember, I had been dating a Frenchwoman and I had decided it was time to end it. Being what is known in social circles as a "coward," I asked her to meet me for lunch at the Café Marley at the Louvre, one of Paris's most glamorous restaurants. It was a very public place. My plan was to have a civilized conversation with her and explain that I just didn't have the time to provide what she needed. I had it all planned; I'd spoken to several world leaders by this time, I'd negotiated contracts with very tough businessmen—certainly I could find the words to end this relationship. Unfortunately, as we sat down I glanced across the restaurant and recognized Bon Jovi lead guitarist Richie Sambora. A few minutes later, as I waited for the right moment to begin my speech, a waiter delivered a bottle of champagne and a note from Richie, which read something like, "You two look so lovely together I couldn't resist sending something to make your lunch even more romantic! Here's to your happiness!"

There was nothing I could say with that bottle sitting on our table.

I also did *not* date Naomi Campbell. I remember how flattered I was when I read about the details of our relationship in the tabloids, because otherwise I wouldn't have known about them. I suppose celebrities get used to this public attention, but there is something very strange about reading details of your life that never happened. I did know Naomi Campbell. She was a guest at the first *Europe Music Awards*, an incredible show held in 1994 to celebrate the reunification of East and West Germany. For this concert we constructed the largest outdoor tent ever built, and set it up in front of the Brandenburg Gate. The highlight of this concert was George Michael singing "Freedom," an emotional moment that anyone who was there will never forget, as several supermodels rose from the stage. Several months before the concert I had flown to Berlin for a press conference to publicize the event. I'd brought with me INXS' lead singer Michael Hutchence and one of those supermodels, Naomi Campbell, because few members of the media would have come to a press conference to hear Bill Roedy, but for a rock star and a supermodel, the room was absolutely jammed. While I was aware of the stories about her volatile behavior, with us she was always gracious and always professional. I actually did get to know her a little bit, but the tabloids reported that she was crazy about me and I had become the stabilizing force in her life. One headline read that she intended to marry "Mr. MTV." Several anonymous people were quoted as saying that since we had become an item she was a different person and therefore I had to be responsible.

I had never been an item before. I had never expected to be an item. But I didn't exactly rush out eagerly to issue a denial, either. I didn't feel a compelling need to deny it to anyone—until it became absolutely necessary. The newspapers wrote that Naomi and I had spent the night of the EMAs together. It never happened.

Actually, by that time I had met Alex Lindemann, the woman who was to become my wife. Because she worked for MTV, we were trying to keep our connection secret. Fortunately, Alex was working in Berlin at the event, so she knew the truth. And she was the only person I cared about knowing the truth.

Even though I encouraged a social culture at MTV, I didn't want anyone to know that I was dating an employee. While I encouraged relationships among our staff, I would never tolerate it for myself. I was mortified by the situation. I was fully aware of the tensions this situation could create in the office. I felt it was completely inappropriate for the boss to date an employee—until I met Alex. Although this took place slightly before sexual harassment had become a major workplace issue, I was well aware of the potential ramifications. One of the first things Alex and I did when it became clear that this was a serious relationship was plan an exit strategy for her. We both quickly realized it was necessary. Within several months our relationship had become public and she was no longer working at MTV.

Every company has to set its own policies regarding social interaction among its employees, but I made my decisions based on the youthful makeup of our staff and the type of office culture I wanted to create. Work hard, party hard. But work hard was always first. So for our company this policy made sense and it helped create a desirable working atmosphere.

But still, I didn't want anybody to know about me.

Alex was a German college graduate who worked originally as a sales assistant in our Munich office. I often admit that she is infinitely smarter than I; her fluency in several languages proves my point. When we needed someone in London who spoke German to work in our sales division with our German-based pan-European clients, she moved to England—but only for one year, she insisted. Our paths would cross naturally and I finally accepted the fact that I was strongly attracted to her. From the very beginning, I was amazingly comfortable with her. We fit together perfectly. But I didn't want to complicate her life, so I didn't pursue it. We got to know each other a little better at a four-day sales retreat at Club Med in Portugal. *Somehow*, we ended up sitting next to each other at dinner on four consecutive nights. By that time she had been offered a job by one of our clients, and was considering accepting it. So she had no hesitation about telling me everything about the office that needed improvement. She unloaded it all on me: There was only one copy machine for three departments, the people who scheduled our commercials were never available, the hours were too long, and there weren't enough people, and . . . she continued, "I just think it would be important for you to take this onboard because it would make a really big difference to us if somebody would address these issues, and since you're in charge. . . . "

As I listened intently to this list of everything that needed improvement in the office I realized I was smitten. The next morning I got on an airplane and flew to Asia.

The next time we had a few moments alone was in my office several weeks later. We had a friendly, casual conversation, without ever mentioning what was really on our minds. I had commanded nuclear missile bases and I was running a rapidly growing international business. I don't know why I was so nervous. We made dinner plans for the following week. She lived in Notting Hill. At that time, Notting Hill was not a safe neighborhood; in fact the night I went to pick her up there had been a murder on the block and the street had been cordoned off. I had to slip under the police crime-scene tape to get to her apartment.

After spending seven years together, we married in 2000 on a beach in Miami. Alex wore a white sari and I wore my formal sneakers, of course.

Our first child was born only days after the assassination of Israeli Prime Minister Yitzhak Rabin, whom I admired. As we watched his funeral world leaders lauded his political accomplishments, but then his granddaughter, Noa, spoke of him with love as her grandfather. We were so moved by her grace and her remarks that we named our daughter Noa. Years later, the two Noas met in Israel.

Liam, our second child, is my namesake. It's the Irish of William. His middle name is Lawless, which Alex worried would prevent him from ever pursuing a legal career, but it is the name of Bono's driver, with whom I'd bonded. Like his sister, Liam was born in London.

Rocky was born in the United States, four days after the attacks of 9/11. We wanted to give him a solid American name. Alex couldn't imagine Rocky Roedy, so officially we named him Max Rockford Roedy, but it's always been Rocky.

It was Alex's turn to name our fourth child. She settled on the name River. My sister, with whom Alex is close, talked her out of it, suggesting instead, Tiger. And so she became Tiger River Roedy.

Through the years, we've had guests from almost every part of the world in our home, and somehow, wherever they're from, Alex and our children make them feel welcome.

Being successful in a business that requires a massive amount of travel requires an independent, supporting, and understanding spouse. Having worked at MTV, Alex knew what that entailed and together we have made a very strong team. She has always referred to our marriage as an "army marriage," because I always seem to be going somewhere while she keeps our home together. People often ask her how she copes with all the traveling I do, and she responds that this is the way our life together has always been, so it's never been a problem. I have learned through the years that it is possible to live abroad with a family. In addition to my own experience as a member of the Board of Trustees of the American School of London, I have seen numerous families move over. Most of the time they are supported by their company, which provides cost-of-living benefits that make it substantially easier. But when you're an entrepreneur, when you're building a business, it is much more difficult. I'm not sure it's possible to be an entrepreneur living abroad while raising a family. What was vitally important to me was that I had a supportive wife, I was doing what I loved, and I loved what I was doing.

At times Alex has traveled with me. One night, I remember, Alex and I were having dinner in Paris with Viacom President and CEO Philippe

Dauman and his wife Debbie. Philippe is someone for whom I've always had a great deal of respect. He's a very decisive leader and a brilliant negotiator. That night he said to me, "You know, I think Alex is capable of running any division at Viacom."

That was completely unexpected. I was immensely proud of Alex and pleased that Philippe had recognized that in her. But then I began thinking about it—and wondering if he was referring to the international division!

■■■

As much as I might have wanted to cut down on travel it just wasn't possible. Building an international business requires being there, wherever *there* is. The problems associated with each launch were unique. While much of the experience I gained each time proved valuable, I discovered that what worked well in one market often had little application to the next market. The infrastructure and the cast of characters were unique. Italy, for example, was our third major launch. It was particularly important because it is the second largest market in Europe and I wanted to reduce our dependence on Germany. Obviously, when you become too dependent on any single market or customer you lose leverage and become too vulnerable to challenges in one particular country. Italy would provide some balance; the problem was that Italy had no cable infrastructure. The eight national channels were transmitted through an extensive network of 800 small terrestrial stations blanketing the country. In Germany we basically had to make one deal with the government-controlled system, while in Italy we literally had to link together our channel region by region, as if we were stringing a pearl necklace, to carry a block of our programming. We started broadcasting on one channel operating on a UHF frequency. It took us almost five years to put together a patchwork network of local and regional channels that enabled MTV Italy to broadcast 13 hours of programming each day to 11 million households.

But eventually we got one of the eight national frequencies, Telepiù 3. It was truly amazing: There were seven general-interest Italian channels and little-ole'-niche-channel MTV. The good news about having a terrestrial frequency was that all we had to do was flip the switch and we had distribution throughout most of the country. The bad news was that we had only one revenue stream, making us entirely dependent on advertising. When the government reduced the number of national frequencies from eight to six, as the only non-Italian company we were an obvious choice, and it created an extremely serious challenge for us. Losing our Italian distribution meant that once again we would be almost completely reliant on Germany, a situation we were trying to avoid. To overcome this problem I spent most of a year commuting back and forth between Rome and Milan, where Managing Director of MTV Italy Antonio Campo Dall'Orto and I met day after day with lobbyists, government officials, and potential partners. The political situation was so complex that at times I felt like I was peeling an onion, I'd get through one layer only to find another layer directly below it. There was never an easy answer, and without Antonio it would have been impossible. Finally, when it became obvious we were not going to be able to reverse the government's decision, we moved to purchase another national frequency. But in that highly regulated market, in order to do that we had to form a joint venture with an Italian company—Italian Telecom—and relinquish half of our Italian business.

In fact, even before we created our original patchwork network the Italians already were getting their MTV.

Almost from the beginning MTV and MTV Europe were being pirated around the world. Almost anyone with a satellite dish could receive our signal. Beyond that, in places that did not yet have their MTV, independent operators would tape the channel and bring it back to their countries. They would run it in clubs, they would show it in their homes, they would use it at parties. Clubs throughout Eastern Europe would play two- or three-hour loops of our programming over and over. Long before MTV launched in Russia, the man who eventually would become our partner, Boris Zosimov, had come to America and recorded hundreds of hours of MTV in his hotel room. He returned to Moscow with VHS players and those tapes, which he played often. But nowhere was MTV pirated more than in Italy. So many small broadcasters stole our unencrypted signal that it was estimated MTV was available in as many as *six million households*—before it was officially launched there. Clearly, a substantial interest in the channel existed. While we participated in antipiracy efforts and did take legal action against some stations that were rebroadcasting our programming, we didn't push it strongly. There wasn't much we could do to prevent it. And although we couldn't include these viewers in our rate card, along with our programming they were viewing our commercials, which provided an additional benefit to our advertisers. I also believed that if we could build a large following even before MTV was officially launched in Italy, we would be able to make a strong case to terrestrial station operators that, like cable operators, they should pay for MTV. Marc Conneely, our extraordinarily skillful network development manager, made several different types of deals with terrestrial stations. It didn't really matter to us how we generated revenue, as long as we got the revenue. In some countries, like Spain, we did receive payment. In those countries where MTV had a 24-hour terrestrial channel our revenue came from selling commercial time. Where terrestrial stations broadcast a block of MTV programming we often kept that commercial time or shared advertising revenue with the broadcaster, which is known as "barter syndication." As in every other aspect of building this business, the situation on the ground dictated the terms of the deal. But in Italy some terrestrial station owners simply pirated MTV and refused to pay for that carriage and there was nothing that could be done about it.

Without question, the most historically fascinating situation in which I was involved took place in Vilnius, Lithuania, in 1990, while it was still occupied by troops from the Soviet Union. One of the joys of my career is that I have so often been able to entwine my business responsibilities with my personal interest in international diplomacy and world history. I've always been a news junkie; I want to know everything that is going on everywhere in the world all the time. As a child I would never miss the 15-minute nightly TV news broadcast; for me, when it expanded to a half-hour that was absolute bliss. And the now the world around me was changing at warp speed, and I found myself right in the middle of it. Eastern Europe had been liberated, the Berlin Wall fell, and we were witnessing the first cracks in the Soviet Union. For me, the opportunity to visit occupied Lithuania was a perfect example of my business and personal interests coming together. In a strange way, once again I found myself on the front lines—but this time to build a business.

Lithuania was too small to ever be an especially profitable market for us, but it fit neatly into my business philosophy of aggressively going after every possible household to increase distribution. Because of my Cold War background, I was inspired by the courage of this small country trying to break its bond with the Soviet Union. In March 1990, I had been in Russia meeting with government officials to try to increase our distribution when Lithuania became the first Soviet Republic to declare its independence. In response, the Russian government instituted political and economic sanctions, and when that strategy failed to quell the uprising, Soviet black-beret troops seized government and public buildings, including the state-run TV broadcasting center.

Lithuanian President Vytautas Landsbergis courageously defied the Soviet Union. He set up his government offices in a building complex in the suburbs, which was completely surrounded by Russian tanks. He managed to get remote broadcasting trucks into the complex, and from there he began broadcasting a second TV signal to his nation in opposition to the Soviet-controlled government channel. I received an invitation to meet with him. I was already scheduled to return to Moscow for meetings, so I decided to go from there.

I had to come to believe that the U.S. government could have saved a tremendous amount of money by aiming TV signals at the Warsaw Pact nations rather than nuclear missiles. It seemed to me that music could more effectively bring nations together than military force. So I certainly couldn't refuse his invitation. The fact that little Lithuania was standing up to the Soviet Union completely captivated my imagination. The Soviet Union was one of the world's two superpowers. In the past, countries trying to break free of Soviet domination, like Hungary in 1956 and Czechoslovakia in 1968, had been brutally crushed. And yet this small country was taking that risk.

Getting there was difficult; the only airline flying to the capital city of Vilnius was the Russian state airline, Aeroflot, whose planes literally were falling apart. I've taken many unusual flights, but this one was memorable. It was the middle of the Russian winter and there was no heat in the plane. It was completely full; people literally were standing up in the back, the only time I've ever seen standing room on an airplane, and the center aisle was crammed with suitcases. To get into my seat I had to climb over a heavyset woman who had a birdcage on her lap, and when I sat down she opened her jacket to let the dog she was hiding get some air. Even more bizarre, over the airplane's sound system they were playing Neil Diamond's "Sweet Caroline." Remaining on an airplane like that requires an optimistic attitude.

When I arrived in Vilnius I was escorted through several checkpoints to meet President Landsbergis. It was an extremely surreal situation. The buildings were surrounded by Russian tanks, protestors were marching and throwing their Soviet army draft cards and military equipment into huge bonfires, while at the same time people seemed relatively free to walk through the barricades. I didn't try to understand it.

Landsbergis was a hero. He was a former professor of music and an accomplished pianist. I remember he had only two pictures hanging in his office, one of Vaclav Havel, who had led the Czechoslovakian independence movement, and the other of Chopin. He also had a piano in his office. He explained the political situation to me. During our conversation, I mentioned to him my belief that music could be a more powerful weapon than missiles and we began discussing the possibility of bringing MTV Europe to Lithuania. We agreed that he would broadcast the channel from his remote trucks. For Lithuanians, he explained, acquiring MTV would be "a step towards democracy, an irrevocable step toward democracy." It also would bring his country closer to Western Europe.

What happened then was truly astonishing. The Russian general in charge of the Lithuanian occupation pirated our signal and began broadcasting MTV to the entire country over the official state channel. Only a few years earlier the government magazine *Soviet Culture* had denounced MTV as a decadent capitalistic tool using sex and violence to capture the minds of young people, and suddenly MTV was being broadcast by both the government and the government-in-exile-in-the-suburbs. Ironically, this was not the only time Eastern-bloc countries stole our signal. Toward the end of the Soviet Union, our pirated signal was being broadcast in several regions. I surmised this might have been a last-ditch effort to appease young people trapped behind the Iron Curtain. But whatever the reasons, when I found out that the occupying force in Lithuania had pirated our signal our attorneys sent them a very strong cease-and-desist letter. Events were moving so rapidly that we never took any additional legal action; freedom came to Lithuania.

Incredibly, freedom also came to Russia. While I suppose it's advantageous to have a strategic plan that you can follow, I've always been a big believer in taking advantage of opportunistic situations.

That's the "aggressive" aspect of my business philosophy. Taking risks is an inherent part of the growth process, especially in the international marketplace. When you recognize an opportunity you have to seize it. I've had great success simply by moving forward toward my goal, even if the path to get there wasn't particularly clear. Sometimes, at the beginning, all the pieces necessary to reach the end aren't obvious, but I have found that most of the time they reveal themselves along the way. There is no question in my mind that if I had followed a sensible expansion plan when we began, we never would have achieved the level of success that we did. I just wanted to be everywhere, it was my business instinct. I often thought about General Patton, whose army drove through Europe before anyone realized what was happening; Patton actually outran his supply lines. Patton was fast and decisive, which had always appealed to me. I wanted to be in as many countries in the world as possible before people could question that strategy. By the time those questions were asked, we were already there.

Being opportunistic requires the support and trust of management, because there are going to be setbacks and even failures; but if you have a good product to market and good people working with you to do it, the successes will greatly outweigh those failures. While initially Eastern Europe had little impact on our bottom line, I believed it was essential to our long-range success that we be there as early as possible with as large a footprint as we could make.

The Soviet Union had always intrigued me. At West Point I had studied Russian and spoke what I described as "menu and taxi." I wouldn't have dared negotiate in Russian. In fact, throughout my career I've tried to learn bits and pieces of several languages; and in addition to my two years of Russian at the academy and five years of high-school Spanish, at various times I took lessons in French, German, Italian, Mandarin, and Japanese. While my approach when I accepted my job was that it made no sense to master any one language because the world is simply too big, my advice now would be to learn Mandarin or Spanish.

When I was serving in the military, the Soviet Union was our enemy. I read and studied as much as possible about the people of Eastern Europe, and from the moment I joined MTV I looked in that direction. I knew that the Soviet Union had done a reasonably good job keeping out that "decadent" western rock and roll. In fact, in the 1970s and early 1980s it was so difficult to get western records there that someone figured out how to turn X-ray films into playable records. You would be able to see the original body image, so these "records" were known as "ribs." The few black-market records available cost about half a month's salary. When I moved to Europe one of my dreams was to bring MTV to Russia, although I never mentioned it to anyone. It seemed impossible. I certainly didn't overlook the fact that it was a vast and completely untapped market. All we had to do to work that potential goldmine was absolutely everything. Of all the channels and properties we've launched, this certainly was one of the most difficult—with the most satisfying results.

It was impossible to have a realistic business plan when I first went to Moscow in 1989, because there was no existing business structure. It truly was the Wild Wild East, where almost anything was possible. For example, I never would have expected to be wrestling with the deputy mayor of Leningrad on the floor of the Czar's Winter Palace. But while bringing MTV to the Soviet Union might have seemed like Roedy's Impossible Dream, we already were on the air in Hungary and Yugoslavia and people with satellite dishes in Czechoslovakia and Poland were picking up our signal. Why not Russia? I went there for the first time presumably to attend a peace concert. In reality, this was one of the biggest cold calls in history.

Among the people I met there were Jon Bon Jovi and Ozzy Osbourne. Eventually I would visit all the historic sites of Russia and I would stand in Red Square in subzero temperatures watching several hundred people wait patiently in line to get into Lenin's Tomb, but one sight I will never forget is Ozzy Osbourne drugged out in Soviet Russia.

At that time the Soviet government highly restricted meetings between western and Russian businessmen. Almost every aspect of my trip had to be approved by my Russian host, from whom I would meet to where I would stay. Originally, I was assigned to a room in a rundown hotel on the outskirts of Moscow. It was ringed by barbed wire and looked more like a gulag than a hotel. I took one look at it and said "No, thanks." I threatened to leave, so my guide arranged for me to stay in the Ukraine Hotel, a monolithic Stalinist building with all the charm of a concrete wall. I learned very quickly how to prosper in Soviet Moscow: Make certain I brought cigarettes and makeup. While the cigarettes went to government officials, the makeup went to the *babuska*. On each hotel floor there was a woman, usually resembling a fireplug, who had control of everything that happened there. A tube of lipstick would get me as many towels as I wanted; rouge would get me toilet paper. The commonly heard joke was that the towels were as soft as sandpaper and the toilet paper was worse. I ended up bringing my own on subsequent trips.

Eventually I managed to get permission to stay on a large boat docked on the Moscow River. It was modern and well-kept, and it was difficult not to notice that many beautiful Russian women also were staying there. I learned quickly from a Russian minister that this boat was "a honey trap," used by the government to entrap and compromise western businessmen. Welcome to Russia.

The government official assigned as my guide loved American culture and Marlboros and was particularly proud of the fact that he knew every word to "Chattanooga Choo-Choo," which he proved by reciting it incessantly—*every single word*. Ironically, whereas in many countries my military background was of little value (working in the rock-and-roll world I usually kept it off my resume), in Russia it proved very valuable. Many of the people I spent time with loved discussing the Cold War. I spent a lot of late nights talking and arguing about it and toasting it. The Russians love to toast. We consumed massive quantities of vodka. And at every opportunity I would explain why the government should allow MTV into what was then the Soviet Union. "If you really want to open the USSR to Western trade," I told anyone who would listen, "there is not a better signal you can send than allowing MTV in Russia. If you want to show people you're serious about *glasnost* and *perestroika*, this is a good way to do it."

Getting distribution anywhere inside Russia was seemingly impossible. As we did when entering any country, we spent a considerable amount of time making cold calls, trying to understand the market. In the beginning you have to have raw ambition and sheer determination that nothing is going to stop you. You have to believe that whatever hurdles are placed in your path, you'll find a way of getting over them. During one of my first trips to Moscow, Howard Smith, who was running our distribution at that time, and I had an 8 A.M. appointment with the owner of a small cable system who lived in the suburbs. We got up very early in the morning, got dressed in fashionable blue suits, white shirts and red ties and drove out of Moscow. We got terribly lost (all of the massive, Stalinesque apartment buildings looked exactly alike), but we managed to get there precisely on time.

We knocked on the door and eventually it was opened by an overweight, unshaven man wearing only skimpy red thong underwear. That sight is permanently etched in my mind: bright *red thong underwear*. Clearly, Howard and I were considerably overdressed. The fact that we were wearing *pants* made us overdressed. In his broken English, he asked what we wanted. We responded in our broken Russian that we were there to discuss a cable distribution opportunity. He remembered the appointment, invited us in, and excused himself to get dressed.

We sat waiting for him at his kitchen table, which was piled high with dirty dishes and cat food. At one point his girlfriend came in, also dressed in her underwear, to offer us coffee. We declined. It was clear to me as we sat there that he was not going to be our future partner in Russia.

I wish I could say this meeting was unusual. Perhaps it was extreme, but when I was looking for a foothold, not just in Russia but in so many other countries, I attended hundreds and hundreds of meetings and met an unusual variety of people. In Russia, we eventually realized that we were wasting our time trying to find a partner, if we were going to be successful we had to make a deal with the national government.

It took me at least 10 trips, but finally the government agreed to take a tentative first step. We invited the producer and host of the most popular Soviet program for teenagers to spend a week in London hosting one of our programs. In return, the government permitted the state-operated station, Gosteleradio, to feed our programming to tourist hotels and foreign embassies. In addition, an hour-long taped version of the *Top 20 Countdown Show* was broadcast every Friday night on the national network. This channel went to 88 million homes. While it was only an hour a week, this was potentially a tremendous opportunity. In Russia, the show became known affectionately as "The Kitchen Show," because everybody would gather in the kitchen to watch MTV. For Russians, this program opened the window to the West just a tiny bit.

The government paid for our programming with millions of rubles, which had absolutely no value outside the Soviet Union, but they also gave us eight minutes of advertising time we could sell for hard currency. We had absolutely no difficulty selling that time. Western companies like Benetton, Wrangler, and Renault wanted to enter that market—even though their products weren't available at that time. It seemed obvious that a huge new market was about to open and everybody wanted to have a presence there. It's probable that this was the first western advertising to be shown to the general population.

We didn't know what type of programming would be permissible. In many cases we produced two versions of our shows, the regular version and a watered-down version for our more conservative markets. I was afraid the Russians would reject anything that was too provocative, so I debated which version to submit to them for their approval. Finally, I decided to go for it and showed them the program as it had been broadcast in Europe—and they didn't blink. They wanted the western program—not just wanted it, they were desperate for it. Throughout Europe I was always careful to identify MTV as *European*, not American. But as we were to learn, Eastern Europeans had had the sterile Russian programming jammed down their throats for so long that they demanded more *American* programming.

In 1990, I was at a sales conference in Munich during Oktoberfest when Marc Conneely leaned across the table and said casually above the noise, "Hey, I think I might be able to get us a channel in Leningrad."

MTV Europe in Leningrad? That was unheard of. There were only four television channels in Leningrad, which within a year would revert to its historic name, St. Petersburg. How in the world could a rock and roll channel showing primarily music videos get on one of them? I've always believed in offering rewards for work well done. On the spot I told him, "You get a channel and I'll give you a £5,000 bonus."

Somehow Mark was able to work out a five-year contract with a joint venture formed by the city council and a U.S. communications company that allowed us to broadcast 24 hours a day over Leningrad cable TV, which reached about half-a-million viewers. This deal made us the first western channel in the Soviet Union. It was revolutionary—and I greatly appreciated the irony that I was bringing a revolution to Russia.

There are times in business when you find yourself in an unusual situation. For example, to celebrate the launch city officials hosted a reception in the magnificent Winter Palace, which had been the official residence of the czars for almost 200 years. It was a spectacular night in that magnificent palace. In front of each place setting was a bottle of vodka—not every other place setting and not a glass of vodka—a full bottle for every person at the table. It turned out that we needed it, as there were many, many toasts. And when Deputy Mayor Yuri

Gerasimov ripped off his shirt and challenged me, I soon found myself on the floor holding him in a half-nelson; I recall wondering if perhaps this time I had gone too far.

Later in the evening Gerasimov offered the single most memorable toast of my career: "St. Petersburg was built in the marshes of the Baltic by Peter the Great three hundred years ago, and more than thirty thousand people died to build the city, with the express purpose of opening up Russia to Europe. And now you are the latter-day Peter the Great, once again opening Russia to the West."

Within another year, the Soviet Union was ripped apart and a new media world opened up. Throughout the entire country hundreds of small cable networks were created, some of them broadcasting pirated videos and amateur programming to a single building or one block in the large cities. One of those channels was owned by a Russian music promoter named Boris Zosimov, who wanted to bring MTV to the new Russia. He had seen MTV during a trip to New York and had fallen in love with it. Zosimov had been a fervent young Communist until he'd discovered rock and roll and dropped out of politics to manage underground bands. To promote one of his concerts in 1989, he spoke about it on his channel. As he once told me, "It was my band, my television channel, my air time. I put this band on many times during the day." When more people showed up than had ever attended one of his previous concerts, he discovered the value of advertising.

Boris was a dreamer, as well as a doer. Eventually, he even managed to bring the Monsters of Rock concert featuring Metallica and AC/DC to Moscow, a concert that drew an estimated half-million people. Our partnership, and our friendship, began when he called MTV in New York and introduced himself as "Boris from Moscow." Somehow, he managed to contact Marc Conneely, who introduced him to me. Over the next few years I met with him many times and eventually we became close friends. This was not normally the way I conducted business, but at that time there was a media land-rush going on in Russia and anyone who hesitated missed staking a claim. I wanted to extend our presence in Russia and met people who wanted to make that happen. I recognized that Boris was aggressive, relentless, and creative—and well-connected—and in 1993 we agreed to a one-year syndication deal that licensed him to broadcast MTV throughout Russia. Under this arrangement he was able to distribute our feed but was not permitted to alter it in any way—with the exception of providing a Russian translation. Russia received the same programming as the rest of Europe. To celebrate this deal, I brought the Pet Shop Boys to Moscow for a spectacular party held at the Moscow Olympic complex. The Pet Shop Boys walked through Red Square wearing enormously high pink hats—and literally brought traffic to a standstill. People just stopped and looked at them in awe. Inside the complex, Boris had constructed the largest MTV logo I had ever seen. The *M* was made of logs, and instead of launching the channel by cutting a ribbon, we sawed a log in half.

I did not have a tremendous amount of confidence that Boris would ever be able to pay us the agreed-upon fee. It was to be paid both in hard currency and in rubles. To my surprise, by syndicating MTV for three hours each day to channel 1 and for another five hours per day on channel 6, he managed to scrap together enough money to make that payment. While this multichannel arrangement may seem unusual, every deal we were making as we grew the channel had unusual aspects to it.

At that time Boris was also negotiating a joint venture with Polygram, and as part of our contract, he remembers, "To make this agreement I swore to MTV that I would not promote Polygram artists more than others. I swore to that. Which was not true, of course."

We took the hard currency but left millions of rubles in a bank. I left them sitting in an account somewhere and no one in New York objected. The time it would have taken to collect them and find something to do with them seemed more valuable to me than the rubles. Only later did I realize that we could have used that money to buy property in Moscow, which at that time was unbelievably inexpensive—and now is among the most valuable property by square foot in the world. But in the early 1990s the ruble was essentially worthless. There wasn't even a decision to be made. No one wanted them; no one had any faith that the ruble would survive as a viable currency. There was no way to exchange or convert them into dollars, pounds, francs, or yen.

When I first met Boris he knew nothing about "making business," as he would describe it. "Bill, we make good business together!" But Boris learned quickly, as all Russians learned quickly. The Russian economy, which basically didn't exist, has become a hyper-capitalistic system. Russia is now considered one of the world's emerging economies. When I first started traveling to Moscow it was almost impossible to buy a new shirt. Today it's possible to drive out of a dealer with a top-of-the-line Maybach. It seemed like they went from communism to capitalism in 24 hours. The country had been a drab gray, and suddenly it seemed as if someone had colored in the entire nation. Boris grew from asking me, "What is this HR?" to owning or co-owning 13 companies, including band management, magazine publishing, record labels, and TV stations. And, as he admits quite accurately, "Now I am not the worst businessman in Russia." Boris knew how to succeed in Russia, he knew how to work the system, and when the system collapsed, he knew how to prosper. Boris was the perfect example of the importance of finding the right people and working with them. It would have been impossible for us to go into most countries without having local expertise. If there is a secret to identifying those people, I've never learned it. It's a combination of research, intuition, and sometimes a little luck. All partnerships are challenging, but some are more challenging than others. We partnered with both large and small players. A big player can be difficult because its agenda will be different than yours although generally it will be able to fulfill its obligations; in a deal with a smaller partner you generally can get the terms you want but there is always the risk of not getting paid. I did make deals with the wrong people. We had partners who didn't meet our expectations, partners who refused to pay the bills, partners who took advantage of our brand credibility, partners who were inept, and even occasional partner who was less than honest. Fortunately all of these problems have occurred in smaller markets.

In those situations the most important thing was to recognize it early, admit it, and extract ourselves from the deal. It isn't always easy to get out of deals and often there are important personal and political considerations, but it has to be done. In one Asian country, for example, our partner in a joint venture was a former government official. He named his son, who was too young and too inexperienced, general manager of the channel. When his son failed to make several substantial payments, we took action to remove him. In return, his father used his government connection to have the channel turned off. That got the owner of the cable system involved. It was a difficult and complex situation that took several years to sort out, all because we picked the wrong partner.

But Boris was the right person at the right time. Whatever had to be done, Boris got it done. Boris had tremendous entrepreneurial spirit.

There was no advertising industry in Moscow—on Boris's first channel his initial advertiser was a financial company offering to pay investors 250 percent monthly interest—so he helped start an advertising agency to service his channels. Russia had its MTV Europe, but we wanted to localize. Boris kept pleading with me, "Please let me make MTV Russia."

Perhaps because of our attitude, MTV rapidly became an important channel in Russia, so much so that we actually played a role in their 1996 presidential election. MTV domestic had created the "Choose or Lose" campaign, which encouraged our viewers to get involved in their local election process. In the States, it may have contributed to Bill Clinton's victory in 1992. I thought it was tremendously important, so I took it and spread it around the world. It was an entire program that included on-air material as well as supportive marketing. In 1996, we used it in elections around the world, including Taiwan; India; believe it or not, Palestine; and Russia. It was very specifically a non-partisan campaign and we were careful not to support any person or political movement. In Russia, though, it appeared that the Communist Party candidate was going to be democratically elected. The incumbent president, Boris Yeltsin, had lost his popularity, but through Boris Zosimov he was able to get hold of the materials we had created for the Choose or Lose campaign and co-opted it for his own use. There is a famous photograph of Yeltsin dancing on a stage with young girls, which was his attempt to connect with young people by bringing pop culture into his campaign. What was not generally known was that soon after this picture was taken Yeltsin suffered a heart attack and there were serious questions about his health. But that was kept secret. Like Clinton, Yeltsin's success in forging a bond with young voters, primarily through our campaign, may have contributed to his reelection.

I was in Russia on election day and went with Boris Zosimov to the polls. For me, this was an extremely meaningful event and I wanted to be there. To participate, even as a spectator, in the building of the Russian democracy, was extremely gratifying.

When we made the decision to focus on developing local channels throughout the world, it was natural for Boris to be involved. He formed a joint venture with Russia Partners, the first private equity fund in Russia. Russia Partners was created by the U.S. firm Sigular Guff to take advantage of the extraordinary potential. Sigular Guff had already invested in several Russian TV stations when Boris approached Drew

Guff to finance what was to become MTV Russia. Drew must have seen similar qualities in Boris as I did, and eventually MTV Europe's general counsel and later COO Greg Ricca negotiated a partnership arrangement for us with Russia Partners.

MTV Russia was scheduled to launch in September 1998 as a free-to-air Russian channel. It had been a tremendous effort to put this business together. It was the first western channel to be localized in Russia. But several weeks before our launch a massive credit crisis caused the Russian economy to collapse. What would my day be without a challenge? In this case, though, there wasn't much I could do. We debated postponing the launch, but Drew urged me to go ahead. There was nothing to be gained by waiting. But I did cancel the lavish launch party we had planned and, although I didn't feel it, continued to give optimistic interviews to the media. Clearly, we had launched our new business at the worst possible time. Russia's embryonic advertising industry was devastated, drying up our primary revenue source. I tend to be an optimist, but even I had to wonder if MTV Russia could survive in that environment. It was Drew Guff who insisted, "We couldn't have launched at a better time. Bringing MTV to Russia is a show of confidence in their future." While a sense of doom pervaded the country, we made a glorious, glamorous splash. We received a great deal of attention in the media.

Boris ran the channel, which allowed him to become known as the man who introduced *Beavis and Butthead* to Russia. "When I saw *Beavis and Butthead* in America, at first I didn't understand what's going on," he admits. "But in six months I fall in love with them. I put it on in Russia because I knew that the kids love it and it's stupid and it would give a bad time for our political people. When I put it on the politicians spoke about it badly in our Duma, our Senate. For the first three or four months in Russia they didn't get it. What is this? What is that? But then the whole country started to laugh. It became a popular hit."

Within a decade we were reaching 35 million Russian households or about 100 million viewers through a network of 21 TV stations around the country that we had bought and were operating, as well as 650 affiliates, including cable and satellite systems. The fact that we owned 21 TV stations, much of our distribution network, was extremely unusual. This was the only time we owned our distribution. It was a matter of recognizing an extraordinary opportunity and taking action. TV stations in Russia were selling for bargain prices and we agreed with Guff to buy them. This network of stations added substantially to the value of MTV Russia.

It had become an extremely profitable venture, so profitable that in 2007 Russia Partners decided it was time to monetize its investment. This was not something I wanted to do. Given all the time I'd spent in Russia, I had an emotional attachment to the channel. This was the first time we considered selling one of our channels. Under our agreement with Russia Partners, we were "dragged," meaning we were compelled to sell. We had two options: We could purchase its 42 percent stake and become the sole owner, or join with them in selling to a third party. Without knowing the channel's actual market value it was difficult to determine a fair price for their 42 percent, making it impossible for us to complete that deal. Phillippe Dauman, who had replaced Tom Freston as Viacom's president and CEO, made the decision to sell it. In retrospect, it was the right decision as it brought an immediate and substantial return.

We sold the channel and our stations to Prof-Media, Russia's largest privately owned media group, in 2007 for $360 million. It was a substantial return on our investment. We had come a long way from our 8 A.M. meeting with a nearly naked man wearing red thong underwear. For Prof-Media it was like buying beachfront property. It had the right to do whatever it chose with the stations. There was a fear, because MTV Russia was considered a niche channel, that they might transform it into a general-entertainment channel. But the strength of our brand is so strong that the highly respected Rafael Akopov, the well-liked GM of Prof-Media, agreed to make a licensing deal with us, so it remains MTV Russia.

In Russia, as we do in many other parts of the world, we had kept Nickelodeon separate from MTV. There are a lot of reasons for that. But because we retained ownership of Nickelodeon, we continue to have a presence in Russia. Nick is on cable in Russia. And while it is a small channel there, there is an expectation that it will continue to grow.

■■■

By 1994, MTV Europe was successfully established and profitable, but it was becoming clear that our horizons were limited. First, in terms of attracting advertising, we had about 500 advertisers and had pretty much tapped out the market for multinational companies. It had become increasingly difficult to find additional advertisers willing to buy the Continent. The real opportunity for growth was vertical, with country-specific clients. Second, after the initial excitement of a united Europe a backlash had developed, and home-team spirit was growing, especially in Germany. For several years the Germans wanted to be considered Europeans, but after unification of East and West Germany there was a growing pride in their new nation, which translated to pride in German music. Third, the number of music channels was exploding, many of them in the national language. Because they were much smaller than MTV they could attract local advertisers who couldn't afford MTV's rates and were not interested in pan-European coverage.

We spent a lot of time debating internally whether to shift strategies. It is a difficult decision for a company to make. MTV Europe had been founded to create one program in one voice to the entire continent. I had been the biggest pan-European cheerleader in our office; I had been on an emotional mission to unite diverse audiences throughout Europe, to connect nations, and to provide the vehicle for young people to experience other cultures. Pivoting would require finesse. There were valid arguments to be made for both positions. After considerable debate, the decision was made to localize our channels. As far as I was concerned, MTV was already local to Europe, but now country by country we were going to bring it down to the national level.

We also were seriously considering launching VH1 as a national channel in Germany, as what is known as a *flanker* brand. VH1 originally had been created in the States partly because John Malone's TCI had decided to launch a music channel to compete with MTV. In this instance, its existence would protect MTV Europe from being undercut by a competing local music channel, but because it attracted an older demo than MTV it would not cannibalize MTV's audience or advertising. This would have been MTV's first localized channel in Europe, although rather than having local management it still would have been part of MTV Europe.

I waited, and that was a mistake. We moved too cautiously. We didn't do it soon enough, for which I take the responsibility. While instinctively I thought it was a good idea, I didn't push hard enough over the internal objections.

In hindsight, I should have launched VH1. Had I done so, it might have prevented what became a very costly situation for us. In August 1993, we'd filed a lawsuit against VPL to break its monopoly. This is a decision I've looked back on numerous times through the years, knowing the consequences and wondering if I'd had any alternative. Unfortunately, lawsuits are part of every business, but if it is possible to avoid a lawsuit, avoid it. The time, the money, and the energy a lawsuit drains away is rarely worth the victory. But I felt I had no choice; I had run out of options.

Video Performance Limited represented more than 350 record companies in the U.K. alone, including the five major labels that controlled an estimated 80 percent of the world market. Almost 90 percent of the videos we ran were produced by those five major labels. As MTV had grown, the up-to-20-percent-of-gross-revenue deal we'd been forced to make with the VPL when we'd launched our pan-Europe channel simply was no longer viable. It was devouring our revenue. Throughout 1992, I had embarked on an exhaustive process of trying to convince VPL to renegotiate our agreement. When that failed, Greg Ricca and I tried to convince any one of the major labels to break away, knowing that would shatter the monopoly. When that also failed, we looked at scenarios that involved moving forward without using their music and tried to find a way to survive without it. It's questionable at best; no one will ever know if it would have been possible, but clearly it wasn't the best path to take. We finally accepted the reality that we had to take VPL to court. There are times when you simply have to stand up, look your adversary in the eye, and go to war. We went to war. It was to be a long and very difficult process, but fortunately we had Mike Fricklas, our general counsel, leading the battle.

It's never a positive step to sue your primary supplier and largest client. I had established strong relationships with many of the people I would be fighting in court, and during our legal fight the situation often got very intense. I remember having dinner one night in Dublin and getting into an argument about the VPL deal with the head of Polygram, Roger Ames; Roger, who would later become head of Warner Music, to this day remains a friend of mine, but that night our voices got louder and we started shoving each other and making schoolboy threats. Eventually we had to be separated. When Greg and I made the decision to go to court I was aware that even if we won, and that was questionable, my relationship with the labels would never be the same. And although under Mike Fricklas' direction Greg and I had reviewed our options numerous times and tried to anticipate their response, in fact we never saw what was coming next.

We began by lodging a complaint with the European Commission accusing VPL of maintaining a monopoly and using it to demand excessive fees for music videos. We still hoped that this action might convince the labels to negotiate with us sensibly or perhaps individually, as they did in the United States. But there was no movement from them at all. Our lawsuit moved excruciatingly slowly through the bureaucracy. I flew to Brussels numerous times to meet with the Commission. While it had become clear that the Commission was sympathetic to our argument, we had no indication as to when it might announce a verdict. Eventually, we decided to bring a lawsuit against the VPL in the U.K. While I am almost always confident in my decisions, on the day we filed I was more frustrated and anxious than angry or confident. The whole thing made no sense to me. Our success translated into increased record sales for the labels. The videos we were running meant free advertising to a massive audience they could not otherwise reach. And even with a modified deal they would have continued to profit. Why fight a battle that could be avoided?

We were certain the VPL couldn't use its strongest weapon, withholding music videos from us. We had a strong contract from which they were continuing to profit, the videos sold records, and most importantly, the artists and their managers understood our value to them. Artists were desperate to be played on MTV and might have fought their labels if those companies had responded with a boycott. The artists also believed that the record companies were incredibly fat organizations supported entirely by their work. In this legal battle the musicians were our strongest ally.

While VPL's attorneys fought the legal battles, four of the major labels launched a new offensive. It is my opinion that as a direct result of our lawsuit they created their own music channel. They knew they couldn't succeed initially in the United States because MTV was too popular, so they launched a locally based and programmed channel in Germany named VIVA. Eventually, they intended to expand globally. It was run by Dieter Gorney, a brilliant, enthusiastic German. That situation was difficult for me because Dieter and I had long been friends and suddenly we were bitter enemies. He turned out to be an extremely effective competitor. While we already had competition from music channels in several countries, none of them had the creativity, the buzz, or the resources to compete with us. VIVA was different; it was a cartel formed by the record companies to promote their products.

I realized quickly that it could become a dangerous competitor. Germany was our largest and most important market. In November 1993, before the record companies announced the creation of their channel, I had attended the annual German music industry convention, Pop Com, with our head of marketing, Peter Einstein. We issued a press release that we were going to make a major announcement at the convention. The media expected MTV to announce the creation of a German-language channel or, failing that, to add an entire block of German-language programming to the MTV Europe feed. And that would have been a very big deal. In anticipation of that announcement the media crammed into the conference room and overflowed into the hallway. Cameras were rolling. A major technological advance, digital compression, suddenly allowed broadcasters to transmit more channels on their existing satellite transponders. When we announced that we were going to provide a separate two-minute feed to Germany to attract companies interested only in advertising to that market, the journalists stood there absolutely stunned. *That's it? That's all you're announcing, local advertising for Germany?* Yes. MTV's programming didn't change at all. It was still the MTV Europe feed; we just inserted German-language advertising.

Had we announced the launch of VH1 in Germany or even the creation of MTV Germany at that conference, it's possible VIVA would not have succeeded. The record companies might have concluded they couldn't compete with us and abandoned their plans. But we didn't, so on December 1, 1993 VIVA was launched.

The best way to deal with competition is to produce a better product, market it thoroughly, and encourage brand loyalty. We had a very popular product, our marketing was excellent, and certainly we had brand loyalty. As I had hoped and preached, MTV had become a unifying force throughout Europe.

Ironically, VIVA had the advantage of size. When it was launched VIVA was a shabby imitation of MTV. It had been thrown together as cheaply and quickly as possible. But the fact that it was so much smaller than MTV enabled it to become an all-German music channel. VIVA's VJs spoke only German and it played more technopop, which had become very popular there, than we could. Their program director outlined VIVA's strategy when he told *Time* magazine, "It's cool to throw in three or four words of English. It's not cool to do it all in English. It's an illusion that everyone in Europe is speaking English."

I tried to be magnanimous when VIVA launched. I actually made a public statement wishing them well. And perhaps I underestimated their capability. MTV Europe was already far more successful than had been predicted, achieving the goals of our five-year plan in only three years. MTV had several hundred advertisers, it was in 60 million homes in 37 countries, with a potential audience of more than 200 million. The original pan-Europe concept had succeeded beyond anyone's expectations. We'd taken a questionable business model and through aggressive, relentless, and creative execution had made it work.

But VIVA had successfully targeted our weakness. The feedback we got was that it was awful—but that it spoke German. We had underestimated the power of national pride. Each country had its own music and its own identity and wasn't ready to give that up, whether they were part of the European Union or not. VIVA also had the advantage of being the underdog, which young people admired. It grabbed a foothold and started growing. While the record companies continued to provide videos to us, it was clear they were working hard to favor VIVA. Within a year VIVA had passed us among German high school students, a demographic that spoke little English. While Germany was still MTV's biggest market in Europe, VIVA had made an impact on the bottom line.

The European Commission refused to issue a decision, but when a preliminary order instructed the major record companies to negotiate individually with MTV, there was no longer any question what that decision would be. Sony was the first company to finally break away and negotiate a deal with us. Within months, EMI, Polygram, and BMG followed, making the court case moot. We'd won. We'd busted the cartel, which was imperative to our long-term profitability. But in many large ways it was a Pyrrhic victory. The result had been the creation of the first serious competition we'd ever faced. While competition is healthy, in this case our competition was also our primary supplier. Once

VIVA was successful, these record companies decided to launch music channels around the world. The landscape quickly became crowded with music channels, although few of them other than VIVA offered us any competition. But all of them followed VIVA's model of programming in the national, or in some cases even regional, language, hiring local VJs and focusing on local tastes in music. The irony, of course, was that while VIVA successfully positioned itself as a local German channel, it actually was owned by these same global record companies. MTV and VIVA would compete for the German music market for the next decade, with VIVA often winning the battle.

When we had originally launched MTV Europe the concept of a pan-European channel had given us several advantages; in particular, it required a smaller initial investment and offered potentially the largest audience. The transmission systems available at that time also limited what was technically possible. When we were criticized for being too general for local tastes, I responded that we were a local channel; we were local to one-Europe. I didn't hire Americans; I didn't originate the feed out of New York; I created a completely unique product. More than 85 percent of the programming on MTV Europe was created in Europe, which was even greater than the amount of British-produced programming on the BBC in England or French-produced programming on France's TV-1. When I claimed we had always preached local, I meant it. But the success of German-speaking VIVA demonstrated we'd gone about as far as possible with the one-Europe concept.

In 1994, I was also given the assignment of duplicating our success in Europe throughout the world. That immediately put a global set of problems in my lap. In addition to Europe, suddenly I was responsible for running MTV Networks Latin American and Asian operations. In Asia, MTV was facing a different but equally serious problem. For almost three years, through a licensing arrangement, MTV Asia had been broadcasting on STAR TV, a satellite system launched in 1991 by Hong Kong media tycoon Richard Lee. Rupert Murdoch's News Corp bought a majority stake in STAR TV in 1993, which created a problem for us. Sumner Redstone and Murdoch were competitors and we did not want to license our channel to Murdoch. Also, we believed that Asia was potentially such an important market that we elected to start over because it gave us greater control over our destiny. For those and other reasons, when we had an opportunity in 1994 to opt out of the contract then held by Murdoch, we exercised that option.

When MTV Asia went off the air, Murdoch did a very smart thing. News Corp scooped up most of our staff, retained our overall look, dropped the *M* and the *T*, and launched the new music channel *V*. Our problem was that we were not immediately able to fight back. We had leased space on a new Chinese satellite and expected to be back on the air within months—but that satellite blew up on launch and left us without the means to transmit our signal. V was nothing more than an MTV clone, but we were off the air and there was nothing we could do about it. It took us more than a year to form a joint venture with Polygram and relaunch MTV Asia, a lifetime in the memories of our young audience. And during that time, just like VIVA, V became a success.

In addition to divorcing Star in Asia, I had to deal with our Latin American operation, which was in chaos. It had just suffered through a management shakeup and morale was terrible, so I had to spend time there. And with VIVA successfully establishing itself in Europe and threatening to expand, I had to pay close attention to Europe. I had learned in the military that it's very difficult to fight a war on two fronts and impossible to fight on three fronts. Forget it—you're outmanned. But I thought I could do it all.

And in addition to fighting those battles, we finally had made the decision to go local. We had begun experimenting with increased local control in 1994, when we had successfully launched a local version of VH1 in the U.K. We were also already country specific in Australia and Brazil. But it was a huge decision. Unlike opening a new branch office in the next town, for us, establishing local operations throughout the world would require a massive investment of resources, and it would take us years to get firmly established.

Surviving in any industry requires flexibility. Technology has compressed time, and decisions have to be made more rapidly now than ever before. The world changes every day—a decade ago there was no Google, Facebook, or Twitter—so adapting to the constantly changing business environment is essential. The longer you stay with the same strategy, the more vulnerable you become to your competitors. When you recognize that a strategy or a product is reaching the end of its effective lifetime, you have to be able to abandon it and move forward. But sometimes it's hard to make that decision; in addition to changing the entire business structure, there is an emotional attachment involved: Doing it this way has always worked before; it has made us profitable, it's still working, so why give it up? The tendency is to stick with what's working until it stops working, and by then, it's too late. There certainly is no guarantee that the changes you make will be successful. MTV Europe was still successful, but its seams were fraying. Business history is littered with the logos of companies that failed to recognize the realities of the changing marketplace.

We had been *local in Europe* for five years; it was time to adapt to the changing market conditions and go *market specific.* VIVA exposed our vulnerability.

As Tom Freston said, "Competition is a good thing in that regard; you tend to try and get better. It makes life a bit more difficult, but in the end it's good. You keep competitive and you don't lose that edge. There are a lot of growth opportunities in this business. We're just getting started."

Now all I had to do was fight VIVA in Germany and V in Asia, convert MTV Europe to local operations, bring some order to Latin America, and then build a worldwide network.

The hill we were charging had become a mountain.

Chapter Five

Get the Party Started

Who would have thought that one of the world's strongest brands would get crushed by Kyonki Saas Bhi Kabhi Bahu Thi, *which means "The Mother-in-Law Was the Daughter-in-Law Once"?*

—*Fortune*, August 2004, referring to MTV in India

Before joining MTV, our top executive in India, Alex Kuruvilla, had brought Kellogg's corn flakes to that nation. Apparently, Kellogg's had seen a vast untapped market for its breakfast cereal. What its marketing people did not consider was that traditional Indian breakfasts are hot, fresh, pungent, and cheap, while Kellogg's corn flakes were cold and crisp. Those first brave Indian women who tried corn flakes poured boiled milk over this strange dish, which turned it into a tasteless mush. It was a dismal failure.

Kellogg's eventually figured it out and became successful by importing cereals that appealed to local tastes. As Alex explained to *Fortune*, "The mistake a lot of multinationals have made in India is looking at the size of the middle class, multiplying by *x* . . . and seeing a business that looks enormous—until they discovered, to their horror, that you had to do things differently. You need to reflect the local culture."

My objective was to reflect the local culture—in every country in the world. To our traditional mantra, "relentless, aggressive, and creative," we added the phrase, "respect and reflect." MTV's new business strategy was simple: Learn the local culture and reflect it in every decision we make. For example, originally the launch of our Mandarin Asian service had been scheduled for April 15, 1995, but it was postponed when a *feng shui* master warned that the fifteenth was "one of the worst days possible to launch a new channel." Instead, it launched a week later on what he saw would be "a great day." Consulting a *feng shui* master before making a significant and expensive corporate decision like postponing a launch was not something I had learned at Harvard Business School, just as we hadn't covered the rationale for eating snake gall bladder when in China, but if we really were going to go local, we had to genuinely respect and reflect local beliefs, traditions, and practices.

The stories of mistakes made by American companies trying to expand internationally are many and occasionally funny. Funny, that is, if it isn't your company that is losing millions of dollars. Pepsi had a difficult time in parts of Asia because its vending machines were light blue, a color associated there with death and mourning. Revlon marketed a camellia-scented perfume in Brazil, a scent used in that country primarily for funerals. FedEx lost more than a billion dollars in Europe because its hub concept just didn't work there. It struggled in Spain because workers there love to work late into the night rather than in the morning, and in Russia when employees took home truck-cleaning soap for personal use. Yahoo! and eBay couldn't compete with Chinese companies in that country and Google has struggled to survive there. Wal-Mart's clerks were taught to smile at German customers—which some male customers misinterpreted as flirting. KFC realized only too late that in Mandarin Chinese its "finger-lickin' good" slogan was translated to mean "eat your fingers off," but it successfully adapted to local cultures, selling tempura crispy sticks in Japan and potato-and-onion croquettes in Holland, and adding more spices to its chicken the further inland it expanded into China, and by adapting to the local markets it has become globally successful. Even McDonald's, whose global success had been based on one all-beef hamburger for the entire world, had to create a new menu for India, offering a vegetarian pizza, vegetable McCurry pan, the vegetarian McAloo Tikki Burger (a no-beef patty that includes potatoes, peas, tomato, onions, vegetarian mayonnaise, and spices), and the grilled chicken Maharaja Mac.

It was inevitable that just like so many other companies we would make mistakes as we expanded. When we launched in India, for example, we pictured that country's flag in our logo. We intended it to be a compliment. When we included the Union Jack in our U.K. logo it worked very well, but we didn't know that many Indians considered this disrespectful and we were forced to change it. Mistakes happen, which is why the time spent building the personal relationships that allowed us to respond to those mistakes was so important.

We were the pioneers in going local globally. I know of no other company that changed its products as rapidly and completely as we did while we expanded. By creating programming content that appealed directly to the local audience we captured the diversity of the world. This was a conscious decision that I believed was necessary. There are many people who disagree with me, pointing out correctly that if we could have distributed one channel throughout the world our margins would be much higher. Pan-regional businesses offer the advantage of building up a sizeable distribution base rapidly. Great savings come from scale, whereas localizing a product requires a substantial investment and results in shrinking profit margins. But I felt the pan-regional vision was not sustainable over time or beyond borders. One channel could not possibly work across all nationalities and languages. I've traveled the world and I have learned that one size does *not* fit all, and personally, I do not believe it ever will. My intention was to be local globally.

When I announced this strategic shift I explained, "There is a tremendous passion for cultural identity . . . . We've been plotting this for many months. We're going to empower local management to define creativity in local terms. Each channel is going to be created from the ground up in terms of content, brand interpretation, and music. We will reflect the diversity of our global audience. It constitutes a major investment in programming, technology and organization."

Even the most brilliant strategy is only as successful as its execution. My strategy, which at the time was revolutionary, was to create independent, autonomous operations—totally separate and responsible for their own profit and loss—fully integrated functional businesses that reflected the tastes of their audience. I intended to put in place a structure that allowed us to combine local expertise with an international infrastructure. While the spirit and style of each channel would be consistent throughout the world, meaning it would be immediately recognizable as MTV, everything else, including the VJs, the advertising, and the videos broadcast would be run by local management to meet local tastes. Each local channel would eventually report to me. We were the first U.S. company to give this level of control to local management as part of a global strategy. The word we coined to describe it is *glocal*—think local, act global. It was a *tremendous* risk. No company had given local operating units this level of autonomy. Basically, we were trusting people with our extremely valuable brand—as I was reminded that memorable morning when I learned that MTV Taiwan was broadcasting wrestling, nude wrestling, male nude wrestling. I decided to go local as a sustainable business model, and eventually this became our USP. CNN, which primarily targeted traveling businessmen, women, and expats, had one feed throughout the world. We were unique; we were the only media company going local throughout the world and it was the key to our success.

My objective was to create an international structure molded after what I had learned in the military. I wanted small operating units at the local level, similar to an army company. The military is structured to permit command and control. Troops at the ground level are the most knowledgeable about the enemy, in our case the competition, and equipped to deal quickly and effectively with local issues without having to wait for a decision from a distant headquarters. Small units can establish local relationships, make and implement decisions rapidly, solve problems faster and more creatively than large operating units, and are capable of exploiting weaknesses or victories. In our case that meant that when we saw a channel was working we could double-down on that business. Also each unit can be small enough to define its own culture, work together as a team, and have everyone be on a first-name basis with every one of their co-workers. But in any situation, it is essential that the lines of communication be kept open. In our case, because each unit would be responsible for its profit and loss, each also would have its own accountability.

Tom Freston warned me that by decentralizing I risked losing control of my brand. My response was that we would hire good people, provide the tools they needed, and trust them to do their job. Everything started with the employees. My belief was that local people would best reflect the needs, tastes, and desires of the local audience, and because their jobs would depend on the bottom line, they were much less likely to make risky or destructive financial decisions. In Vietnam, I had seen over and over the benefits of dealing directly with the local population on their own terms, rather than trying to impose our beliefs on them. Good people are always difficult to find, and this was especially true as we moved around the world into developing countries. How do you find a salesperson in Russia who has never sold before? In China, we hired an executive from Shanghai Television to head our distribution. He was a member of the Communist Party who left a relatively secure position in the state media system to join MTV. But it was rare to find someone like him. For several years, I interviewed almost everyone we hired, especially at the senior level, but eventually that became impossible. I learned that the enormous amount of time I spent interviewing people and developing relationships was the most valuable investment of time I could make. In many countries, there was strong competition for young, educated workers. After we hired and trained our people they became in demand and it was difficult to retain them.

With the whole world as my portfolio, the question was, where to begin? I probably could have thrown a dart at a map and started wherever it landed. My goal was to see MTV and VH-1 in every household in the world, so eventually we'd have to plant our flag in every country. I began by looking for the most economically and technologically developed markets, especially in those places where we already had a strong presence. Some of the choices were obvious, and we launched local channels very quickly in countries like Germany, Holland, Italy, and the U.K. We certainly looked hard at Scandinavia, Brazil, Russia, Kenya, and even further east to Japan and eventually India, China, and Africa.

We began that expansion by gathering as much information as possible about each market. We looked at the GDP, the existing distribution infrastructure, the level of technology, the potential audience, and the regulatory situation. Where traditional distribution was limited, we looked at the possibilities for creative distribution. And no matter how we looked at the world, it was obvious Europe had to be first. It had the most mature infrastructure and offered the best financial return. Asia would be next because it had the most exciting growth potential, then Latin America and the Middle East would fill in nicely, and finally the emerging nations, which would include the African continent.

I wish it had worked out that easily. But there was a lot of variability in that strategy. Every country presented unique difficulties. In Germany there was little demand for pay-television because movies and sports were on free TV. In Asia, there was limited infrastructure. In China the government was especially concerned about the potential influence of foreign media companies. They examined every word, every look, every feel, so MTV, which possibly could have an impact on their culture, faced more regulatory problems than an automobile manufacturer. On the other hand, countries with growing economies (such as throughout Africa) want to develop, so they wanted media expertise and encouraged financial investment. Kazakhstan, for example, reached out to us several times. They wanted their MTV because it would be good for the national image and because they wanted to forge a closer association with the West. And there are other countries with local media interests they wanted to protect, so they put up regulatory barriers that shut out MTV—Israel, for example.

To create and manage this business, I've spent more than two decades traveling around the world. I counted it up once: I've been to more than 150 countries. I've met about 30 heads of state and nine Nobel Prize winners. I've done the karaoke clubs in Asia and the four-star restaurants in Paris. It's fair to say that I know every food stand open late at night in every major airport in the world. I've even been back to Vietnam—about six times. It is considerably more enjoyable bringing entertainment to that country rather than artillery.

One particularly memorable day in 2001 began at 3 A.M. in Beirut. From there I fled to Istanbul, and from there to Nice. From Nice, I took a helicopter to Monte Carlo for a client party at the Grand Prix, and finally drove from there to Cannes for our Film Festival party, finally getting to bed at 5 A.M.

I've probably traveled at least once on every commercial airline operating a regular schedule in the world—outside North Korea. I can tell you that American Airlines offers the best musical selection in the airline industry, and the food on the Asian airlines is far superior to that on the U.S. and European airlines. I've lost suitcases on every continent. Once, I remember I had about 10 meetings scheduled in Tokyo and my bags got lost. It is considered poor manners to conduct business in Japan unless you are wearing a suit, preferably a blue suit with a white shirt.

I spent an afternoon and evening going to every possible shop to find a suit that fit me, but it proved impossible. Finally, in desperation I bought a suit several sizes too small. I spent the next two days squeezed into this suit, my arms folded to cover the fact that the sleeves were about halfway up my forearms. Fortunately, the Japanese were too polite to show their amusement.

It was a lot easier when my bags got lost on the way to Havana. I had been invited to dedicate a hospital with Castro. Not only did I not have my clothes, I didn't even have time to shave before the ceremony. I showed up unshaven and dressed in wrinkled clothes. Fortunately, nobody even noticed—it turned out that was the way everybody with Castro looked.

I've been jetlagged for more than two decades. People seem to assume that someone who flies as frequently as I do has discovered the secret of traveling around the world without suffering from jetlag. Here's the secret: There is no secret. I have often found myself sitting in meetings fighting desperately to keep my eyes open. To combat fatigue, I drink coffee and diet soda. It helps, until it doesn't. I am an expert at cat-napping, falling deeply asleep for a few minutes in a car while going to a meeting or between meetings. I learned that art in the army, where you grab a few minutes' sleep at any opportunity. In the military we slept anywhere and everywhere—waiting on the chow line, in a foxhole, even standing up in an airplane with a parachute on your back flying toward the drop zone. But the only remedy for jetlag I've ever found is *sleep*.

Surprisingly, considering the millions of air miles I have flown, often on dubious airlines, I have had very few dangerous flights. I remember an Aeroflot flight landing on an ice-covered runway in Moscow and slipping and sliding mostly out of control down the runway. And I remember being forced to land at London's Heathrow in what was essentially a hurricane because, as the pilot informed us, we were running out of fuel. I have been on many planes that were flying considerably lower than the peaks of the mountains we were passing. I've been in severe turbulence and in impressive storms. But in Vietnam I was awarded an Air Medal, which means I spent more than 50 hours on a helicopter in combat, so, compared to those often-terrifying hours, the flying that I've done for business has been a flight in the park. (Helicopters are a whole other thing; I haven't flown in a helicopter since the day my first child was born. I happen to believe they are very dangerous—although they probably land well on ice.)

But all that travel was necessary to build and expand MTV. Any business has to keep growing and evolving to survive. There is always another country, another product, another partnership, and new programming. As new technologies develop, there is always a new way to grow. One such tour I took in the early 1990s I will never forget. I refer to it as "Bucharest to Beirut." It was on this trip that I learned a great lesson. Right after the Iron Curtain fell, I visited Bucharest, Romania, to see if it was possible for us to syndicate a block of programming to terrestrial TV. On these trips I usually traveled with an associate, but this time for some reason I was alone. I was taken to a cavernous building, which until several months earlier had been the headquarters of the state-controlled TV station. I opened the door of a large control room to discover a group of people sitting there smoking cigarettes and staring intently at monitors with nothing but snow on them. They looked dazed. There was no energy at all. To me that symbolized the toll the years of communist rule had taken on them.

From there I went to Beirut, Lebanon, where a war had been fought less than a year earlier. Beirut had been devastated. Even with my military background I had never seen more destruction. There was tremendous damage everywhere; on every corner there were mounds of broken buildings. I had been there before the war and had seen what a wonderful city it was, so to visit this city in ruin was heartbreaking. It seemed like everyone in the city was carrying a weapon; members of Hamas stood guard outside the airport. At night, an armed guard sat in front of each hotel room. But in the middle of all this rubble stood a modern building, a new TV broadcast center. In contrast to the government center in Romania, this building was alive with young people moving rapidly through the corridors; a sense of energy and excitement pervaded the whole place. Appropriately, it was called "Future TV."

It suddenly became clear to me that the *psychological* destruction wrought by the communist regimes in Romania was much worse than the physical destruction caused by war. Eventually, we syndicated blocks of programming to both countries. We announced the launch of MTV programming in Beirut in the ruins of the once-great Hotel Phoenica, and when we did, Prime Minister Rafic Hariri, who is credited with rebuilding that country after 15 years of civil war, said, "The music of MTV will help us forget the war and unite the Sunnis, Shiites, and Christian Maronites."

With the possible exceptions of China, Cuba, and, surprisingly, Canada, we successfully navigated the maze of government regulations around the world. Launching MTV Italy, in particular, was difficult and time consuming because of their regulatory system. In every situation we needed clever lawyers, people who are familiar with the complexities of both international law and the local laws. The great irony was that we were in Communist China, the Soviet Union, and Eastern Europe before the Berlin Wall came down, but the one country that would not allow us in was Canada. The Canadian government wanted to protect its own music channel, *Much Music*. Eventually we were permitted to launch a channel, but we were prohibited from broadcasting any music videos. In Canada, we don't even bill ourselves as "Music Television"; we're just plain-old "MTV." Dealing with these regulations can get very complicated. No company has those resources in-house, so even from the first day at MTV Europe we've had to have experienced legal help. But any barrier can be overcome with the right strategy and by forming the right relationships.

Government regulations also prevented us from starting a business in Cuba—although in this situation it was the American government. Americans are prohibited from doing business in Cuba. I have seen a pirated version of MTV in Cuba and I'm certain we would be successful there. At one time I actually developed a strategy for getting around the ban. The largest number of visitors to Cuba come from Canada, but Italians are the second-largest group. One of our most creative executives was the managing director of South Europe, Antonio Campo Dall'Orto, and we had figured out what appeared to be a legal way to use an independent channel to bring MTV to Cuba. We intended to expand into Cuba through MTV Brazil or MTV Italy. I made two visits there and spent a considerable amount of time with Fidel Castro. At one of those meetings he spent five hours at lunch with my group, which included Tom Freston, *Vanity Fair*'s Graydon Carter, and Paramount's Brad Gray—four hours and 45 minutes lecturing us and 15 minutes listening to our response. He did tell me that he wanted to use MTV to teach English to Cubans and loved the concept of MTV Cuba. I wanted to do it—I wanted to be everywhere—but when I was fined $5,000 by the U.S. government just for visiting that country (I never quite understood how that was legal, and I never found out because it would have cost me considerably more than the fine to hire an attorney to fight it), it was obviously going to be a lot more complicated than we had anticipated and I dropped the idea. It wasn't going to be a great business opportunity for us, but the wonderful musical tradition of Cuba would have enriched the network.

We never let constraints stop us from moving forward. Government regulations in China have proved to be very difficult to overcome. Brazil has no cable infrastructure and protective policies, and its vast stretches of jungle and the Amazon River made it difficult to find a terrestrial frequency, but our partner was able to link together a chain of small stations that provided distribution to most of that vast country.

In Russia there are 12 time zones, so we had to figure out how to transmit from multiple satellites, which allowed us to shift our programming so our primetime block would be seen at the desired time throughout that country.

Although India has a large, educated, and growingly affluent middle class, when we entered that market most Indian households had only one television set for the entire family, and more than 75 percent of those TV sets were black-and-white and capable of receiving no more than eight terrestrial channels. While that has changed slowly, it remains a problem. So a niche channel like MTV, which appeals to a younger demographic, often is the second or even third choice behind more family-oriented programming. Making the situation even more difficult for us, India has as many as 25,000 "cable *wallahs*," or cable system owners and the cable industry is extremely competitive and sometimes violent. Those system operators collect fees in cash and won't risk losing a customer who refuses to pay. All of that makes the ad sales market in India very soft. After launching MTV India in 1996 with Bob Geldof, it became apparent that we would never be able to get sufficient penetration in a market dominated by one-set households. We had never faced a problem like this before. We could either be satisfied to remain a niche channel in a potentially huge market, or adapt to the situation. In 2008 we formed Viacom 18, a joint venture with a strong Indian company, TV18, using MTV India as part of our investment in the partnership. Viacom 18 launched Colors, the first general-appeal channel in Viacom's history. Colors was created to appeal to the entire family. Our goal has been to make Colors the default channel for all age groups.

Programming included everything from soap operas to *Khaton Ke Khiladi*, a show similar to *Fear Factor*. Colors was an immediate hit; it exceeded our expectations and during several periods has been the most popular channel in India.

We went into every market knowing that eventually we would face some type of problem in distribution, revenue, programming, or even government relations. But no matter how complicated the situation became, I tried to remain optimistic. I believed there was an answer to every problem—we just had to find it. Sometimes, it involved finding a partner who had access to a frequency; sometimes, it was finding the right programming formula; in some places it meant making a friend in the government or hiring a good lobbyist or lawyer. Finding a solution often took time. Sometimes, we have had to make multiple attempts before succeeding. Surprisingly, for example, whereas Japan is so advanced in producing consumer electronics for the whole world, it has limited cable distribution; and while western movies are popular there; it has been very difficult for media companies to succeed there. So for us it has been a challenging market; while at times we've been successful, it has yet to meet our expectations.

Just as we did when founding MTV Europe, in many countries we also had to directly confront strongly held suspicions that our hidden objective was to bring American culture over international borders. On numerous occasions I met with national leaders to reassure them that we were launching a channel that would reflect their culture, and that rather than importing American culture we wanted to export their musical culture to other regions of the world. Among those leaders were Israeli Prime Minister Shimon Peres, Singapore founder Lee Kuan Yew, Chinese leader Jiang Zemin, South Korean President Lee Mung-Bak, South Africa's Nelson Mandela, and Fidel Castro. I told everyone who asked the same thing: "We are not in the business of exporting American culture." One of the more skeptical leaders we had to convince was the mayor of Mecca, the religious center of the Islamic world, whose permission we needed to launch MTV Arabia. The Arab world was potentially another huge market for us, offering the possibility of reaching more than 200 million people. But any company doing business in that region must be extremely sensitive to the conservative local standards. Many people doubted MTV would ever be permitted in that part of the world. It was the real test of our commitment to respect and reflect to find a way to adapt the spirit of MTV to their local standards.

Eventually, we formed a partnership with the Dubai-based Arab Media Group, the largest media company in the United Arab Emirates. One of their representatives and I traveled to Mecca to meet the mayor. That was a hugely important meeting. Mecca is the most important city in Islam—Muhammad was born there—and the mayor of that city is extremely powerful. We couldn't launch without his permission. We stayed in Jeddah, Saudi Arabia's second largest city. While we were there, to get a taste of the local music scene, I went to a recording session to hear the region's most popular rap group, the Jeddah Legends. Perhaps surprisingly, the rhythmic structure of Arabic translates easily into rap. The Jeddah Legends are a talented group, although fittingly for that culture, rather than rapping about street cred and sex, they rap about how much they love their mothers, their concern about their marriages, and respect for their elders.

Our meeting with the mayor took place in his massive marble palace. While it looked and felt as if it had been built many decades earlier, I later found out it was less than 10 years old. When doing business in that region of the world symbolism is very important, and your place generally is determined by your importance. As in China, large formal chairs are arranged in the shape of a horseshoe, with the most senior people sitting at the top of the U. Rather than facing each other, as in the West, the seating is arranged to face the open end of the horseshoe. When people address each other they lean in their direction. It's all choreographed and it does take some getting used to.

There is an art to conversation. When speaking, it's best to complete one sentence, then pause, and then continue. I had to learn how to be comfortable with silence. While westerners like to fill silences, and meetings proceed steadily, in most other parts of the world, and especially in Japan, long periods of silence are common and perfectly acceptable. It's important to appreciate the silence. In some countries the brash American has become a cliché, so it is always better to listen when another person is speaking. It's often a temptation for a western business executive to start talking; if not right away, quickly. And interrupting when someone else is speaking is a major error. When you do speak, never hesitate to tell your hosts how much you're enjoying the crunchy live fish special, but while doing so weave in the key messages that move directly toward your objective.

From missiles to music: After two years in Vietnam, I spent four years commanding missile bases in Italy. It was a very different world than the one inhabited by Bono (*below left*) and Mick Jagger (*below right*) at the MTV Europe Music Awards.

I broke my personal rule by dating an employee—and then I married her. Alex and I, seen here on a boat in Greece, have four children together.

At Nickelodeon's Kids' Choice Awards in Los Angeles in 2007: Tiger, Alex, Noa, I'm holding Rocky, and Liam (*from left to right*).

Here at a dinner honoring my service as Chairman of the Global Business Coalition Against HIV/AIDS in 2001. Alex and I are joined by former President Bill Clinton (*between me and Alex*) and the late Richard Holbrooke (*far left*), who succeeded me as head of the Global Business Coalition Against HIV/AIDS.

Sumner Redstone, my boss for more than two decades, was the visionary who built Viacom into one of the world's leading media companies.

Among those many people who were essential to that effort were (*from left to right*) Philippe Dauman, Judy McGrath, Tom Freston, myself, and Tom Dooley.

Among the many world leaders with whom I've worked are Chinese President Jiang Zemin . . .

. . . the Dalai Lama . . .

. . . Nelson Mandela (*center*), who with the help of Will Smith (*left*) formally launched our African channel MTV Base from a mountain in Johannesburg . . .

. . . and former British Prime Minister Tony Blair (*center*) with me and Bob Geldof (*right*).

My career has also allowed me to work with some of the world's most popular performers, including Beyoncé, Naomi Campbell, Paul McCartney, and Pamela Anderson, seen presenting with me at the MTV Russia Music Awards.

Among the countless trips I've taken was a journey to Cuba with (*from top left*) Tom Freston, Graydon Carter, (*second row*) Jim Wiatt, Brian Grazer, and Brad Gray. To the right of me is Les Moonves, and to the left of me are Jonathan Brandstein and a second person who helped facilitate the trip—for which we were fined by the U.S. Government.

Few business leaders gave more to others than the late Anita Roddick, who founded The Body Shop and campaigned for environmental and social issues.

I've been invited to address the UN General Assembly several times. Here I am speaking to 2,000 students at the Model UN.

Secretary General Ban Ki-moon presenting me with the UN Correspondents 2009 Global Citizen of the Year award.

Me with an Afghani soldier, showing our preferred weapons.

Generally in these meetings I would sit next to the most senior official with an interpreter between us, but in Mecca my local partner sat next to the mayor and I sat next to him. My partner did most of the talking. But in response to the mayor's questions, I assured him we would create programs that emphasized the importance of education to young people, which we knew was extremely important to them; we would hire only local employees; there would be no risqué programming—in Arabia that meant no bare chests, including men; and we would be pleased to broadcast a call to prayer five times each day as required by the Muslim religion. It was essentially the same message I had delivered to other leaders: We would respect and reflect their culture; we would do nothing to offend anyone; and our long-term goal was to export their culture rather than importing western values—bring out as opposed to bringing in. If there was a political statement to be made, it was done by exposing young people around the world to diverse cultures. I said it, I meant it, and we adhered carefully to those dictates.

When we launched MTV Arabia, we made the controversial decision to bring the rappers Ludacris and Akon to Dubai, as well as the Canadian-Lebanese singer, Karl Wolf, who was popular in that region. I love Ludacris and Akon, they're amazing artists, but their lyrics are not about loving their mother. We would never be able to play all their music on MTV Arabia. But young Arabians wanted to see major recording stars and the two of them were a big hit just by showing up. When MTV Arabia went on the air we followed through on the commitment we'd made to reflect and respect their local culture, as we do in all Muslim countries, among them India, Indonesia, and Pakistan. We broadcast the call to prayer on the channel five times every day. For Ramadan we produced an animated film explaining the meaning of that important religious holiday to young people in a creative way and refrained for a month from showing any music videos. As our station manager in Saudi Arabia, Samer al-Marzouqi, explained, "Though part of a global brand, MTV Arabia is conscious of regional sensitivities and we are keen to respond to the needs of viewers in the Middle East, the vast majority of whom will be fasting and focusing on their spiritual lives." While the programming was similar to that of other countries, consisting of reality shows, celebrity news, music and pop-culture programs, long-form programming, and concerts and awards shows, the content of those programs was determined by the local staff and met the local standards. In fact, a government official there lauded us in the media for doing a better job respecting local sensitivities than their regionally owned channels.

The night following that meeting with the mayor, my Arabian partners hosted a lavish celebratory dinner in a large tent set up near the Red Sea. No matter where I traveled in the world, sharing a meal is an extremely important symbolic gesture, it is a way of actively participating in the local culture. That means eating whatever is served—even if sometimes you're not quite certain what it is. To build relationships, I've eaten fried scorpion, snake gall bladder, ants, ox penis, and live fish, as well as many unidentifiable foods I can't accurately describe. Ox penis is not pleasant; its consistency is just what you would expect. I didn't like eating the swimming fish in Japan, either; the tradition there is to catch very small fish with your chopsticks and then decide whether to crunch or swallow. I tried both; swallowing is easier than crunching. I also didn't enjoy eating fugu, or blowfish, in Japan, which has to be prepared by people specially trained and licensed by the government to remove the poison or it can kill you. As the platter was placed on the table I was told how many people had died from eating fugu that particular year. Through the years I've learned just to be polite and eat it, on occasion forcing myself not to think too much about what *it* is. I remind myself that if my hosts are eating it, it must be safe. Fortunately, our Saudi feast consisted of more traditional foods.

A similar celebratory dinner I will never forget took place in the back room of a karaoke bar in Thailand. It was a long night and included numerous toasts to fellowship, partnership, and practically every other type of 'ship. My Thai partner was a big martial arts fan, and late in the evening the swords came out. These were very real and very sharp swords. He and another man started demonstrating martial arts moves with swords. I'd seen enough Quentin Tarantino movies to know what could happen next. What started as fun suddenly became serious. They started puffing up their chests and pushing against each other, and I thought, *in one second this is going to get out of control.* But no one else in that room seemed concerned about it; mostly they ignored it. I was greatly relieved when they put down those swords to have another drink. That was an accepted aspect of their culture.

■■■

The first thing we did when deciding to enter a market was to develop a business plan that predicted how long it would take us to become profitable. These blueprints were created by our business development people and usually included elaborate charts and graphs and an analysis of several different scenarios, which invariably concluded with a set of numbers that projected profitability. In our early days, I preferred conservative business plans that would show we would be profitable in four years, even though I believed we could be profitable in fewer years, just as were at MTV Europe. If we already had a channel up and running with an existing infrastructure and simply were launching another channel on top of that, our breakeven point could be instantaneous.

That long-term plan is a little game that many corporations play. What I did (probably what most executives do) is try to get a business plan approved by MTV Networks and Viacom that I knew I could meet or exceed. My philosophy in writing a business plan or a budget was *UPOD*: *Under-promise and over-deliver.* I may have picked up that terminology from someone else, but I've embraced it. The UPOD needs to be balanced. It is always important to set high objectives for your internal sales team, especially on the revenue side, otherwise they may be lulled into lowered aspirations; but it is equally important to set expectations for the parent company that clearly can be met.

Whereas years ago long-term business plans were acceptable, business plans now have to be updated constantly, at least every six months. As everyone realizes, a business plan is simply an extended projection that is subject to every possible fluctuation. But the worst thing an executive can do for his own career is approve a business plan that is almost impossible to meet or exceed. Unfortunately, I've had experience with that, too. Missing projections can dampen enthusiasm for an entire market. For example, I've always believed Korea is a strategically important market for us because it is on the cutting edge of digital technology and its youth-oriented culture influences the rest of Asia, but because it didn't meet financial projections there has been pressure to exit that market.

I knew that our business plan for MTV Asia was wrong. We went to Asia early in our expansion strategy and the initial financial projections were overly optimistic. The business plan showed earlier breakeven points than I suspected were possible. But after our success in Europe, there were tremendous expectations that we could conquer the world. They couldn't be met and had to be continually revised. Just as in Europe there was limited infrastructure and difficult regulatory issues to be overcome, so originally MTV Asia was a pan-regional channel. That concept proved much more challenging than it had in Europe because the cultural differences were so great, which led to the launch of more national operations.

A lot of western corporations have invested in Asia, in China particularly, in preparation for a future that never quite seems to arrive. Apparently since the days of Marco Polo the potential of the huge Asian market has masked the huge challenges: Like just about every other U.S. corporation, I looked at Asia and saw the Fertile Crescent. I was seduced by the potential and convinced we would be able to do what nobody else had yet accomplished. Somehow, I figured, we would make it work. In fact, I have been quoted as saying that there is no such thing as an international strategy that does not include China, and I continue to believe that. There is the possibility for a large and profitable business there. Our plan for Asia was growth, growth, growth, so I approved a business plan that was overly optimistic. Still, I was disappointed when we didn't meet it. As a result we spent the next few years making numerous course corrections. Several media companies have left China; Time-Warner got out and Murdoch got out, but I believe there is a way to succeed in China. Like MTV, Disney is making the necessary investment. I remain a firm believer that if you have the right people in place and you execute a well-conceived strategy you will find a way to be successful. MTV has had mixed results in China, but it has become a multipronged business. MTV is still in the investment stage there. It has four offices in China and in addition to the TV channels it produces programming, digital operations, and consumer products. As it has throughout history, China remains a long-term investment.

Much of the tremendous pressure I felt to continue expanding, I put on myself. I had completely embraced Sumner Redstone's business philosophy—as summed up by the title of his autobiography, *A Passion to Win*. I knew we had a unique, and popular product to sell. The "New World Teen Study" conducted in 1996, which included 25,000 young people, reported that in our target demographic MTV had become the most-recognized TV channel in the world. Throughout the world, even those young people who had never seen MTV were increasingly becoming aware of it. They wanted their MTV, and we wanted to find a way to get it to them. We couldn't wait; more than a hundred music channels had sprung up around the world, and in those countries where we weren't available they began to take root.

As we had done when building MTV Europe, when we entered a market we had to determine the best possible business structure. The market generally determined whether it was best, or possible, to own and operate the channel, whether we needed to find a partner, or whether we simply licensed programming to an existing channel. After launching more media properties than any person in history, I can state with conviction that there is no single right answer. In Singapore, for example, we didn't need a partner because that government has established one of the most business-friendly environments in the world. But because there was limited cable infrastructure in Indonesia, we needed to find a partner with a terrestrial station.

Whatever our initial decision, it rarely was permanent, as changing circumstances forced us to adapt. For example, we had launched MTV Brazil in 1990 as a licensing deal with Abril, the nation's biggest magazine publisher. That decision had been made because the market simply hadn't been developed. But as I got to know Roberto Civita and his son, Giancarlo, the principle owners of Abril, I realized Brazil was potentially a great opportunity for us. Roberto and Giancarlo were dynamic, well-respected, and very successful business leaders in Brazil, precisely the type of people with whom we wanted to be in a partnership. So I decided to exercise our option to convert the licensing agreement into a joint venture with Abril. For almost a decade this proved to be a good relationship for both partners, but the government tightened its regulations in 2005, prohibiting foreign-owned companies from owning more than 30 percent of a terrestrial network. That forced us to reduce our stake. Two years later we decided to return to the original licensing arrangement.

In Korea, we have gone through several different corporate structures. Korea has become the most advanced broadband market in the world, the second largest music market in Asia. Tom Freston and I first went there in the early 1990s to negotiate a licensing agreement. It was a highly regulated country and we had been offered one hour of broadcast time a day. We met with the minister in charge of foreign media, and 30 seconds after "Hello" we were drinking what they referred to as "Depth Charges." A Depth Charge is a beer stein with a shot glass of whisky. After 10 minutes and several Depth Charges, we were offered a second hour.

Beginning in 1999 we formed a partnership with Korea's largest cable music channel to broadcast five hours of daily Korean-language programming. When we couldn't agree on renewal fees, they cloned our channel, creating their own music channel that looked just like MTV. We responded by syndicating four hours of daily programming to another cable channel, OnGameNet, which until then was basically a gaming channel. Eventually MTV Asia took control of the programming of that channel. We now have a strong presence in Korea—Nickelodeon is particularly popular—but it remains a very challenging market.

Joint ventures can be very complicated. Partners often have different objectives and different interests. For example, after leaving Rupert Murdoch's STAR TV in Asia, we relaunched MTV Asia as a joint venture between us and Polygram, while at the same time in Europe (as part of our action against VPL) we were suing Polygram. But in Asia, Polygram was run by Norman Cheng, who had built it into the number one record company in the region. We also were battling Murdoch's News Corp–owned Channel V in Asia, but in Britain News Corp had a financial stake in both our Nickelodeon and Comedy Central channels.

Operating as many channels as we do, it is inevitable that sometimes we end up with the wrong partner. In 2006, we formed a joint venture in Turkey, for example, but we had to withdraw our channels from that country when our expectations were not met. Sometimes, the economic circumstances change. MTV Arabia was immediately successful; a strong partnership enabled us to reach 30 million households. It was a great success—until the economy of that region collapsed. Then we had to extract ourselves from the existing partnership and look for a new opportunity. It can takes years and be very expensive to end a partnership and it sometimes ends up in court. Although it may take a long time at the beginning of the process to select a partner, it is time very well spent.

Many of these deals were difficult to negotiate at times because the people on the other side of the table were too demanding, but on occasion because they simply didn't know how to negotiate. I loved negotiating; it was so much a part of my life that at times I couldn't stop. When I walked into a store to buy something. I'd pick out what I wanted and ask, "What's your best price?" Then we should start negotiating. At times the sales clerks would look at me like I was crazy. During my years at HBO it was all I did. But as my responsibilities at MTV Networks grew, I was no longer involved in the day-to-day deal making. Negotiating is an art form and when it is well done it is extremely satisfying. "Well done," of course, is subject to interpretation. The question you always have to ask at the very beginning of a negotiation is where you want to be at the very end.

For years my negotiating strategy was to begin by finding out what the best deal is and then push for more. I would keep pushing and pushing until I got the best possible deal. In our licensing deals, for example, we included all types of fees. In addition to receiving a percentage of revenue just for the brand (a trademark fee), we would get a programming fee and then a management fee. We could do that because our brand was so strong. But I've learned; I didn't get softer, I got smarter. My evolving objective became to make a deal relatively equal, as close to a win-win situation for both sides as possible. In the early days, we negotiated some deals that simply weren't sustainable for the other side; when the contract expired after three years they would walk away. Three years of an extraordinarily good deal is not as good as a 10-year deal that works for both parties. We found that when we negotiated a deal that was too good, we not only had burned through a relationship, but we probably had negotiated ourselves out of the market.

That's what happened in Spain. We had spent months negotiating a joint venture with Antena 3, a terrestrial station. Those negotiations literally went down to the *last minute*. We were scheduled to flip the switch and go on the air at 12:00 A.M.; all the marketing materials had been circulated, there had been a substantial amount of publicity, and everything was in place except a signed contract. At 11:59, we were still negotiating. We signed the contract exactly at midnight and went on the air. It was a great deal for us—*too* good. The contract was so much in our favor that at the end of the term our partner didn't want to renew it. It had enabled us to earn a good profit, but in the end, it was not sustainable and we had to begin the process of finding a suitable partner all over again.

A contract that is too good can be bad in the long run. In 1998, our Japanese partner, Music Channel, decided not to renew our agreement, claiming the fees we were requesting for renewal were too high. Instead, it set up a competitive music channel, called "Vibe," which never really worked. We were off the air in Japan for two years—until we were able to reach an agreement with the investment firm H&Q Asia Pacific, which had purchased Music Channel, to transform "Vibe" into MTV Japan. In 2006, after the channel had become profitable, we decided to buy out the investment firm, making this our second largest acquisition behind only VIVA.

We had to learn not to be greedy. A little advantage is always nice, but the best possible contract is one that's as close to equal as possible. Eventually, we developed a standard licensing contract, so, theoretically, all the other side had to do was read it and sign it. For licensees, the agreement set out clear contractual obligations on the use of our brand and logo, and we would manage the relationship through our servicing department. In return for fees and a share of the profits, we worked with our partner in every area of the channel from the look to ad sales. They would have access to all of our strengths. We would provide all the training and resources they needed to operate successfully, at times even implanting a creative person in their organization for a long period of time. But we would negotiate every aspect of the arrangement.

When it was time to launch a new service we sent an experienced launch team, a business version of a SWAT team, headed by Rebecca Batties, to that country. When possible, we'd include some expats from that country on this team. The team literally would live there for months, teaching the new employees our corporate culture and operating principles until the channel was successfully on the air. Brent Hansen, who had started as a junior producer but by the mid-1990s had become our programming director, explained,

> When we set up a channel we always provide a set of parameters in terms of standards of things we require. At every network group around the world we have creative heads whose job it is to bring people up to speed, to help coach people, to hire

people locally and, if necessary, to make sure that if there is a weakness in an area, we can cover that. Obviously an MTV channel that doesn't look good enough is not going to produce business for us, let alone satisfy the audience. There's a high expectation factor.

■ ■ ■

We were extremely aggressive about launching channels. It seemed like every month we were launching a new service. Once we started expanding we were seemingly unstoppable. We launched channel after channel after channel. Every week there was another launch, another two launches. We raced through our penetration goals: 5 million households, 10 million, 25 million, 50 million, 100 million, 125 million. Five years earlier we had celebrated getting on a small service in the Ukraine; now we hardly paused when we added five new countries. My strategy was, simply, to be everywhere. MTV raced across the entire world: 20 countries, 50 countries, 100 countries, 150 countries. Within a decade we had created a potential audience of more than a billion people.

Over a few months in 1995, for example, we launched our Mandarin channel in Taipei. MTV Asia signed a distribution deal with a strategic partner in Thailand. We launched in Singapore. We launched an English-language channel in Jakarta, Indonesia. We launched service to the Philippines on a patchwork of satellite and terrestrial systems. MTV Asia began terrestrial distribution in Sri Lanka. We opened an office in Hong Kong. In January 1996, we launched our 24-hour service in India with a party in Bangalore, which was blessed in a Pooja ceremony that offered positive energies. By late 1997, our three 24-hour Far Eastern channels reached 57 million households.

We were launching so many services so rapidly that on occasion I would joke that there were channels launching that I didn't even know existed. Among my favorite names was MTV Adria, for the Adriatic countries. Looking back, that may have been the first hint that I was overextending myself, that I was stretched too thin. But I didn't want to slow down. This was the decision I had made and the results had been astounding. We were successfully building the largest media network in the world. Some people later argued that we could have been even more successful by carefully targeting specific countries based only on their potential profitability, but this was the strategy I had embraced and pursued. I wanted to be everywhere and I had faith that every channel eventually could be successful. We were relentless; we didn't take time to pause or even slow down. Expanding aggressively was in our corporate DNA. Admittedly, it was a somewhat controversial strategy, but this rapid expansion eventually made it difficult to exercise command and control. I accepted the reality that mistakes were going to be made as an inherent part of the growing process. And when a mistake was made I dealt with it, and then I told the person who'd made it, "It's done. Let's not waste time talking about it. Let's just move forward." And we did.

There also were doubts about the value of launching MTV in smaller countries that we knew would never generate substantial profits. I argued that while they didn't provide a great return, neither did they require a lot of time to manage them. In most smaller countries we made licensing deals that required no investment. When I saw an opportunity, I took it. I wanted to be everywhere.

In countries that couldn't support their own national channel we distributed existing channels. That was the strategy in Africa for a long time, where until 2005 there was limited infrastructure. I always wanted to be in Africa because the roots of all forms of music can be traced to that continent. There is no place else that has the diversity of music found in Africa, but very few countries had the distribution network to support a local channel. Instead, MTV France was in West Africa, MTV Arabia was in northeast Africa, MTV India was on a powerful satellite so it was received in parts of Africa, and other countries there received MTV Europe. Finally in 2005 MTV Base was launched, which is a pan-African channel primarily in English featuring local VJs. It's called MTV Base for complicated legal reasons and has the type of patchwork distribution network similar to what was originally created for MTV Europe.

As I had done at HBO, I tried to attend as many launches as possible. At every single launch I would make a speech and admit, "I'm so excited to be here. This is my favorite country." In fact, I loved working in the international market so much that at any given moment, *wherever* I was, *it* was my favorite country. As we grew it became impossible to be at every launch, so I had to start picking and choosing. One I did choose to attend was the 2006 launch of MTV Pakistan.

I felt strongly Pakistan was an important cultural market for us. Many people disagreed with me. Pakistan has a small but powerful extremist element. A couple of years earlier one of these groups had burned a pile of television sets, calling them "Satanic devices that corrupt people and society." To be certain we did not offend these Muslim traditionalists, we spent several months before the launch test-marketing the channel. We made a licensing deal with Ali Ghazanfar, the owner and CEO of Indus Music Group, a satellite channel that broadcast to 64 other countries. Indus hired an all-native-born-and-bred Pakistani staff. Since the murder of journalist Daniel Pearl, Pakistan generally has been perceived to be an extremely dangerous place for westerners to visit. My wife, Alex, and several of my friends tried to convince me not to go. They reminded me that the Taliban would make international headlines by successfully kidnapping the head of MTV Networks International. In fact, on several previous trips to unsettled regions Sumner Redstone would joke that I was so valuable that if I was kidnapped the company couldn't afford the ransom that would be asked for me, so I would be there forever. I understood the potential dangers, but I had never been to Pakistan and I thought it was important that we were forging a link between young people in Pakistan and the rest of the world. The value of launching MTV Pakistan was questionable, but I felt young Pakistanis deserved their own MTV.

I decided not to tell too many people, including executives in New York, that I was going to attend the launch in Karachi. In retrospect, that probably was a mistake. I'm not naive; I recognized that there was at least some danger, so I did make one compromise: In my previous travels I had never hired security. Either I didn't believe it was necessary, or I felt it might attract more attention than I wanted. But in this instance I decided to take this precaution. I hired a trained English-speaking driver who also served as my security guard. He came with the requisite sunglasses and certainly looked the part, but as I got to know him I realized that I had a lot more military experience than he did. In fact, he was mostly a very expensive tour guide.

When I arrived in Karachi, the streets were filled with weapons for sale. Major arms-trading bazaars are held periodically in different countries around the world. Coincidentally, one was taking place in Karachi while I was there. It was possible to buy anything there from bullets to tanks, and in my hotel I saw every type of military man, from four-star generals in uniforms bedecked with medals to men in semi-military fatigues. As a result of this arms bazaar, security was incredibly tight. I had to pass through several checkpoints just to get to my hotel room.

The launch party was an impressive event. It was held outdoors and was attended by about 3,000 warm, generous, and successful people. Karachi was not at all what many westerners believe. At the launch I went onstage and made my usual speech, which I always ended by thrusting my fist into the air and, trying to be inspirational, promising, "MTV Pakistan will be the best MTV in the world!" This time, though, as I walked offstage, the entire audience stood and began singing, "I want my MTV." A week earlier, I'd been a bit anxious about being kidnapped; instead, I'd received one of the warmest welcomes of my entire career.

One launch I particularly remember was MTV Israel. Government regulations had made it extremely difficult to launch there. Before I delivered my usual speech, I asked our partner, Udi Miron, the president of Ananey Communications, if he could think of a quote that might be appropriate. He paused only briefly, then perhaps remembering all the problems we'd had to overcome, suggested I quote David Ben Gurion, who said, "In Israel, miracles are part of the planning." I used it that day, and subsequently have incorporated it into many of my speeches.

Probably the most difficult place to get a foothold was China. That's a lesson taught by history—and it proved to be our experience. I spent almost two decades traveling to China to build strong relationships. In that time no nation has changed so drastically. When I first went there it was very drab, a monochromatic country, with countless bikes and virtually no cars on the roads. It's impossible to accurately convey the magnitude of the change. There are now traffic jams at all hours; the skyline of every city seems to go on into the horizon. It's bright and colorful and exciting and loud and very creative. And since China hosted the Olympics, Beijing has turned green; there have been thousands of trees planted. The transformation of China has been stunning—with the exception of access to its markets. That hasn't changed very much. While certain corporations have been successful in China, like General Motors, Volkswagen, Wal-Mart, and the National Basketball Association, the same has not been true for media companies.

To protect its own media, as well as its cultural integrity, China severely restricts foreign media companies. Numerous media companies have gotten very impatient waiting for that future to arrive, including Viacom. Time Warner sold its interest in a Chinese satellite company in 2003. Murdoch's News Corp sold control of its Chinese TV channels in 2010. Everybody has tried—Google, Yahoo!, eBay—but no American media company has been able to take full advantage of the lucrative Chinese market. That didn't stop us from trying, though. In some ways, several of those media companies had attempted to circumnavigate the system, but I decided we were going to play by the Chinese government playbook. I was going to deal with all the red tape, all the roadblocks, all the headaches. The key was finding the right person to lead our effort; our first GM in China was a Chinese-born college professor we'd found teaching Mandarin in New Jersey. He returned to China for us and, tragically, for reasons we've never learned, he was murdered in Shanghai. We then hired a man named Harry Hui, who had earned his MBA in the United States and then returned to Asia to run Warner's music business there.

The first challenge in China was getting distribution. There were several different distribution platforms from which to choose—terrestrial, unencrypted satellite, encrypted satellite, basic cable, or pay cable—and each of the other media companies had made different decisions. I knew we weren't going to be able to secure a 24-hour channel outside of hotels—that was the impossible dream in China—so instead we focused on syndicating hourly blocks of programming. At one of our meetings with the director of the Chinese state regulatory commission he suggested that we should consider basic cable. A suggestion from a Chinese government official was more than a helpful hint. That turned out to be the right choice, although it resulted in only partial carriage. But just like I had seen two decades earlier at HBO, as the number of homes with cable access grew, so did our distribution.

We also had to assure Chinese officials that we were going to respect and reflect their standards. In China, this was more important than anywhere else in the world. It meant that in addition to nothing violent, nothing sexual, nothing religious, and nothing political, we could never refer to what is known as the "three *T*s: Taiwan, Tibet, and Tiananmen Square." In later discussions with government ministers it was explained to me that to the Chinese, Tibet is like Texas; I was asked how I would feel if Texas suddenly declared itself an independent nation. I was also told that what happened in Tiananmen Square was an internal issue and not a subject for discussion or debate. We assured the government that we had no political agenda, and at various times we actively supported Chinese initiatives like its bid to join the World Trade Organization and to attract the Olympics and the World Expo. Whether I personally agreed with all of this was not the point. If we were really going to be a local channel, we would support the local view of the issues.

Music plays a very important role in Chinese culture, and in those early days, many government officials assumed MTV was going to feature popular Chinese classical music. While it took us a long time, we finally secured a one-to-three-hour block of programming time on Beijing cable TV, which at that time probably had fewer than a million subscribers. Eventually, we were broadcasting as many as six hours of programming a day on about 40 cable systems with a potential audience of 100 million households. We were so popular that when we announced open auditions to find new VJs more than 10,000 young Chinese came from all over China.

We had successfully created programming that attracted the youthful audience we wanted, while demonstrating our commitment to adhere to their standards. As in some other countries, in China we broadcast about 85 percent local music and 15 percent from the rest of the world. In fact, Ricky Martin's "Livin' La Vida Loca" became popular there before it was a hit in the United States. We built strong relationships with several government officials, so when we had a problem—and we did have problems—or had a request, I knew to whom and where to go in the bureaucracy. I continued to lobby for increased distribution. What I really wanted was a 24-hour channel.

Yifei Li, who had replaced Harry Hui as Viacom's General Manager in China, was able to arrange a meeting for Sumner Redstone and I with Chinese Premier Jiang Zemin in the Forbidden City, the former Imperial Palace dating back to the Ming Dynasty. Like Harry, Yifei Li was well-connected, tenacious, and able to navigate a path for us through the often complex Chinese bureaucracy. There was very elaborate protocol and essentially it was a meeting between Jiang and Sumner. I said very little, but as we were introduced to the premier, who was dressed in a western suit, to my surprise, the first words out of his mouth were "MTV." He complimented us on how well MTV was doing in China and pointed out that music played an important role in the Chinese culture.

Sumner visited China several times and became greatly respected there. He appeared on national TV and lectured at leading universities. And while he often repeated our respect-and-reflect mantra, in one instance he got into an argument with the minister of propaganda, Minister Deng. In China, propaganda is not considered a bad word, and this official ran the Propaganda Department of the Communist Party While the Propaganda Department is not formally considered to be part of the government, in fact it strictly controls the media throughout the country. Minister Deng was upset by the fact that CBS, which at that time was owned by Viacom, had broadcast a *60 Minutes* interview with Jiang Zemin that the Chinese felt was unnecessarily hostile. At this meeting Chinese officials asked Sumner why he had allowed it. Their point was something like, "You're the owner of the news channel, why would you tolerate something like that?"

Sumner then explained the American concept of freedom of the press. Basically he replied, "I may disagree with a journalist, but I am not going to tell him what to say." The Chinese couldn't understand that. Their belief was that he controlled the journalist; if he didn't agree with his words, he should change them. It became quite a heated debate and voices really got raised. Sumner didn't back off at all.

His visits to China proved invaluable. While meetings with high-ranking government officials mostly are ceremonial, the fact that Jiang Zemin met with Sumner made Chinese bureaucrats take MTV Networks very seriously. The credibility we got from these meetings was extremely important.

Eventually, we were informed it might be possible for us to secure a 24-hour cable channel in Guangdong province, China's most densely populated and prosperous region. This was a giant breakthrough; there are only about 35 cable channels and to provide access for MTV one of them would have to be cleared. It was a difficult negotiation and the terms to which we eventually agreed were unlike any other deal we'd made. The Chinese have long been concerned that "the average American does not know nearly as much about China as the average Chinese knows about America." The belief in China is that Americans, and by extension westerners, hold stereotypical images of China, many of which are false. The Chinese government wanted our help in countering that. That's when I was introduced to the concept of *reciprocity*.

After prolonged negotiations, we were offered distribution for a 24-hour channel in Guangdong in return for distribution of a Chinese channel, CCTV 9, to 76 American hotels. The Chinese believed CCTV 9 offered Americans an insight into Chinese culture. The deal actually came down to a formula: They would give us access to a specific number of households in Guangdong province in return for distribution to precisely 76 American hotels. We were able to provide that exposure through MTV Networks Affiliate Operations division. Eventually, we were able to reach an agreement that made MTV the only 24-hour non-Chinese-branded service permitted to broadcast outside hotels and compounds in China. Ironically, Minister Deng, who had debated with Sumner about a free press, met with us in Hawaii to finalize this contract. The fact that he traveled to Hawaii was an indication of how important this was to the Chinese. At that time this was a mutually beneficial deal that was good for both sides. But in the ensuing years the Chinese attitude has changed. China feels much more emboldened now so exposing their culture to the west is less of a priority. But when we were negotiating this arrangement the government was very concerned about the world's perception of China.

Among the Chinese government officials with whom I forged a strong personal relationship was the leader of this province. We bonded over the fact that he had attended the Chinese military academy and was fascinated by West Point. When he visited the United States, I was able to arrange a private tour of West Point for his entire entourage. I never could have expected that my military background would prove to be more valuable than my Harvard education in establishing a relationship with a top official of the Chinese Communist Party.

The good news was that we had permission from the central government; the bad news was that we still had to reach agreements with the cable systems. While the Chinese government exercises control over the flow of information into the country, in several parts of the country there is also a strong capitalistic ethic. In some ways it seemed to me that China was more capitalist than any other country I'd visited. Chinese cable operators are just as tough as cable operators anywhere else in the world. They will fight for pennies. Many of them live a great distance from the central government in miles as well as ideology. And they didn't like being told what to do. To build MTV's distribution we had to negotiate with each of them. We've had reasonably good success doing that, particularly compared to other media companies. In addition to a 24-hour channel in Guangdong, MTV has been able to claim partial carriage distribution in China to about 100 million households. We also syndicated blocks of Nickelodeon programming—including *SpongeBob Square Pants* and *Dora the Explorer*—on CCTV, which has provided nationwide distribution. But the reality is that, considering the size of that country and the potential market, MTV's overall coverage is still limited.

Harry Hui has become a very recognizable figure in China. After he left MTV Networks he appeared on the Chinese version of *American Idol* and has become their version of Simon Cowell. His picture now appears on giant billboards and he has remained a good friend.

In China, as elsewhere in the world, one of the initial decisions I had to make was whether to encrypt our signal. If a signal is unencrypted, any viewer with the right equipment can receive programming for free; when it's encrypted they have to pay a fee for it to be unscrambled. We knew we had to encrypt in China and go on the China satellite, Sinosat. That was less a business decision than abiding by the wishes of the Chinese government. MTV actually had no choice. Encryption was the means the government used to restrict access to programming to those people or places who were permitted to receive it. No media company would be allowed to transmit its signal into the Chinese mainland without government supervision.

Making the decision to encrypt was more complicated in most other markets. The choice is between remaining unencrypted, which provides the largest possible audience and therefore the greatest advertising revenue, or encrypting the signal, which diminishes the size of your potential audience but offers the possibility of subscription revenue streams. On basic cable, which is the whole slate of programs that a cable operator offers to subscribers for one monthly fee, channels like MTV are paid by the cable operator for the right to include it on that slate, but these channels also can sell advertising. There are also tiered channels, like HBO, for which subscribers pay an additional fee. But while those channels are paid substantially higher fees by cable operators, they are paid only for those subscribers who choose specifically to receive it, rather than being paid a few cents per home for the entire cable subscription base.

The beauty of the cable business has always been the dual revenue stream, and for that reason cable distribution has always been more desirable for us than terrestrial channels. Creating that dual revenue stream has been the objective of every cable programmer. It has proven to be especially important during recessions, because advertising is vulnerable to swings in the economy while subscription revenue is more reliable. The recent recession has given programmers a much greater appreciation for the subscription side of the business. "Free" has never been part of our mantra. Cable has always been more desirable to us than terrestrial.

But desirable is not necessarily practical. Cable distribution throughout the world remains spotty, and where we could not get sufficient cable distribution we turned to terrestrial systems. Italy, for example, did not have a cable infrastructure when we launched MTV Europe there. Getting terrestrial distribution provided instant distribution throughout the entire country. The advertising revenue we received by gaining national distribution more than compensated for what we lost in cable subscriber fees.

Because of its popularity MTV is the only cable programmer that also operates a profitable terrestrial business around the world. In addition to Italy, MTV is on terrestrial stations and supported primarily by advertising in Indonesia, Brazil, Russia, and several other nations. That additional exposure is one reason the brand has become so well known everywhere in the world.

Getting cable distribution has not always been easy. When MTV was launched in Europe there was little demand for it, so we couldn't attract sufficient subscribers to make us desirable to cable operators. Additionally, leaving our signal free-to-home meant that anyone who bought a satellite dish would be able to turn on their TV set and receive our programming. So out of necessity we relied primarily on advertising revenue. But my experience at HBO had taught me the value of a steady, reliable income stream paid by cable operators rather than having to rely on the volatility of the advertising market. As far as I was concerned, it was never a question of *whether* we would encrypt our programming, just a matter of *when*.

■■■

By the early 1990s MTV was firmly established throughout Europe. While we were adding as many as 500,000 households or more each month, I was concerned that we had come close to maxing out our pan-European advertisers. While I knew we would lose subscribers if we encrypted our signal, which would also reduce our advertising base, I was confident that the additional revenue stream would more than make up for it. As a media analyst with a major London financial company told reporters, "By going subscription, they can literally double their revenues overnight." But then he added, "It will result in some loss of direct-to-home viewers. It's a risky prospect because it's difficult to predict at the start how many subscribers you lose—and as you lose viewers so you lose advertising revenues."

In 1995, I made the decision to encrypt the entire channel. I was confident we would quickly be able to replace those households we lost. But as it turned out, encrypting the channel at that time was a sound business decision because it gave us control of our signal throughout Europe, but in the short-term turned out to be costly. This was the first year our revenues did not exceed our projections. As I discovered, people resisted paying for the same programming they had been receiving for free. In Germany, in particular, the free-to-air stations are so popular that people do not want to pay additional fees for encrypted channels. Even today Germany does not have a strong pay-TV universe. Throughout Europe, by encrypting our signal we lost an estimated 2 million cable homes and as many as 8 million direct-to-home households.

When we decided to localize MTV Europe we had an opportunity to take a second look at our decision country by country. Throughout most of Europe encrypting our signal had proven to be successful as we created a reliable revenue stream, but in Germany it had become obvious that we were not going to be able to generate enough subscription revenue to replace what we had lost in advertising, so we flipped the switch and put Germany back in the clear. But we did keep the rest of Europe encrypted. It got even more complicated when we were able to create packages of our own channels, including a selection of MTV, VH1, Nickelodeon, and Comedy Central. Subsequently, we've decided to take MTV off basic cable and make it a pay service. While our subscriber base has diminished, we were paid substantially more per subscriber. One reason we made that decision is because we have VIVA, so we'll still have a music channel in Germany with national distribution.

This will always be a market-by-market decision. In Asia, for example, our English-language channel originally was unencrypted, while our Mandarin-language channel was encrypted. We did that because the English-language channel was also going to India, where at the time the 25,000 cable *wallahs* didn't collect significant fees and whose payments to programmers are at best unpredictable.

In the end, as it should, the decision comes down to the bottom line: Which strategy gets you to sustained profitability the most rapidly? It requires adaptability to each individual market conditions. In China and India, for example, as the Indian cable industry developed, we were finally able to encrypt our English-language channel.

In less than two decades we have been successful in bringing MTV and our other channels and digital properties to at least 175 countries, although that number seems to change when the sun comes up each morning. There have been only two countries in which I really wanted to establish a channel and could not, Afghanistan and Cuba. I can't justify Afghanistan as a sound business proposition; it would require some creativity to draw up a realistic business plan that showed how we could be profitable there. But I would have loved the cultural significance of MTV Afghanistan. It would have added to our mix. We found a partner, a talented entrepreneur named Saad Mosheni, an Afghan who was educated in Australia and has worked in television. For a time it appeared that we might be able to launch there. But there was insufficient support for it, and because of the obvious dangers, few of our people were willing to relocate Kabul.

There was one more way of expanding our distribution—buying existing successful properties. We have built up such a strong global infrastructure that in certain situations it made great sense to buy additional media properties. We already had incredible local management talent, an office, skill sets, and a sales force. We had creative resources that could be easily layered over another cable company. So while we prefer to grow organically, there have been times when it just made great business sense to buy an existing property.

Ironically, the largest acquisition we've made was VIVA, the German channel that I believe the record companies created in response to our lawsuit against VPL. VIVA was purchased in 2004 for about $400 million. VIVA was a very attractive property. It was a strong brand with universal distribution in Germany; it also had expanded into several countries, including Holland, Hungary, Switzerland, Austria, and Poland. VIVA was our strongest competitor; for several years it actually beat us in the ratings in Germany. I don't believe it makes sense to buy a property when you're in an unleverageable position because you'll be forced to overpay for it. But finally, we hired a skilled programmer named Catherine Műhlemann as our managing director; she deserves the credit for MTV once again becoming Germany's leading music channel. The fact that VIVA had lost some of its luster made it easier for us to acquire it. VIVA gave us several strategic advantages. It operated two universally distributed channels, so we immediately transformed one of them into Nickelodeon. Nick had been in Germany previously, although at that time it had been operated independently of MTV and had been unsuccessful. When Nick became my responsibility I knew the German market had great potential; we just didn't have distribution. After we acquired VIVA which provided the potential national distribution Nick needed, it quickly became a large and very successful business for us, in programming as well as consumer products. As Catherine Műhlemann explained, "This expanded programming offer will create enhanced advertising revenue opportunities for the family of MTV and VIVA channels in Germany, since advertisers will be able to reach a wider range of audience demographics."

For many of the same reasons, we acquired the Dutch channel TMF (The Music Factory), which had been founded to focus on local music in 1995, like VIVA, as a response to our pan-European strategy.

Throughout my entire career, the philosophy I had learned at HBO has never changed: whatever it takes—relentless, aggressive, creative *distribution*. If you can't get your product in front of your potential customers, you have no business. We took every opportunity to expand, and as technology changed we changed with it. We never stopped.

As we learned, the whole world wanted its MTV.

Chapter Six

We Will Rock You/We Are the Champions

When I was growing up I dreamt of being a pop star and I would like to thank MTV for my three houses, my five cars, and my supermodel girlfriend. Live the dream!

—Robbie Williams at the 2000 Europe Music Awards

Christina Aguilera was the host of the 2003 *European Music Awards*, which was held in Edinburgh. Kelly Osborne was the host of our *Red Carpet* show, which covered the arrival of the stars at the event and has itself become a popular and important program. I did not know that Christina Aguilera and Kelly Osbourne did not get along. The night began when Christina refused to walk the Red Carpet if Kelly was there. In response to that, Kelly called Aguilera's music "crap" and referred to Christina as a "cow." In a sketch during the live broadcast, Christina threw darts at Kelly's picture pasted on a board, to which Kelly responded, "I take it as a compliment. If Christina has to resort to throwing darts at my head after everything she's achieved and everything she's done, then she's a really sad, sorry person."

I was backstage while all this was taking place. I had just watched the Black Eyed Peas give one of the greatest performances in the history of the EMAs; Justin Timberlake had jumped onstage to sing with them and the arena was still shaking from the ovation. I didn't know this feud was going on until Harriet Brand, our head of Talent Artist Relations, told me that Kelly Osbourne wanted to see me. That didn't surprise me; at our major events I often spent considerable time backstage making our artists feel welcome and resolving any problems. Kelly's dressing room was mobbed. She was surrounded by handlers and as I walked in I saw that she was in tears. I hadn't met her before; after we were introduced and through her tears she told me basically what was going on. The first thing I did was tell her how truly sorry I was that this had happened. I had no problem apologizing to her, even if I had no idea what I was apologizing for. Kelly seemed to need an apology and I had one to give her.

Everything seemed fine and I started to leave. Beyoncé was about to go on and I was eager to see her perform. We were in the middle of a great show. The energy factor was through the roof. I had already put this problem behind me. But as I started walking away, Kelly ran after me, handed me a cell phone, and asked me to speak with her mother. I took the phone and started walking, and Sharon Osbourne, who was in Los Angeles, said to me, "I don't know who you are and I haven't met you. But I promise you this: I'm going to fly back to London and I'm going to track you down and I'm going to cut off your balls and I'm going to eat them."

The only thing I could think of saying, and perhaps it wasn't relevant, was, "As a new parent I know exactly how you feel." That was absolutely true; my daughter Tiger had been born less than a month earlier. Then I said a few more words, handed back the phone, and kept walking. Quickly.

MTV needed pop culture stars as much as they needed MTV. Even the most extensive distribution system in the world, which we had, would do no good if people didn't want to watch the channel. It was MTV's unique ability to program glocally that set it apart from every other media company. My input into day-to-day programming decisions had become more limited, but I had established the revolutionary structure that gave so much power to local operations, and, as in this situation, got involved when there were difficulties. It was like a balancing act, making certain that everyone at the management level felt empowered to make programming decisions, while retaining corporate responsibility for those decisions. My management philosophy was the same here as it was in every other area: Be quick to take the blame, but be slow to take the credit.

In the initial stages of our expansion we tried to monitor programming on all of our local channels. Taped "air checks" would be sent to New York from around the world. We had a team there, which I referred to affectionately as the "brand police," that would watch them to see if there were any problems. Eventually that became overwhelming and we were almost entirely dependent on the local management to protect our brand. In a lot of situations programming decisions were being made by relatively inexperienced people, so it had the potential of being dicey. But generally, they created a programming environment relevant to their specific audience.

Initially, it was the highly stylized look, the innovative design, and the brash attitude of MTV Europe, as much as the music videos, that made us successful. MTV was fresh, creative, brash, and very exciting—and equally important, it was instantly recognizable. We were the *one and only*. But the competitive home-grown channels that quickly sprang up all across the world had access to most of same videos, and at first some of them did a better job than we did focusing on their local market. In response, we began focusing on nonvideo programming. These channels lacked the budget, creativity, or talent to match us. Our competitors couldn't copy our popular programs, like *Remote Control*, *Real World*, or the awards shows that featured performances by the most popular artists in the world. Eventually, we discovered that our long-form programming generated higher ratings than straight music videos. And more recently, with the exception of the chart shows such as the Top Ten, music as a television category was losing its appeal. So we listened to our audience and gradually replaced music videos with programming.

After we went local, our regional channels were expected to produce a substantial percentage of their own content, hosted by local VJs. Our strategy from the beginning was to take the best of our international programming and marry it to the best of locally produced programming, and then customize it for market so the blend in each country was very different. In Taiwan, for example, the blend of the channel might be 75 percent local and 25 percent international, while in the Philippines, whose history has a much stronger American influence, the channel might be 60 percent international and only 40 percent local.

Each of those channels had access to all of our programs, but the decision what to broadcast and when to broadcast it was entirely under their control. Our premise in going local was that these people knew their market much better than we did, both commercially and artistically, and would create a mix that would appeal to their audience. We weren't marketing the same hamburger around the world; local management was responsible for creating products that appealed to local tastes. The decision on whether to broadcast shows like *A Shot at Love with Tila Tequila* or *Jackass* was made at the local level. In certain parts of the world these shows obviously are too radical for the local audience, but those decisions were made on the front lines by each local operation.

As we learned, that assumption that local management best understood local tastes wasn't always correct. In India, for example, our local team believed that young people there wanted to connect strongly with American kids and ran American-produced content almost exclusively. It was a local station with a heavy American influence. It didn't work. Not only did Indian teenagers reject hard rock and rap, they were dumfounded by shows like *The Osbournes*. They had absolutely no idea what that show was supposed to be about, they couldn't understand a word Ozzy Osbourne said, and apparently they didn't care. "We read the market completely wrong," the general manager admitted. "It completely bombed."

In that situation I had to step in and change the local DNA. The new team hired only Indian VJs who spoke the local Hinglish, a blend of Hindu and English, and focused almost exclusively on Indian music, dance, fashion, cricket, Bollywood films in local languages, and the great Indian movie stars. Eventually, MTV India had the most glamorous VJs anywhere in our world, including a Miss World runner-up, a former Miss India, a Bollywood star, and other nationally recognized personalities. The redesigned channel exuded the colorful persona of the country. The redesigned channel connected strongly with our young audience, which increased an astonishing 700 percent!

As I had hoped, and intended, the channels reflected the personality of the local culture. In Italy, the emphasis was on great style, romance, and good cooking, and programs included *MTV Kitchen*, in which musicians were interviewed while cooking, *Loveline*, a talk show about the subjects that most interest teenagers—love and sex, *Sexy Dolls*, which allowed audience members to interact with pop-star impersonators, and the fashion show, *Stylissimo*, which had guests like Giorgio Armani, Domenico Dolce and Stefano Gabbana. The culture of MTV Brazil was sexy and athletic; viewers could feel the beaches of Rio as they watched *Rockgol*, a soccer tournament that pitted teams of musicians against record company executives, or *Megaliga,* an animated show in which their VJs had superpowers. MTV India was bright and colorful; it successfully captured the street culture, and had a self-effacing sense of humor. In addition to music programming like *MTV Supersonic* and *brand:new:tour*, which featured new artists, among our most popular shows were *MTV Cricket in Control*; *MTV Housefull*, which visited Hindi film stars in their homes; *MTV Bakara*, a *Candid Camera*–type show; and *Roadies*, which tracked the adventures of four boys and three girls as they crossed India on motorbikes. Russians, who were exploring their new freedoms, were watching *Twelve Angry Viewers*, a talk show in which a panel of teenagers argued over their favorite videos, drawing on their history. The most popular show on MTV Arabia was *HipHopNa*, in which a popular Saudi rapper auditioned aspiring rappers in cities throughout the Middle East. One of the most popular shows on MTV Indonesia, *Salam Dangdut*, celebrated that nation's traditional music, which until that show became a hit had basically been ignored by the local recording industry. In Japan and Korea, the channels were oriented toward the techies and included considerable anime. MTV Australia created a series of surfing programs, including *Girls Get Out There*, about female surfers, and *Surf Shorts*, featuring short surfing film-clips. The U.K. emphasized its rich music history with nine different music channels. The concept of glocalization had taken root and was growing.

In addition to reflecting local culture, the channels were careful to respect local sensibilities and customs. MTV Arabia, for example, realized that risqué shows like *Dating My Mom* and *Parental Control* weren't right for its audience, but created local versions of the extreme-sports show, *Barrio-19*, which featured young Arabs racing ATVs through the desert, and the dream-fulfillment show, *Made*.

One of the formats we successfully took around the world was *Total Request Live*, a daily live show that had originated in Times Square and included music videos, performances, and celebrity interviews. While it became iconic in the United States, it was even bigger in Italy, primarily because it moved around the country. They did *TRL*, as it became known, in Rome, in Milan, on the beaches, and wherever young people gathered. In addition to being great on-air programming, it became a very successful marketing event on the ground and these broadcasts would draw thousands of young people.

Our music programs always traveled well. We often could get a popular artist to perform by promising exposure throughout a region or large parts of the world. While I rarely insisted a specific program be run, when there was a strong business reason for doing so I didn't hesitate to communicate that. No program has ever worked universally, *Pimp My Car*, in which an old car is transformed into a hot ride, is popular throughout Europe and the Middle East. A pan-European version, but *Pimp My Ride International*, was taped in the Netherlands. The British, French, New Zealanders, Brazilians, and Arabians all do their own versions. MTV Italy created *Pimp My Vespa*, which transforms beaten-up motor-scooters and motorcycles into flashy bikes. MTV Germany broadcasts three versions: *Pimp My Bicycle* is a whimsical parody of the original; on *Pimp My Whatever*, anything imaginable from a person to a bathroom is completely renovated; and the American version with German subtitles is also broadcast there. *It's My Life* was the Asian attempt to recreate *Real World*.

Channels from Africa to the Philippines broadcast the American version of *Cribs*, essentially a tour of a celebrity's home, while several other countries, including Indonesia, created their own local versions. The animated show, *Beavis and Butthead,* which was first broadcast in the early 1990s, became one of our first international hits; more recently, *Jersey Shore* has been picked up in more than 30 countries around the world. In fact, all of MTV's popular shows, among them *The Hills, Punk'd,* the animated *Celebrity Deathmatch, Paris Hilton's My New BFF, Jessica Simpson's Price of Beauty, A Shot at Love with Tia Tequila, Date My Mom, 16 and Pregnant, Teen Mom*, and *Jackass*, run on selected channels around the world.

In addition to MTV programming, Nickelodeon's animated shows, beginning with *Rugrats* and including *Dora the Explorer* and *SpongeBob Square Pants,* have proven to translate easily and inexpensively to local channels, as these children's characters were universal and dubbing into the local language was simple. By 2009, *SpongeBob* was sold into more than 171 markets and had been dubbed into 25 different languages, becoming the most widely distributed show in our history. Dora, who in the original version speaks English but teaches viewers common Spanish phrases, speaks Spanish in Latin versions and teaches viewers English. The show has been syndicated to 135 markets in 24 languages from Chinese to Turkish, but throughout the world her second language is English.

Dora and *SpongeBob* have become extremely valuable stars, accounting for as much as $2 billion in retail sales annually. I remember the concept of putting Dora in a headscarf or a burka was brought up at a meeting in Los Angeles during our *Kids Choice Awards*. We were about to launch Nickelodeon in Arabia and invited our Arab partners to this event. During this meeting, in perhaps the height of local sensitivity, someone suggested putting Dora in local dress. We weren't considering full cover of the character but rather the type of headscarf made popular in *Aladdin*. It was immediately dismissed, but later I began wondering about it. I mentioned it a second time, but there was little support for the idea. It was an economic decision, not a political one.

Nickelodeon, under the direction of Cyma Zarghami, has done the best job connecting the dots between programming, Pam Kaufman's marketing department, and Leighanne Brodsky's consumer products division. They work very closely with International COO Pierluigi Gazzolo to expertly and very successfully market Nick's programs and products throughout the world.

In 2010, we acquired Winx, an Italian company that produces products, especially dolls, patterned after the characters on the popular program, Winx Club, which has been running on Nick since 2007. Our strategy for merchandising has always been to introduce the character on the air, and then market a variety of products.

Nickelodeon also has produced our first show created by a local channel to become a successful international format. It has always been my dream that the production pipeline would run in two directions, from America to the rest of the world, and then from international back to the United States. *Telenovas*, which are basically multi-episode romantic soap operas, have been extremely popular throughout Latin America for decades, although until recently they haven't been equally popular in other parts of the world. But *Isa TKM*, a series about the difficulties of teenage romance made in Venezuela, became a huge hit and was eventually syndicated to more than 50 countries—including Tr3s, our Hispanic channel, and Korea and Southeast Asia. But it was another telenova, *Annubis House*, a scripted thriller about eight teenagers living in an unusual boarding house, that became our first show from International to be remade for the U.K. and America. It originated in Holland and has been hugely successful in the United States.

I have often been asked how we've dealt with government censorship. While from the very beginning that has been a concern, I believed strongly that if we did what we said we were going to do, meaning respect and reflect, it wouldn't be a problem. And that has been the case. Our local employees understood local restrictions as well as local tastes far better than we did and we supported their choices. In each country our employees reviewed videos and programs, looking specifically for things that might insult local sensibilities; in Asia, for example, any image of Buddha with crossed eyes offends the Thais, while bullfights upset Hindus, and anything to do with the feet is considered an insult in Arabia. In Indonesia, we followed the government's *4-3-2-1 rule*, which stipulated that in a video, a closeup of a woman in a bikini was acceptable for 3 seconds but not 4, and that a shot of a woman in a bikini moving was allowed for 1 second but not 2. In China, of course, the three *T*'s were absolutely forbidden, but there were other areas of sensitivity our local operation had to recognize. One of the more difficult decisions that had to be made occurred when an episode of *South Park*, shown in the United States, featured a representation of the prophet Muhammad as a character. As a result, Viacom received serious threats from religious fundamentalists. It was a potentially dangerous situation. In 2005 a series of editorial cartoons depicting Muhammad published in a Danish newspaper sparked violent protest rallies in several Muslim countries and reportedly resulted in as many as 100 deaths. The cartoonist also received several death threats and at least one attempt was made on his life. In fact in May 2010, less than a month after the episode of *South Park* had been broadcast in America, a car bomb had been parked directly in front of Viacom's New York City headquarters. Fortunately, that bomb failed to detonate, but law enforcement authorities wondered if that attempt was related to this program. We had to decide whether we would run the show in other markets throughout the world. Obviously, we had no intention of showing it in Muslim countries, but *South Park* was popular in several European nations, and I was very reluctant to bow to threats. MTV International President Bob Bakish and I discussed it at great length and finally decided not to run it. For us, the risk outweighed the point we would make by standing up to those threats. There are crazy people in this world, and we recognized that we were responsible for MTV employees in 164 countries. It was a difficult decision and the principle of standing up to threats is absolutely correct, but this was the prudent path to follow.

We also had a problem in 2003 when MTV domestic ran an animated series for one year entitled *Clone High*, in which the clones of legendary world leaders were depicted as high school students. Among those clones was Mahatma Gandhi, who was portrayed as a typical 16-year-old. Even though the show was not broadcast in India, it caused tremendous outrage there; 150 people, including several members of the Indian parliament, protested and began a long fast. This show did not run internationally, but because we were corporate siblings we were blamed for it. The Indian government was upset and threatened to suspend our channel. We issued an apology, which said, "MTV U.S. wants to make it clear that *Clone High* was created and intended for an American audience. We recognize and respect that various cultures may view this programming differently, and we regret any offense taken by the content in the show." The fact that the last few episodes of that series were never broadcast domestically helped resolve that situation. But it also required an apology in Mumbai, which was offered and accepted.

In the past I have resisted government pressure when I believed we were right. For example, when we participated in an anti-whaling campaign, Save the Whales, the government of Norway immediately took us off the air. Whaling is an important industry for that nation. In that instance, the first thing we did was try to lower the volume, then we tried to negotiate without backing down. Although those negotiations failed to find a compromise, after six months we were allowed back on the air.

■■■

The most popular programs that MTV produces, the shows that get the most play throughout the world, are our major events and awards shows.

These always-exciting shows are elaborately staged and star the most popular artists in the world—often doing outrageous things on camera. Our award shows have become you-don't-want-to-miss-this TV. On these shows our audience has come to anticipate the unexpected; we've had everything happen on these shows from full-frontal nudity to a political attack on the president of France. MTV in the United States broadcast the first *MTV Video Music Awards* in 1984. Our first regional version, the *MTV Europe Music Awards*, was created in 1994 and is hosted by a different European city each year. In addition, many of our channels eventually created their own local awards shows, ranging from China's *Mandarin Music Honors* to the *MTV Romania Music Awards*. By 2010, we were doing 35 major events and awards shows annually, including VIVA, TMF, and local versions of Nickelodeon's popular *Kids Choice Awards*. That was too many.

These awards shows fulfilled several objectives: First, they are what is known as "tent-pole events," usually special programs that attract an audience to the rest of the programming schedule. Second, they generate very high ratings and produce substantial sponsorship advertising revenues. These shows have evolved into a major revenue source for us. Third, they are popular client events. In the domestic television industry every broadcast and cable channel holds an annual event called an "upfront" to generate excitement about the upcoming season. These are highly produced events for clients and ad agencies that include appearances and performances by top talent. But in the international environment, we don't have upfronts. We invited all of our clients, ad agency executives, corporate types, our biggest distributors, and even government officials to these spectacular shows to remind them how important MTV is to the youth demographic. It isn't so much a chance to get work done as to solidify relationships. And finally, these shows are huge marketing events that bring a flood of attention to the brand.

Probably the best example of how we achieved our multiple objectives was the Mile High Party that Dave Sibley arranged for the 2009 Australia Music Awards. It was the most innovative marketing promotion we'd done in my career. I couldn't believe we pulled it off. This was a flying concert to bring about 100 people from New Zealand to Australia for the show. We rigged an Air New Zealand flight with speakers, hired popular rappers and other artists, including the U.K.'s number one rapper, Dizzee Rascal and Scribe, and threw a party at 30,000 feet. We invited important clients and music journalists, and the station held a contest in which the prize was a seat on the flight and tickets to "the best awards show in the world."

The party started at the gate. Passengers were greeted by bands playing loudly, drinks were served, and it continued on board. Our VJs were the flight attendants, one of them a former Miss New Zealand. The artists performed in aisles, literally climbing over the seats. It was an unbelievable show—as least for a while. Unfortunately, the business class section was being used as the greenroom, so it was closed. That left only the restrooms at the rear of the plane. The beer began to kick in once we got over the ocean, and the long line to the only rest room snaked along the same aisle that the performers were using. That's when one of the speakers started burning, filling the plane with smoke—and no one was even slightly upset. The event was unbelievable: great music, long lines to the bathroom, performers climbing over the seats, and a smoking speaker. It was a perfect MTV party.

On the negative side, these shows are massive and expensive productions that often require months of time and energy. Many of our local channels wanted to produce their own awards, but in smaller countries these shows were losing a considerable amount of money. In addition, the major artists were very much in demand and could receive 20 or more invitations from various MTV channels around the world, which made it more difficult for us to get them to attend the most important events. Sometimes, for example, it was a struggle to convince major artists to appear on MTV's live shows. Michael Jackson, for example, whose early videos were credited with helping establish MTV, could be difficult. Overall, MTV had a strong relationship with him, and after he was acquitted of child molestation charges, his first public appearance was at the MTV Japan awards. But he agreed to appear in Japan only if we gave him an award. So MTV created the Legend award for him. While for us it was kind of tongue-in-cheek, he took it very seriously. I think he considered it to be an important step in reclaiming his career.

Michael Jackson certainly wasn't the only star to ask for recognition. Being in the music business I had have heard many of these stories concerning bizarre and extreme contractual demands made by stars, from cases of champagne to one color of jelly beans. But in fact that generally was not our experience. I've always thought asking for a working shower was quite reasonable, and that was the type of demand we would get. But there were artists who wouldn't appear on an awards show unless they knew they were going to receive some special acknowledgment. Elton John, for instance, who has been an amazing leader in the fight against AIDS, would want to be certain he was going to receive an award before he would agree to make an appearance. To get around having to guarantee awards we created the People's Choice awards, which allowed us to explain to managers who really wanted these awards that we have nothing to do with the decision. To get around that, they began asking for Icon awards. Paul McCartney is one of the least demanding stars in the industry—we live near each other and I sometimes see him just walking down the street—yet we had to give him an Icon award for him to appear at the *MTV Europe Awards* in Liverpool.

Our first *Europe Music Awards* show took place in Berlin in 1994, *five years to the day* after the Berlin Wall had come down. In many ways this was our coming-of-age party; it was so much bigger and more elaborate than anyone imagined we were capable of producing. The decision to hold it in Berlin was made primarily because Germany was our biggest market, but it was also symbolic of the fact that MTV Europe had successfully united the young people of the continent. In the former East Berlin we constructed an outdoor tent large enough to seat several thousand people on the spot where the Berlin Wall had divided that city. At that time it was the largest outdoor tent ever constructed; it may still be. The only restriction the government placed on us in constructing that tent was that we could not make any holes in the ground, so we weighed down the tent poles with massive water tanks. The show opened with a group of supermodels, led by my non-girlfriend, Naomi Campbell, rising from below the stage to surround George Michael as he sang "Freedom." While he was singing, the massive canvas curtain that covered the entire back of the stage dropped to the ground to reveal the Brandenburg Gate to the audience. For the German audience, that was symbolic of the Wall coming down on that spot five years earlier and was extraordinarily emotional. Then the Gate, which represented all of Europe coming together, was dramatically illuminated in green, the color of hope. No one who was there has ever forgotten that moment. In so many ways, it was also representative of the emergence of MTV Europe as the creative force that had helped unify Europe.

The show was hosted by Tom Jones and featured Aerosmith, Bjork, and Prince, who ended his performance by diving into the audience. We encountered very few problems putting on this show, although one supermodel (not to be named) did threaten to walk off the show when she was told she could not dance with George Michael. And just about the only demand we had from our performers was from Aerosmith's Steven Tyler, who wanted a private shower built in his dressing room—or, in fact, his dressing *closet*. That was a difficult problem, as we'd pieced together a maze of pre-fab structures for the offices, press rooms, and dressing rooms we needed—and there was no running water. We finally located a fold-up shower stall and made sure we had hot water.

Ironically, our production office was in the former Stasi Building, the abandoned secret police headquarters. The building basically had been untouched for five years. It had no heat, so we were always freezing, and inside some of the offices we found ID cards and discarded paperwork.

Our second awards show, held in Paris in 1995, was hosted by fashion designer Jean-Paul Gaultier, who appropriately changed his clothes nine times during the show. We had learned our lessons from the first show, bringing in a 400-person production crew and building private showers for each act. The most serious problem I had to deal with was P.J. Harvey's refusal to perform a scheduled duet with David Bowie because of "creative differences." We had spent months preparing for the show. It was extremely important to us, and I was confident we had prepared for any eventuality. The one factor I forgot to take into consideration was the fact we were in France.

The day of the show I was informed by the French police that a credible terrorist threat had been received; supposedly a bomb was set to disrupt the show. Security was extraordinarily tight and we were advised by the authorities that this was not unusual. They advised us to stage the show as if nothing had happened. That was a difficult decision. Although I seriously considered canceling the show, I accepted their advice. In response, we increased security and had a massive police presence, we designated access routes and escape routes, and then we went forward. Everything was great right up until the show began.

The show went on the air in Europe as scheduled at 8 P.M.—precisely the same moment all of France's public-sector workers went on strike.

Public transportation immediately was shut down and the streets quickly became gridlocked. But inside the Zenith sports stadium we were secure.

We had our first fight that year. For whatever reasons, the bands Oasis and Blur hated each other; they intentionally had launched records on the same day, and Oasis' Liam Gallagher had publicly threatened to knock out Blur's Damon Albarn. At the after-party, our security guards kept the two of them separated—Gallagher couldn't get near Albarn—so, instead, he punched out the lead singer of INXS, Michael Hutchence.

We also had the first of many political controversies. While U2 was accepting the award for Best Group, Bono spoke out against French President Jacques Chirac's recently announced decision to test nuclear weapons in the South Pacific. "What an evening!" Bono told a worldwide audience estimated at 250 million people. "What a city! What a bomb! What a mistake! What a wanker you've got for president—do something about it!"

As much as I would have liked to ignore that, when 250 million people are watching it's impossible to pretend no one noticed. That marked the first time I'd had to apologize to the president of a nation, but unfortunately it was not the last. With practice, I got very good at it. Admittedly, I give a great apology.

I made one of my best apologies to Sarah, Duchess of York, or "Fergie," as she is better known. Richard Godfrey, the producer of the 1998 show being held in Milan, asked me to invite her to present the award for the Best Video that year. It would be fun, I told her, and good publicity. Finally, she agreed. She had only one or two lines to read, then announce the award. It was a simple task. Before the show I went to see her, and was surprised to discover she was terribly nervous. I started pumping her up, telling her how great she was going to be, and perhaps that's when I made a mistake. I happened to mention that this was going to be very good for her various businesses and charities, because "a billion people are going to be watching and they're going to be enchanted by you." I don't think she heard very much after "a billion people are going to be watching."

Truthfully, I knew our audience wasn't really going to be a billion people. My argument was that a billion people had access to MTV and could watch the show. For promotional purposes I often exaggerated the potential size of the audience. While several hundred million is a substantial figure, it just doesn't have the ring of "a billion." Once I even claimed that "over nine billion people would see the show," which was several billion more than the entire world population.

Eventually I discovered that the phrase "a billion people" made some artists very nervous before they performed, so I stopped saying it. But with the Duchess of York I already had made that mistake.

At the venue, to make sure she remained calm, I decided to sit next to her. She was repeating her few lines over and over, getting more and more anxious as the evening progressed. The winner for the Best Video was Massive Attack. Unfortunately, when she announced their name as the winner she mispronounced it.

The band was not happy that she was the presenter, as opposed to someone in the music business. And then she got their name wrong. "Someone's having a fucking laugh," a member of the band said as they accepted the award, and they refused to shake her hand. And then, just when I was sure the situation couldn't get worse, it got worse. As the band left the stage one of them said clearly to Fergie, "F—k you very much."

It was a disaster, but, surprisingly, Fergie did not seem at all perturbed. She attended the after-parties and never said a word about the show. *Okay*, I thought, *it's over. We got through it.* Maybe we got lucky; maybe the crowd noise obscured that slur. In fact, maybe I had misheard him. I could hope.

I got back to my hotel about 4 A.M. My phone rang an hour later. It was Fergie and she was distraught. I went right over and tried to soothe her, but there wasn't much I could say. Our awards shows are rerun numerous times both locally and internationally. I was able to get the worst of it edited out before it was rebroadcast around the world, but it was still rough. There wasn't anything more I could do, and fortunately we have remained friends.

We learned how to do it better every year. Our third year we were in London, and we decided it would be good for business to put record industry executives and reporters right up front, close to the stage. What we forgot was that the record industry is the most cynical audience in the world and that reporters are not supposed to get involved in an event they're covering. On television, it looked like the people sitting in the front rows had been embalmed. Onstage, Metallica, Smashing Pumpkins, and the Fugees were rocking, but judging by the reaction of the people in those front rows, they just as easily could have been at a weather-forecasting seminar. The VIPs were like a river flowing serenely between the stage and the real fans.

We realized that for viewers the audience played an important role in the show, and we made sure to put attractive and interesting-looking people in front. For MTV's 2010 EMAs in Madrid, for example, Head of Events Dave Sibley wanted to bring 20 transvestites to the show and the after-party. He had someone from that community conduct interviews to select those people to be invited. It became a very hot invitation. The 21st person was put on the waiting list, which made her so angry that she was caught on a security camera pouring rat poison into the drinks of several people on the list ahead of her, hoping she could get a spot. It became a big scandal in that Spanish transvestite community!

It seemed like there was some type of problem that had to be resolved every year. For the London show I was sitting in the audience, next to George Abrams, a member of Viacom's Board of Directors, and his wife. While not officially my boss, within the company George Abrams was a man I greatly respected and over the years I have come to rely on his advice. Before the show had gone on air a British comedian entertained the audience. We wanted them in their seats early so we staged a pre-show event of lesser-known performers. When you've spent more than a decade in the music industry you accept foul language as part of the business. I thought I had heard it all. As the British comedian performed early in the show, after only a few jokes I understood why he was lesser known. He turned out to be the single most unfunny and foul-mouthed comedian I'd ever heard. Obviously, he had failed to learn the difference between being merely outrageous and being funny. Worse, he was getting angry at the audience. As he told yet another joke that got no response, he got even angrier. It was embarrassing. This was the only time in my career that I ordered a director to yank someone offstage—and even the director couldn't get him off. When he finally finished, I leaned back in my seat and thought we'd got past the worst of it. As it turned out, I was wrong about that.

The show moved along without incident right up until Metallica performed. This part of the show was being broadcast live to a billion people—more or less. They were scheduled to sing "King Nothing," a song about greed and losing the things that matter in life. "King

Nothing" was the song they'd rehearsed and it was the song we expected them to sing. Instead, when they got onstage they sang "So What," a song that makes a passing reference to bestiality. On worldwide television, even a passing reference to bestiality is probably too much. As I sat there, I wondered exactly how I might deal with that problem. Moments like this made me welcome normal problems—like losing distribution in Greece or Italy.

After the London show we always put our VIPs in a special section to the back and to the side. And rather than risking another passive audience, we would bring in screamers. A week or so before the show, we would hold an audition for screamers, and put them right up next to the stage. If necessary, we would even bus them in. For example, there is a cliché that people in the north of Europe are less outwardly enthusiastic than those from the south. So for the 2000 awards being held in Stockholm, we bused in several hundred Italian screamers.

It seemed like each year the show became visually more spectacular. Host Robbie Williams opened the London show by running through the venue wearing a straitjacket and being chased by police and police dogs. In Stockholm, Jennifer Lopez landed onstage in an airplane and Ricky Martin performed surrounded by dancers in giant water tanks. In 2003, in Edinburgh, Beyoncé entered hanging upside-down from the ceiling and our host, Christina Aguilera, opened the show dressed in a nun's habit. A year later in Rome, Gwen Stefani was brought onstage suspended from a giant clock.

In the spirit of rock and roll, we always waited for that unexpected event of the night to take place; we rarely were disappointed. P Diddy hosted in 2002 in Barcelona, demanding a bathtub filled with milk and a double bed with Egyptian silk sheets in his dressing room. During the show he offered to give away his diamond-encrusted pinky-ring to the first woman who would come onstage and get naked. Instantly a woman leaped up out of the audience and took off her dress, standing topless onstage in front of perhaps a billion people. She grabbed his diamond ring and ran backstage. While Travis was performing in Edinburgh a year later, a group of nude women pushed their way onstage, carefully covering themselves with their signs—which they lifted when he finished his song.

At the 2006 awards in Copenhagen, Kanye West was named Best Hip-Hop Artist, but when Justice and Simian won Best Video he interrupted their speech and in an expletive-filled rant screamed at the audience that he deserved the award because his video for "Touch the Sky" had "cost a million dollars, Pamela Anderson was in it, and I was jumping across canyons." And then he added, perhaps humbly, "If I don't win, the award show loses credibility."

All of these antics added to the buzz about the show and every year it grew bigger. Each year, the night before the show I hosted a dinner for the artists and I would give a welcoming speech, during which I would reel off an array of impressive statistics. This is where I began pointing out that as many as two billion people would either watch or read about these awards, that as many as 1,300,000 people had voted for the winners; if the time spent by people voting on the Internet was added up it would come to 15 years. To house our guests we would rent all the rooms in as many as 23 hotels, arrange more than a thousand flights, and employ 500 makeup artists. At the site we had 50 dressing rooms containing 150 mirrors, 90 makeup lamps, 75 clothes racks, and 17,000 square meters of red carpet.

The awards originally were held on Thanksgiving, so I began hosting a turkey dinner for American artists. It became a major event, so much so that we even had a red carpet. In 2002, in Barcelona, I held this dinner at Gaudi House; Sumner Redstone was there and I wanted the event to be perfect. At the suggestion of Pino Sagliocco, a legendary figure in Spain's music industry, I hired Chef Ferran Adria of El Bulli, which *Restaurant* magazine had declared "the greatest restaurant in the world," to cater it. Things started to go wrong early. Although I had planned for 115 people, about 150 showed up, several of them world-famous artists whom I could not turn away. As we were setting up additional tables, P Diddy came in with his entourage, took all the liquor from the bar, and then left. So I was stuck with too many guests and not enough liquor, but it was about to get worse. As I gave my traditional speech, I watched in dismay as Chef Adria storm out. I later learned he was incensed because no one was paying attention to the small cones of caviar he was serving. In a snit he had thrown down his toque and left. I felt like I was living in the middle of a comic strip. Fortunately, the junior cooks stayed and we managed somehow to get through the evening.

These shows got so important that several governments actually offered MTV subsidies of as much as $10 million to bring them into their country. It's a very good situation for a company when nations are bidding for your product and it's definitely worth it for their tourism; the EMAs are seen by more young people around the world than any other program. Young people travel, and this show is a unique opportunity to draw the attention of that valuable demographic to a city. I remember meeting in Ankara with Turkish President Recep Tayyip Erdoğan and the first thing he said to us was, "We would really like you to bring the MTV Europe Awards to Turkey." Not a bad way to start a conversation.

What has always made these awards unique is that we hold them in a different city every year. As flattering and lucrative as those million-dollar offers may be, we can't make our decision based primarily on that. Our biggest concerns are security, logistics, and infrastructure—in addition to revenue. But we've learned that for several reasons the size of the market matters. We have two levels of sponsorship—one of them multinational and European advertisers, the other national advertising in the country where the awards are being held. As a result, larger nations like Germany offer a bigger universe of potential national sponsors than are available in Denmark, for example. And we take that into consideration when picking our site.

The only city that has hosted the EMAs twice is Berlin. To celebrate the 20th anniversary of the Berlin Wall coming down we returned to that city in 2009. That had not been our plan, but in Munich a year earlier I'd had dinner with Berlin Mayor Klaus Wowerit. "Why don't you come back to Berlin?" he asked.

I pointed out that Berlin had grown so rapidly since we'd been there that it would be almost impossible to get permission to build a venue in front of the Brandenburg Gate. Wowerit smiled, and said confidently, "I can get you that permission."

"If you can do that," I offered, "I'll get U2 for the show." This was one of the few times I got involved in selecting talent for the show. If we were going to return to Berlin, I thought U2 was the perfect group to perform. They would sing the song "One," which had been written shortly after they watched the Berlin Wall being ripped down. While I'm not sure if it is well known, in 1990 U2 had been on the verge of breaking up when the band went to Berlin to work on the album *Achtung Baby*. As only rock-and-roll artists can do, they had gone to a divided city to get back together. "One" has since become an anthem of unity.

As it turned out, closing the center of a great city for several days and building a stage there was easier than getting U2. I had known and respected all of the members of U2, in addition to Bono, The Edge, Adam Clayton, and Larry Mullen J., as well as their band manager, Paul McGuinness, for years. Paul agreed to reduce their fee for this show. But only for this show. In addition, Beyoncé, Jay-Z, and Shakira accepted our invitation. "This will be the largest show in the history of MTV Europe," I confidently told the media. "The broadcast will be available globally to around two billion TV viewers."

Notice, I did not say it would be *seen* by two billion people. It would be *available* to *around* two billion. When we announced that we were returning to Berlin there was a huge demand for tickets. Tickets to these events are always free, and are very valuable for promotional purposes, but in this instance we had a problem with people offering obviously counterfeit tickets for sale on Internet auction sites. They were asking as much as a thousand dollars. The city government actually was worried that so many young people would descend on the city for the show, without having places to stay safely, so we appealed to people without tickets to stay away. "There are no tickets available," we announced. But still they came and on the night of the show they stood happily outside the venue.

Our music and artist relations director Bruce Gillmer put together a fabulous line-up. Katy Perry hosted the show. U2 performed "Sunday, Bloody Sunday" with Jay-Z, a collaboration that worked so well that two months later they appeared together again in London, at our Hope for Haiti Now concert to raise emergency funds for Haitian relief.

While the main venue was at the 02 Center in East Berlin, as Mayor Wowerit had promised we were able to do our remote from the Brandenburg Gate. These remotes had become an important and exciting part of the show; it was another unique aspect of our awards show. On the regular show we had time for only 10 performances and sometimes we'd have to knock that down to eight. We usually had more artists than slots for them. By adding segments from a remote location in the host city we were able to bring in more artists. We also had been criticized for taking over a city for as long as a week and failing to provide sufficient tickets for the residents of that city. There wasn't much we could do about it, our venues rarely seated more than 5,000 people. Doing remotes allowed us to invite local residents to be part of the show.

We picked iconic locations. In Edinburgh, for example, our remote was Edinburgh Castle. For our 2010 show from Madrid featuring Katy

Perry and Linkin Park, in addition to the main venue Bruce Gillmer staged a remote in the Plaza de la Independencia. In Rome, the main venue was a tent erected at the Tor de Valle racetrack, while Anastacia, The Cure, and several popular local acts performed at the Coliseum. This was the first time the Coliseum had been used for this type of event. It was an extraordinary setting. We lit it to make it appear as if it was on fire. We expected about 50,000 people to show up; instead an estimated 400,000 were there. This time I'm not exaggerating. This was the largest crowd we've ever drawn. It was the largest crowd almost anyone has ever drawn.

In addition to the EMAs, for several years many of our local channels held awards shows to celebrate their music industry. As often as possible I attended these events, and some of them were truly spectacular. For our first *Russian Music Awards* show in 2004 we got permission to hold it inside the Kremlin, another huge breakthrough for MTV. The show celebrated the Russian culture that had become so familiar during the Cold War. It began with Russian soldiers goose-stepping ominously right outside the walls of the Kremlin, which certainly brought back memories—but suddenly those soldiers burst into a raucous hip-hop. Within seconds, gymnasts, astronauts, and legions of laborers joined them in this performance, representing all of the various aspects of the Russian Cold War culture. For that show we brought Queen, without the late Freddie Mercury, to Russia. This was the new Russia on display for the world. Unfortunately, elements of the old Russia still existed. Security inside the Kremlin was so tight that the international media were not permitted inside. They were unable to report it, and this became the greatest show nobody outside Russia knew about. There was no coverage at all.

The Russians took great pride in these shows. Several years later the Russian Space Agency gave us permission to have a cosmonaut announce the Best Song of the Year from the International Space Station. One especially emotional moment in Russia was the singing of the new national anthem. When the Soviet Union had collapsed the militaristic lyrics were cut out of the national anthem; for several years it was performed as a hymn. New lyrics had finally been added but almost no one knew them. So we taped every major Russian star singing those words, then played it on the show as those stars lip-synced. It was actually the first time many young Russians had heard their own national anthem. And the fact that it was performed on MTV Russia made it acceptable to them.

With so many different awards shows, problems were inevitable. At our Asian awards show in Singapore, Donatella Versace was to be honored as a Style Icon. What we hadn't prepared for was the inevitable clash of cultures. Generally, at these events I parked myself at the beginning of the Red Carpet to greet our guests. On both sides of the Red Carpet, fans and the media squeeze together to see their favorite celebrities, shout questions, and take those photographs that appear in newspapers and magazines around the world. The photos are particularly valuable to the head of a stylish brand like Versace.

Unfortunately, in Singapore everything is done as scheduled to the minute and Donatella arrived fashionably late, in the Italian style. She was dressed beautifully, perfectly made up, an absolute style icon, but by the time she arrived the Red Carpet had been closed, the media had gone into the venue, and the fans had left. My job was to walk her down this abandoned Red Carpet.

She was not a happy icon. Just to make the situation worse, she had requested that Enrique Iglesias present her award. Unfortunately, Enrique did not want to do it, so we arranged for Pink to do it. In fact, Pink was a much better choice, but Donatella didn't think so. As I sat with her, it actually made my memories of the night with Fergie seem not quite so bad.

Without question the most difficult show to put on has been the *Mandarin Music Honors*. It was called that because in China we were not allowed to refer to it as an "awards show."

A few years after we had started broadcasting in China we began getting hints that Chinese artists wanted recognition from the international community. That's when the idea of an awa—an *honors*—show was born. Our managing director in Asia, Harry Hui, along with Frank Brown and me, wanted to do a co-production with CCTV, the largest television station in the world and, basically, the government station. CCTV was run by the Communist Party and served as the government's propaganda outlet. We emphasized to their representatives that this would provide the cultural exchange they so badly wanted—as well as being profitable. It took us more than a year and a half to work our way through the government maze; it required endless lobbying, the submission of proposal after proposal and revision after revision. This was considered a very risky step for CCTV and there was a lot of skepticism to be overcome. Harry was there, doing the heavy lifting; my job was to remind him we were dreaming the impossible and we knew it wasn't going to be easy. But finally, in early 1999, we got the permits to put on a show. This was highly unusual and a major breakthrough for us.

Those permits were difficult to get and very valuable. On another occasion we had had to cancel a concert literally minutes before it was scheduled to begin because the permit we had anticipated receiving wasn't issued. Our managing director in China, Yifei Li had had to get onstage and explain to several thousand people that we had not received authorization to present our show to a live audience and had to cancel.

So we understood that everything about the *Mandarin Music Honors* had to be negotiated. This was the first time the Chinese government had collaborated with a western media company on a major broadcast. It was a highly unlikely and unexpected partnership, MTV and Communist China. Every decision we made had to be scrutinized, every artist and every lyric had to be approved. When the Chinese government told us it wanted to recognize types of music not usually associated with MTV, marching bands for example, we agreed enthusiastically. We agreed to most of their requests. From that moment on, we had *always* loved marching bands. They wanted gymnasts, we agreed to gymnasts. We agreed to give honors that never would be seen in the West. This was the price we paid to do business in China.

We invited Alanis Morissette to perform (although Harry pointedly asked her to sing but not speak to the media), as well as The Atomic Kitten, the Danish group Michael Learns to Sing, Aqua, and Hong Kong and local Chinese artists. The show was taped at CCTV's studios on May 7, 1999, and when it was finally done, when the venue had been cleared and cleaned and the tape was safely stored, we celebrated. After all the struggles, the close calls, the doubts, after all the meetings and negotiations, it was done. The show was in the can. Nothing could go wrong. We partied through the night.

The next morning I was awakened by loud, angry organized chanting outside my hotel. I had no idea what was going on. But as I soon learned, the night before, NATO aircraft fighting in the Balkans had mistakenly bombed the Chinese Embassy in Belgrade, killing three people. Within hours, the government had organized massive protests—and we were the most visible Americans in Beijing. All scheduled American programming was immediately canceled, and MTV was removed from the cable system.

The *Mandarin Honors* tapes were locked up at CCTV. There was absolutely nothing we could do. Within hours I had gone from an extraordinary high to a deep and anxious low. Like me, thousands of westerners decided to leave the country. The airport was overwhelmed. In one day I went from euphoria to a mob scene in an airport fleeing the country.

For several months we tried everything possible to get those tapes released. During that time Sumner Redstone and I made an already scheduled visit to Beijing and met once again with Jiang Zemin. Among the many subjects we discussed was getting those tapes released. We couldn't get an answer. Our sponsors began complaining and requesting rebates. It was a complete mess. Finally, five months after the bombing we were informed that the show would be broadcast. With little preparation and no publicity the show was broadcast to more than 300 million households across the country—and incredibly earned the highest rating in the history of CCTV-3, a music and cultural channel. CCTV's executives were elated; this was a great success for them and they immediately began talking about our second show.

With all the channels we were operating in all those countries, it was impossible not to accidently insult some nation at some time. On several occasions we paid substantial fines for our programming. Ironically, because we were located in London and therefore came under British regulations, we paid most of those fines to the U.K. for graphically demonstrating to our viewers how to put on a condom in a documentary about preventing AIDS, for permitting a discussion of sex when children were watching, and for running an ad about teenage suicide prevention.

Problems occur in every business. I've always felt that when a problem occurs the most important thing an executive can do is to be visible. Be out in front, assume the responsibility, take the heat—even when it's not your fault. The best example of executive accountability comes from Japanese business leaders, who are overzealous in taking the blame and accepting responsibility when anything goes wrong. Generally, when one of our local channels had a problem with a government agency I would go there immediately to personally deal with it and, if necessary, issue an apology. I was running an international business, not a foreign policy.

We made mistakes, certainly we were far from perfect. In China, for example, at various times we violated each of the three *T*'s. We showed a video made by a Taiwanese pop singer that included a brief image of Taiwan's flag, a serious violation of one of those *T*'s. The editors at our channel overlooked it and after it was broadcast we were called in by the minister of propaganda to explain what happened. I flew to China to meet with him and explained how the mistake happened. Our explanation was accepted without consequence.

We did have a much more serious problem when CCTV decided to broadcast the 2004 Super Bowl throughout China. That year the game was broadcast on CBS, which at that time was a Viacom subsidiary. MTV was the logical choice to produce the halftime show, and we were going to make it hip and trendy. To take advantage of this huge worldwide audience, I wanted to create and run a brief AIDS-awareness clip. When the NFL objected, at the last minute a junior producer in New York put together a seemingly benign two-minute pictorial celebration of unity.

The Super Bowl halftime show is usually a spectacular display of dance and song, but by Monday morning it's always forgotten. Not this time. The performers were Janet Jackson and Justin Timberlake. At the end of their number, as rockets exploded and the crowd cheered wildly, Justin Timberlake sang, "I'm gonna have you naked by the end of this song," and pulled open Janet Jackson's costume—exposing her nipple to the world for less than a second. If this had been broadcast on cable no one would have cared, but this was the public airways, the largest gathering of family viewing of the year. The nation was shocked! *Shocked!* This suddenly became a historic television event and certainly the most infamous halftime show in history. Janet Jackson's "wardrobe malfunction" was on the front page of most newspapers in the world—except in China. Our problem in China was that for .06 of a second in our diversity clip, less than the exposure time of Janet Jackson's nipple, we had showed the iconic photograph of a nameless Chinese dissident standing in front of a tank in Tiananmen Square. That picture had never been published in China. Officially, that incident never happened. The Chinese government was not happy. We had violated another one of the three *T*'s. While the rest of the world was in an uproar over Janet Jackson's nipple, all I was concerned about was a photograph that was visible for slightly longer than the blink of an eye. Once again, I flew to China to begin another round of apologies. I knew the rules of doing business in China and, whatever my personal feelings, I had accepted them. Accepting the fact that something with little meaning to me as a westerner might be extremely important elsewhere in the world was the daily reality of international business.

My last apology tour to China took place shortly after the 2010 Olympics in Beijing. I was scheduled to attend the opening ceremonies as Sumner Redstone's representative and I didn't show up. The government wanted to know what happened, but equally important, they also wanted to know why the father of DreamWorks' popular character Kung Fu Panda was a duck.

I actually believed there was a third and more significant reason I was invited to meet the Minister of Propaganda. I thought they had found evidence that I had violated the third T, Tibet.

In fact, I had quietly met with the Dalai Lama, the exiled Tibetan leader. There was no political agenda; I had the opportunity to meet with him and I did. Our entire conversation was about as serious as the predictions found in a fortune cookie. My niece Lauren had put a picture of me with the Dalai Lama on her MySpace page and I suspected the Chinese had seen it. Yes, the government does have that capability.

At the meeting I explained that I had missed the Olympic opening because I had been scheduled to attend the international AIDS conference in Mexico at the same time, and then I took a trip with my children on the first Nickelodeon cruise. The question of why Kung Fu Panda's father was a duck was easily avoided. When DreamWorks had produced that very successful movie, it had been owned by Viacom. But by the time of this meeting DreamWorks was no longer part of our operation, so no explanation was necessary. And while I was prepared to explain that I had absolutely no affiliation with the Dalai Lama, the subject was never raised. It was the Olympics and the duck.

Weeks after I returned I happened to see DreamWorks' CEO Jeffrey Katzenberg and told him the story. He assured me there was nothing to worry about. The movie *Kung Fu Panda 2* would explain why this hero's father was a duck.

■■■

Running a business in at least 175 countries, each of which has its own political structure, often required some very fancy footwork. We were doing business at the same time with nations that despised each other, nations that sometimes refused to recognize the existence of our other partners, nations that were at war with each other. We were doing business with democracies, monarchies, dictatorships, and totalitarian regimes, and with nations that practiced every known religion. Avoiding problems required walking the tightrope. I've had to sit quietly through some very unpleasant conversations, listening without responding as one partner spoke angrily about another. And then the following night I'd be at dinner with the other side, listening to their anger about the situation. Wherever possible, I've taken actions to try to reduce the divide by emphasizing unifying themes. When it was possible, I used music to unite people. We've shown videos by a Pakistani singer in India, and by a Taiwanese singer in China, and broadcast AIDS educational programs in countries where supposedly the disease does not exist. But there were times when some contact was unavoidable. I remember sitting in a restaurant in Cannes with our Israeli partners when our Lebanese partners walked in. In addition to having spent time with Lebanese Prime Minister Harari, I had also met several times with Israeli Prime Minister Shimon Peres, who told me how much he wanted to use music to bring together Israel and its Arab neighbors. It was clear this was going to be an awkward moment. I liked all of these people, and I had the strange feeling that I had been caught cheating. I wondered how to respond. Could I ignore them? Absolutely not. Should I invite them to join us? Probably not. Do I dare to introduce them? Well, maybe. In situations like this there is no correct answer. I relied on the fact that each of these men understood the situation. At moments like that the reservoir of goodwill you've established in the path is invaluable. Fortunately, Israeli and Lebanese citizens have found themselves in this situation many times, and they knew from experience how to respond. I greeted the Lebanese warmly and introduced them to the Israelis. And a few seconds later the Lebanese went to their own table.

On another occasion I was in a board meeting in Kuwait in which we were discussing encrypting the pay-TV channel Showtime throughout the Middle East. Piracy is a major issue there and it was costing us substantial revenues. We had done a request for proposal to encrypt our signal, and in response three companies had submitted bids. By far the best equipment had been designed by an Israeli manufacturer for Israel's military. That company had been bought by Murdoch, so the Israelis no longer owned any part of it, but because it once had been Israeli it was eliminated from the competition. There wasn't anything I could do about it.

At times our partners from around the world have been in London and I've invited them to my home. My home is a celebration of diversity (although my wife, Alex, calls it a celebration of confusion). Originally, the building had been a church; during renovations we had installed stained-glass windows from a synagogue, which now are over a prayer rug facing Mecca. The house is filled with remembrances from my journeys and mementos I've collected. I've got pieces representing every culture and religion. There are large Buddhas in the living area, a beautiful Koran, and historic handwritten letters from world leaders of the past. One of our Kuwaiti partners gave me a beautiful painting, which is hanging over the dining-room table directly across from a photograph autographed by all the Israeli political and military leaders during the Six-Day War. So when Alex and I do invite partners from around the world to our home, before they arrive I find a way to describe the diversity they will encounter. And while I never put anything away before a guest visits, Alex may arrange the seating strategically.

Personally, I remember making at least one major cultural error in my travels. In a small shop in Kabul, Afghanistan, I bought a beautiful necklace from which dangled a locket, and inside that locket was a scripted passage from the Koran. There is a lot of street crime in that city, so without thinking about it, I stuck it in my shoe. If I had a problem on the street, I figured, no one would look there. But I had forgotten completely that in that part of the world anything to do with the foot is considered disrespectful. That night I went to dinner with Muslim friends and without realizing the mistake I was making, I told them about this purchase. In fact, I got so excited as I described this necklace that I took off my shoe and pulled it out. I had completely forgotten that to Muslims anything to do with the foot is considered offensive. And they *were* offended. There was absolutely nothing I could do about it. Mistakes happen and you just have to learn how to deal with them and learn from them.

Through the years I have also become very skilled at bowing. Bowing is not part of America's culture, but it is an extremely important gesture of respect in several regions of the world, especially Asia. As I learned, all bows are not equal; different bows for different folks. In Japan, for example, it's important that you never bow too deeply to someone more junior than you, but with a senior executive the deeper the better. While it may seem no more important than a handshake to Americans, elsewhere in the world bowing carries with it several important messages.

After establishing our glocal network, on occasion we would still try to bring all of our channels together to form one vast network for special programming. We had built the largest network in the world, we had access to an audience of a billion people, and at times it made sense to use it. We are the only global network that connects young people and I wanted to use that capability as a positive force in the world. For technological reasons it's difficult to do, and for political reasons it's difficult, but in addition to our international awards shows, on a few occasions we have been able to pull it off. In February 2002, Secretary of State Colin Powell agreed to appear before the young people of the world and answer their questions. In announcing this event I said, "Young people are very attuned to recent events," alluding specifically to the 9/11 attack on the United States. "This MTV Global Forum will give them an opportunity to debate these issues in a frank, public multimedia environment, regardless of political ideology or religion."

There had never been an event quite like this one. While we did not require our regional channels to run this program, we did strongly urge them to do it. I wanted every channel to run it and, almost without exception, they did. It was impossible to determine precisely how many people watched it, but certainly it was one of the largest audiences for a public affairs program in history. It was almost inevitable that the United States was going to go to war, one that would be fought mostly by members of our viewers. I felt we had an obligation to at least present an honest discussion of events and I admired Colin Powell for agreeing to appear. Contrary to the warnings of many people that this event would be frivolous, the questions were far more brutally honest than any I've ever seen a government official asked, or answer. It was clear this was not going to be an ordinary question-and-answer format when a Norwegian girl asked Secretary of State Powell, "How do you feel by representing a country commonly perceived as the Satan of contemporary politics?"

Powell was polite, organized, and direct. "Satan, oh, well, I reject the characterization," he responded, and then continued, "quite the contrary, I think the American people, the United States of America presents a value system to the rest of the world that is based on democracy, based on economic freedom, based on the individual rights of men and women."

Powell proceeded to take provocative questions from a diverse audience that included Egyptians, Afghanis, Italians, and Turks about a diverse range of subjects; among them what evidence the United States had that proved bin Laden was the mastermind behind the attacks on 9/11, why America had ignored Afghanistan for so long, and even the Secretary of State's opinion about the use of condoms. Uh-oh, I thought when I heard that last question. Powell surprised me by breaking completely from the Bush Administration position, replying,

> In my own judgment, condoms are a way to prevent infection, and therefore I not only support their use, I encourage their use among people who are sexually active and need to protect themselves . . . from HIV/AIDS, which is a plague that is upon the face of the earth.

It went on like that for 90 minutes. In many ways, it was my dream coming true, young people from around the world joining together to question a world leader about the topics that affected their lives. We did several programs like this. For example, British Prime Minister Tony Blair appeared on MTV several times to respond to often hostile questions about his controversial decision to commit British troops to the war in Iraq. I always felt he deserved great credit for appearing on MTV to face a young, antagonistic audience. While he may not have changed anyone's mind, he at least gained their respect.

I did invite President George W. Bush to appear on MTV. When the president visited London after the Iraq invasion he was met with massive demonstrations. Perhaps to blunt that reaction, he met with a group of African leaders in the Cabinet Room at No. 10 Downing Street to discuss his AIDS policies in Africa. Whatever people think about President Bush, he is regarded in many parts of Africa as a hero for the work his Administration did for AIDS relief. In addition to Bush, Secretaries Powell and Condoleezza Rice were there and British Prime Minister Blair was there with his aides. Finally, as Blair was bringing the meeting to a close, I raised my hand and said I wanted to make a statement. I knew how undiplomatic that was, but I remember thinking, how often am I going to have the opportunity to be in a meeting with the Prime Minister of England and the President of the United States? The answer was, probably not too often. So before I could catch myself I found myself making a brief speech about condom usage as a means to prevent the spread of the disease, which I disguised as a question. I remember looking at Blair as I was speaking and he was giving me the dirtiest look I'd ever seen. Clearly he was furious, although later we got on quite well.

When the meeting ended, I approached President Bush and introduced myself. "We have a long history of putting world leaders on MTV," I said, naming Blair and Nelson Mandela among others, and then I asked him, "Will you go on?"

The president didn't hesitate; he put his right arm around my shoulders in a very friendly gesture, started patting my chest with his left hand, and responded, "My mother won't let me."

In 2003, we celebrated Nelson Mandela's 85th birthday with a one-hour program hosted by Beyoncé and broadcast globally. After learning the amazing story of Nobel Peace Prize recipient Nelson Mandela's struggles and eventual triumph, I felt certain he would be a strong role model for the world. There is no way to overemphasize how strongly I felt that our audience should know about Nelson Mandela. He was one of the few global heroes that people of all ages could respond to and respect. Coincidentally, our first headquarters in London had been on Mandela Street. If I had any global heroes he certainly was at the top of that list. I always encouraged our people to think big, so when I saw an opportunity to do a program with Mandela, we worked very hard to bring it to reality.

I'm not certain Mandela knew what MTV was when we first met. I was ushered into his small hotel room and we sat there alone for an hour as he told me the remarkable story of his life. But when I explained to him, "Through MTV you have direct communication with two billion young people all around the world," his eyes lit up. Even if he didn't know anything about MTV, he understood the value of speaking to our audience. So much so, in fact, that a year later he also participated in the launch of MTV Base, our African channel.

While we were thrilled to be able to do this show with a historic figure, we also knew the problems we'd face. To bridge the multi-generation gap between Mandela and our viewers we had to find a way to make his experiences relevant to their lives. The theme of the show was reconciliation, so we brought together young people who had suffered terrible misfortunate to question him. This included an AIDS-positive young man from Uganda named Henry Hudson whose father and brother had already died from that disease, a Burmese young man named Min Zin who'd left his family and moved to Thailand to fight to free his nation, an Israeli whose 17-year-old sister had been killed by the first female suicide bomber, and a Palestinian whose father had been shot and killed by an Israeli sniper. Each of them spoke with Mandela about finding a way to forgive their enemy, and Mandela drew from his own experiences to explain to them how it was possible. To provide Henry Hudson with hope he told the story of his own lonely and seemingly hopeless battle against apartheid in South Africa. To the freedom fighter from Burma who had been forced to leave his family behind, he remembered how the government had refused to allow him to leave prison to attend the funerals of first his mother and then his son. And he told the Israeli and the Palestinian who could not find forgiveness in their heart for their enemy how he had been brutalized in prison by the guards, suffering permanent injury, and how when he had been elected president of South Africa the first people he had invited to his inauguration were those guards. Then he went further and convened the Truth and Reconciliation Commission, which was also led by Archbishop Desmond Tutu. This remains one of the most extraordinary examples of forgiveness in history. The commission granted amnesty to South Africans who had committed crimes during apartheid in exchange for their confessing to those acts. When I had lunch with Archbishop Tutu in 2011, I asked him where the concept had come from. To my surprise, he gave credit for it to Chile, which employed a similar doctrine to heal the wounds of the Pinochet era.

Mandela certainly influenced our young participants. By the end of the week in South Africa the Israeli and Palestinian were talking to each other and even went shopping together. It was an incredibly moving program. What could have been a tedious television event was transformed into a program that will remain valuable and touching for decades. Being involved with its production was a highlight of my career. It was thrilling to be able to use our resources to teach young people some very valuable lessons. That show was broadcast globally to a *potential* audience of more than a billion people, including the Chinese.

When I'd joined MTV in 1989 I made three rules for myself: First, in the industry, some media companies listed an executive producer at the end of every show, even though he had nothing to do with the production. So I vowed I would never receive credit as an executive producer. Second, I promised myself that I would never appear on the air; that was the job of talent, not a businessman. And finally, I vowed I would never be a groupie.

At least I've never received credit as an executive producer.

I have managed to avoid many requests to go on-air—many, but certainly not all. On occasion at an awards show a producer would insist that I go on the air, so I'd appear for a few seconds to say something wonderful about the event. At times when MTV was launching a new channel I would appear on local media to promote it, just as I'd done years earlier at HBO. I also have appeared as a presenter on awards shows; in India, for example, I gave the Icon of the Year Award to one of India's leading businessmen, Anil Ambani, which I was pleased to do. MTV Russia asked me several times to co-present an award, which I did with Pamela Anderson. Pamela didn't speak a word of Russian, although no one seemed to care about that. I've also presented with Ronan Keating and Timbaland.

As for becoming a groupie, I admit to that. I have had the privilege of meeting and working with many of the most talented artists in music history, as well as some of the most accomplished people in the world—why would I not become a groupie? If I didn't love watching and working with the people we were putting on the air, then why would I expect my audience to love them? Music has always been an important part of my life; I was fortunate enough to have it become central to my career. And with my fascination with history, how could I possibly resist the opportunity to spend time with legendary figures like Nelson Mandela as well as former presidents, prime ministers, and nine different Nobel Peace Prize winners?

Through the many years I have gotten to know several of those artists very well, among them Bono and Bob Geldof, both of whom have been extremely active in causes that MTV has supported. The one completely unforgettable night I spent with the two of them occurred in Tokyo after the *MTV Japan Video Awards Show.* Bono had come to Japan to present an award and Geldof showed up unexpectedly. I spent much of the night sitting in the Green Room with the two of them. I missed a lot of the show, but how often do I get to spend casual time with Bono and Geldof?

After the show I went out with some of our advertisers, clients, and business associates, among them the former prime minister of Japan. We finished about one o'clock in the morning and I went to meet Bono, Geldof, and several of their friends. We went to a club called the Cavern in the Rapongi District, Tokyo's nightclub area, where four Japanese performers did a spot-on Beatles impersonation. They didn't speak a word of English, but they looked and sounded amazingly like the Beatles. We got the playlist and Bono and Geldof requested mostly obscure Beatles songs, and this group nailed every one of them. From there we went to another club, where a young Japanese woman seemed transformed into Petula Clark. By 4 A.M. I was wearing down and ready to call it quits. But Bono wanted to sing karaoke while in the karaoke capital of the world, and I was not about to turn down the opportunity to see one of the greatest rock stars in history singing karaoke at dawn. Unfortunately, I didn't know where to go in Tokyo. In each of our offices around the world we usually have a person we call our "character." A character is someone with an effusive personality, who is well connected and knowledgeable about his city; the character may even not have an integral role in the day-to-day business—but you need one in your organization. The character is that person who knows where to go to get anything done. So I called Tamon, who in this case is a very important sales executive in the Tokyo office, and explained the situation. "Don't worry," he said.

No more than a half-hour later we were in the state-of-the-art karaoke club in Tokyo. The Japanese take their karaoke seriously. This club even had its own Green Room filled with costumes so customers could dress up as their favorite singer. The character got us started, becoming James Brown. I dressed as the cop from the Village People, and Bono dressed as a nurse. And at five o'clock in the morning I was singing *Born in the USA* with Bono in a karaoke bar in Tokyo. It was a magical moment.

It got better. Two hours later, as the sun was rising in Tokyo, we were all in Bono's specially equipped van listening as he sang along to tracks from his album that would not be released for several months.

At moments like that I wasn't the CEO of an international media corporation; I was a starstuck music fan in a van with Bono at sunrise in Tokyo listening to unreleased tracks from his next album and thinking, *This is really cool.* Maybe it is the fact that I could still get excited about listening to new music, or that I could understand how lucky I was to be able to hang out with the greatest musicians in the world, or that I can be silly and have fun that enabled me to continue doing the job with enthusiasm and genuine excitement for more than two decades. I've always believed that the day a CEO wakes up not wanting to go into the office is the day he or she should stay home for good. If the CEO doesn't look forward to going into the office, there's something seriously wrong in that office. In my case, my office sometimes happened to be a Japanese karaoke bar at 5 A.M.

I am often asked to name the single greatest concert I've ever seen. I've seen hundreds of concerts; I've seen them staged everywhere from Madison Square Garden to the Kremlin; I've seen crowds of several hundred people and of several hundred thousand people; I've attended so many memorable concerts that I've always resisted picking out one. I will never forget the euphoria of the first *MTV Europe Awards* in Berlin, for example, or the night we returned to Berlin 20 years after the fall of the Berlin Wall. But certainly the most emotional concert I've attended was a U2 concert in Sarajevo. And we didn't even broadcast it.

I first met U2 when we brought them to Italy for what was called "MTV Day Italy." It was actually the launch of service in Italy. U2 was going directly from Italy to Sarajevo for a concert. When the concert had to be canceled because of the war, Bono had a General MacArthur moment, promising the people of Sarajevo that the band would return. And when hostilities ended, U2 returned for the concert.

I met them there; this was a gig I did not want to miss. I think the band was shocked to see me. At that time no one was visiting Sarajevo. The city had been ripped apart. There were bullet holes in my hotel room. And the people were hardened, as if they still were in shock. We walked up to the stadium for the concert; the stadium was still half-filled with soldiers.

The event began and the audience was ecstatic. But after two songs Bono lost his voice. Whatever had happened, he couldn't sing. Edge tried to sing a few of the songs but it didn't work. What happened then was one of the most moving events I've ever seen. The audience completed the concert. For the rest of the show, the crowd sang all the lyrics. It was amazing—they had been through a war and survived, and this was their opportunity to express their joy. Then, miraculously, for the final song Bono got his voice back. And together U2 and the entire audience finished that concert.

As meaningful as our public service programming was, as exciting as our award shows were, it was difficult not to be impressed by the size and the power of the viewing audience. We literally were capable of knitting together a worldwide audience of more than a billion people. There was no media company in the world capable of drawing an audience even one-tenth that size on a regular basis. Eventually it became obvious that we were not using the capability we had built in the most productive and efficient way.

I had been an advocate of our pan-European concept until it was clear that localization made more sense for our business, at which time I became an advocate of going glocal. No company had drilled down into local units better than we had, but eventually we began to wonder: How local did we really want to go? How local is *too* local? I had argued that we would never reach that point because technology had made it possible to create narrow local "communities" that were appealing to advertisers. We had the capability of breaking down our audience demographically, by attitude, preference, even language and numerous other criteria. India has as many as 12 recognized languages; for a time we even considered launching a channel in Hinglish. There were many practical ways of going even more local than we had.

But by the mid-2000s it was obvious MTV wasn't taking advantage of its size and corporate diversity. That's when we began emphasizing the concept of *scale*. As a worldwide company, MTV was a huge and powerful force, tied together loosely by the headquarters in New York. It had a centralized command and control—every channel outside the United States reported up to me—but we weren't exploiting that structure. It seemed obvious that the corporation would be more profitable if all the units were working in harmony, rather than as 175 separate and semi-independent national operations. Local channels had been impressively creative in establishing their own unique looks, but in doing so the company had given up many of the economic benefits that were derived from being part of a massive global operation. MTV was capable of knitting together a worldwide audience of tens of millions of people—but with the exception of occasional public service programs and events we were not taking advantage of that. Doing your own thing had gotten very expensive. Basically, scale was defined as giving all of our channels a more unified look through the use of a common programming grid, while emphasizing the use of highly produced programming from either domestic or international. Under this strategy all of MTV's channels would share a common template and management in New York would exercise more control globally.

Bob Bakish, whom I appointed President of MTV International Networks in 2007, began instituting the strategic changes that allowed MTV to take advantage of scale. MTV 4.0, as it became known, involved streamlining our *on-air look* to make it more consistent, meaning how we go into and out of programs, how we present the logo, and all the visual cues that make each of our channels unmistakably MTV. In an effort to create some of the uniformity that had existed earlier in MTV's history, we set up regional design studios to supply materials to many different channels. It's much more cost effective for those stations than maintaining an in-house creative team. We also created an in-house production company, Greenhouse, to try to develop programming concepts that would work around the world. In many ways, technology had allowed us to return to a modified version of our original strategy: producing programming that works across national boundaries.

As challenging as it was to change the culture, it made great sense financially. While we were expanding I was a proponent of glocal programming, but the reality is that small markets lack the resources to create high-quality programs. And producing an expensive show that would run only in one or two markets could no longer be economically justified. MTV Germany, for example, wanted to do an animated show entitled *Famous Last Words*, which fantasized the last moments of rock stars, but it was too expensive to be produced only for that market. Scale gave us the budget to create programming that could run in numerous countries—while also allowing individual channels to dramatically reduce programming costs. Under 4.0, corporate management would select specific shows that all 175 channels would run and then provide marketing support. In actuality, it hasn't quite worked out that way. It's impossible to program the entire network; some shows simply won't work in certain countries. No program can possibly work universally—Asia is just too different from the West—but many shows will play well in multiple markets. But as a consequence of MTV 4.0 a substantial amount of programming produced in America is being broadcast throughout the world. As in the past, some of those shows work very well. *16 and Pregnant*, for example, which has become very popular in numerous markets, sounds like a cheesy exploitation show, but in fact it is well produced, packed with emotional content, and has a great social message for teenagers: "Don't get pregnant." Thanks to MTV International, *Jersey Shore's* Snookie and The Situation are now almost as well-known around the world as SpongeBob and Dora.

This decision was traumatic for the organization because we'd spent a decade preaching glocal, supporting glocal, believing in glocal. But change is essential. I can make a very strong argument about the benefits of glocalization, but I can make an even stronger argument about why scale has become essential. Any business needs constant reinvention, so while initially my heart might have resisted the change, my brain told me to go with it, welcome it, and embrace it. Life is about change. And even though the local channels now have a more unified look, they are still managed locally, meaning the majority of the programming and the music being played is still dictated by local tastes.

What this has meant is that MTV can now mandate that centrally produced programming will be shown in almost every country. The logic of that is irrefutable. Producing for multiple countries makes it possible to spend more money on a single show, as well as allowing for a larger promotional budget. In fact, the most successful show produced under this strategy brought us right back to our roots. It is based on our original premise that young people everywhere in the world speak music. It's actually a show we gladly would have done in the old days at MTV Europe, called *World Stage*, which is essentially an awards show without awards. *World Stage* is a weekly concert broadcast to more than 550 million households around the world. It features a music industry superstar performing in concert, or at a music festival, or at an exclusive venue anywhere in the world. Among the stars we've featured are Bon Jovi, Wyclef Jean, Kings of Leon, Black Eyed Peas, Kid Rock, Shakira, Lady Gaga, Green Day, Nirvana, Beyoncé, Snoop Dog, Foo Fighters, Tokio Hotel, and Katy Perry, stars that no single channel could afford.

But we've taken advantage of scale. Our ability to provide these artists with worldwide exposure they could get nowhere else has made *World Stage* an extremely desirable show for artists and music companies. *Panworld* works for them and it has begun to work for us.

Change is essential to the bottom line. MTV's complexity has continued to grow even as it centralized. Because the local structure has been maintained, each channel still has its local flavor, but now there are times when it works to everyone's benefit to act as a single, large company.

Or, as the Chinese philosopher Confucius reminded us, "When it is obvious that the goals cannot be reached, don't adjust the goals, adjust the action steps."

Chapter Seven

How to Save a Life

I represent the younger generation. And I can say that we learned more about prevention by watching MTV, more so than from our schools and our parents.

—Beyoncé

I believe MTV can save more lives than doctors.

—Dr. Peter Piot, executive director, UNAIDS

From time to time through the years I've been asked what advice I might offer about running a multinational business. That is not an easy question to answer. I have been very fortunate in so many ways and I have learned a great deal, but perhaps there is one thought above all others that I can suggest without any hesitation: Don't get in a fight with the Pope.

In 2009, on his first trip to Africa, where more than 22 million people are infected with the HIV virus, Pope Benedict XVI told reporters that AIDS was "a tragedy that cannot be overcome by money alone, that cannot be overcome through the distribution of condoms, which even increase the problems."

I was stunned when I read his remarks. MTV had spent more than a decade educating young people around the world about the importance of safe sex. We'd even been fined for demonstrating how to put on a condom. Because I was a well-known activist in the AIDS community I was invited by CNN and Sky News to respond to the Pontiff's remarks. It was obvious to me that the idea of MTV criticizing the Pope was a no-win situation, but I believed it was necessary to correct his information. I tried to find an area of agreement, so I agreed that condoms can't completely stop the epidemic. But his comment that the use of condoms made it worse was wrong and potentially very dangerous. In response to that I suggested that maybe he didn't really mean what he said, pointing out that the Catholic Church has been very aggressive and effective in fighting the epidemic in Africa. On the ground, many priests and nuns had quietly ignored the Vatican's position and as a result of the work of so many dedicated people young Africans had finally begun using condoms. But CNN's reporter continued to press me, so finally I said flatly that the Pope was wrong. Perhaps I didn't say it loud enough. But it *is* the Pope.

Amazingly, almost two years later the Pope reversed his position, announcing, "In certain cases, where the intention is to reduce the risk of infection, it can nevertheless be a first step on the way to another, more humane sexuality." However, he did reiterate the church's position that condoms should not be used for contraceptive purposes. This was a huge policy change for the church. This time, though, I didn't say a word.

Initially, I hadn't planned on becoming a leader in the fight against AIDS and there was no corporate strategy to position MTV as the company leading the fight. The question of what is the social obligation of a corporation is complex. A corporation is a business, not a social organization. The obligation of an executive is do as much as possible to generate profits. Personally, I believe corporations also have an obligation to be good world citizens and to contribute to their community. I also believed that the tremendous influence we have with our audience brought with it the responsibility to use it in positive ways. While it has never been our intent, through the years we've found that MTV's commitment to public service also has turned out to be good for our brand. Our audience is directly affected by the issues we've embraced, and becoming active in educating our audience about those areas has allowed us to gain great credibility and strengthen our bond with them. It's also good business to keep your audience alive.

In addition to the work we've done at MTV fighting the HIV virus, we also have become involved in other issues that directly impact our audience; among them are the debate over climate change; the fights against drugs, alcohol, smoking, human trafficking, bullying; and, after massive human tragedies like the tsunami and the Haitian earthquake, disaster relief. Even as a young man growing up in Miami I somehow understood the potential power of television. I realized that anyone with seniority in that industry was going to have great influence. But the question has always been how best to use that power.

Throughout its history MTV Europe has emphasized corporate social responsibility. From the earliest days it was running public-service messages about the dangers of smoking, drinking, and drugs, urging its audience to participate in elections, and combating violence against women and racism and bigotry. MTV had the attention of Europe's young people and took advantage of it by speaking to them honestly, openly, and with respect. As I learned, it's impossible for a company to become regularly engaged in public service campaigns without the active support of top management, and in all my efforts I have been fortunate to have the support of Sumner, Philippe Dauman, Tom Dooley, Tom Freston, Judy McGrath, and Viacom's Executive Vice-President for Corporate Communications Carl Folta.

I also recognized the value of public-service programming; in fact, I thought it was more important for us internationally than it is in the United States. I never forgot that as local as our channels became throughout the world, we still were guests in 164 countries and to be credible it was important to demonstrate that we had a responsible side. In my discussions with government officials I always emphasized that we weren't only a music television service, but we were a channel that could tap in and tap out of issues that were important to their culture. I'd show examples that supported my point. The more success we had with our programs, the more credibility I had in these discussions. I have little doubt that in many countries MTV's proven record of engagement without pushing a political agenda made it a lot easier for us to receive government approval.

Tackling those issues that directly affected people locally helped us gain acceptance as a corporation invested in the welfare of our audience and enabled us to forge a strong bond between the brand and our audience. We couldn't preach to our audience. We never tried to tell our audience what to think, we never dictated, but we covered the issues that affected our viewers and provided responsible information. When skinheads were a serious problem in Europe, for example, MTV dedicated a weekend to discussing fascism. Ultimately, our involvement in these issues helped build tremendous trust in our brand, and the value of that long term is immeasurable.

Kenneth Cole, the incredibly innovative designer, and chairman of amfAR (American Foundation for AIDS Research), was among the very first corporate executives to devote the resources of his company to the fight against AIDS.

> I did it because it was the right thing to do, but I also found it benefitted the company. I always believed corporations would get there with us; either their hearts will get them there or their balance sheets, but eventually they would come to realize that the need to be there is as simple as one hand washes the other. In my company I think at the end of the day everybody feels better about what they do here because of what we do. They understand it's about something other than how much money they are making. We don't impose it on anybody, we never take attendance, we just make it available to embrace it or not.

For me, as well as for MTV Networks, getting there was a process of evolution. It didn't happen overnight—it wasn't as if a switch was suddenly turned on. I didn't wake up one morning and decide to devote a substantial amount of time to fighting HIV/AIDS. Maybe my childhood belief that television could be a force for good, combined with the fact that I had some control over the largest television network in the world, had something to do with my involvement. I had always felt an obligation to contribute to society; while serving as an aide to a general my second year in Vietnam, for example, I had spent nights teaching English to schoolchildren. It seemed to me in the middle of all that suffering and war I could make a small difference in a few lives. But my involvement in the battle against HIV/AIDS probably began with a casual conversation I had with my assistant at the time, Georgia Arnold, rather than with any type of passion. MTV had allotted a small budget to charitable expenses, which was usually spent haphazardly. We'd buy tables at music industry charitable events or contribute to local causes, but there was no master plan. One day, I suggested to Georgia that we probably should be a little more focused on how we used that money and asked her to give it some thought. As Georgia later explained, "We looked around for an issue that was both global and affected young people. It didn't really take a rocket scientist to figure out that was AIDS and HIV."

To give this the attention it deserved, I needed to find the right person to manage it on a day-to-day basis. Fortunately, she was sitting right next to me. Georgia has been my partner in this effort for two decades and the success we've had would have been impossible without her. Having an executive totally focused on social responsibility was critical for me, because I was running an entrepreneurial organization that demanded a tremendous time commitment. It was obvious to me that I wasn't going to be able to give this issue the focus it needed. Not only did I appoint Georgia, whom I trusted completely, I put her desk right outside my office and set up a structure in which she reported directly to me, rather than to another division like HR. We spoke every day; she was completely dedicated, passionate, and tireless. We traveled together to some of the regions in the world most severely affected by this disease, and as my partner she was right there with me on the front lines. These arrangements, which guaranteed access and accountability, were key to making this relationship effective.

Like every other American I was aware of the disease, but I wouldn't claim to be actively involved in fighting it. In the 1980s most of the western world believed it was limited almost exclusively to the gay community and wasn't something heterosexuals had to be concerned about. There was almost a societal don't ask, don't tell, don't talk too much about it policy.

Having lived in Los Angeles for several years I'd known people in the entertainment industry who had died. I knew it was an awful disease, but it was only as I got more involved in the fight that I truly understood that AIDS is the most serious disease of our time. In the United States there is a fairly stereotypical view that AIDS is a gay disease. It isn't. It touches people regardless of sexual preference, demographic, or gender. It kills men and women, young and old, heterosexual and homosexual, people of every race and color. By 2010 it had killed more than 20 million people and 33 million people around the world were living with the disease. It is both preventable and treatable, yet as you read this as many as 8,000 people are still dying from it every day. Ironically, the first AIDS case had been reported only a few weeks before MTV went on the air in America in 1981. By the mid-1990s, about half of all new HIV infections were occurring among people aged 25 or younger, and, tragically, that was our audience profile. Even worse, a high percentage of those cases were occurring in developing countries in Africa, in India, Russia, Eastern Europe, the Caribbean, Brazil, and even China, many of them places where MTV is particularly popular. I was being brutally honest when I described it this way: Left unchecked, AIDS will kill off MTV's audience.

There is no question that linking the MTV brand to an epidemic with a very negative stigma attached was a risky business strategy. But we made this decision because this is an issue that has a tremendous impact on our audience. We have regularly conducted surveys and held focus groups to determine which issues are most important to our viewers, and HIV and education have always registered among the most important global issues of concern. Many other issues were unique to specific regions, but HIV crossed all boundaries and borders. More than half of all the people infected were under 25 years old, that was MTV's audience. When I looked at this response, it was obvious that the fact that we had a global footprint, a strong connection to the audience directly and disproportionally affected by this disease, and that the publicity and education we could provide would make a significant difference.

It was clear to me that there a huge void existed, not only in how the media should cover the epidemic but even in how to talk about it. That difficulty went all the way back to the 1980s, when the Reagan Administration would not even use the word AIDS. In the 1990s, when we began to recognize that this was the worst epidemic in recorded history, there was almost zero coverage, slightly more than zero money allocated to fight it, and about zero leadership in this fight. That huge void was another reason I felt we had no option. In addition to an obligation to serve the audience, it was a huge opportunity to make a difference.

At first it was a lonely fight. Perhaps because two-thirds of the new infections were located in regions that produced less than 5 percent of the world's economic output, few companies felt they had a real stake in this particular battle. Those companies that did get involved in social causes generally picked issues much closer to their own bottom line. Other than

South African mining companies, which were losing their workforce, and the Ugandan army, whose soldiers were being wiped out by the disease, few companies showed any interest in AIDS. But the mantra I have repeated over and over to the business community is that we all had reasons to get involved in this particular fight: First, it is the right thing to do if we intend to be good global citizens. Second, it is important for employees to be involved in issues that directly affect their lives, which translates directly into job satisfaction and increased morale. Third, it may help save the lives of your customers. Finally, it's been proven to be good for your brand. It seemed like the most natural thing for the business community to try to find ways to prevent the spread of the disease, encourage testing, fight against the discrimination or the stigma related to it and provide treatment for their employees.

The HIV virus is spread primarily by sexual contact, intravenous drug use, and mother-to-child transmission. While in the United States there is a strong tendency to consider AIDS a gay disease, throughout the rest of the world it has greatly affected heterosexuals. In some countries, for example, more young women have contracted the disease than men. At MTV, we have recognized and accepted the reality that our audience is interested in sex and is sexually active. We haven't ignored it or tried to hide it. The videos we showed very often had a sexual innuendo. Our critics often have accused us of selling a sexual lifestyle to impressionable kids, and they've questioned how we can continue to show these videos while at the same time preaching safe sex.

It is a fair question and certainly it does appear incongruous. But the truth is that we've won the trust of our audience by responding to their interests and treating them with respect. Young people have been having sex since the beginning of time, and watching a video isn't going to change that. Ignoring the reality that whether or not they are sexually active they certainly are sexually interested would be absurd. My approach has been that we have built our connection with young people because we have a channel they want to watch, and it is that connection that gives us the opportunity to be taken seriously when we discuss safe sex. That phrase we've drilled into our business plan, *respect and reflect*, is just as relevant here as in any other context. Kids know we show it like it is and tell it like it is. Our objective in our campaign against the HIV virus is to make sex safe, make the use of condoms cool, and educate young people about the disease. I always make the case simply and clearly. As I told a Japanese magazine, for example,

> HIV/AIDS is preventable and there is no reason anyone should get it. There are several methods for prevention and safe sex is one of the major methods. I would like to say to boys, "Make sure to practice safe sex," and to girls, "Say 'No' if the boy does not practice safe sex." Girls should be empowered to say "No" and boys should be responsible.

We've emphasized that point in some of the public-service commercials we've done. In a spot aimed directly at girls, for example, Beyoncé tells them, "It's okay to say 'No,' and it's okay to insist on a condom." In other words, we tried to empower young women. And we did another spot, this one with Wyclef Jean, in which he literally shouted directly into the camera, "Use a condom!" Sometimes you *do* need to shout at young men to get through to them.

In 2004, we even launched our own brand of condoms, selling them in Virgin Records Megastores and at some M-A-C cosmetic counters. As I said at the time, "I can remember how awkward it was to buy condoms and I am not sure we've moved so far over the last 25 years. The idea is to try to take the embarrassment out of the purchase."

I just thought it would be easier for young people to buy condoms from their peers rather than the local pharmacist, especially young women. Believe me, I know how difficult that can be. During my Plebe (freshman) year at the then-all-male West Point, I was anointed the "Rubber Rep," *rubbers* then being the term we used for condoms. As Rubber Rep, I was charged with going into the PX before we all left for spring break and purchasing condoms for the entire company. As an 18-year-old inexperienced kid, I had to go up to the attractive young woman at the checkout counter, look her right in the eye, and say as firmly as possible, "I'd like three hundred condoms, please."

Through the years we've even handed out thousands of condoms for free, although there are organizations that do a lot more condom distribution than we do. MTV is in a perfect position to make condoms cool, condom use cooler and conversations about condoms acceptable. When we started this campaign condom use was not considered cool. We've come a long way since then, to the point where we now have stores like Condomania, which sells condoms in a variety of colors and flavors. Young people trust our brand. And that trust has given us the credibility to engage them in a serious discussion about AIDS.

There are critics who point out we rarely make the case for abstinence—the best way of preventing AIDS—and that's true. That debate can get pretty heated at times. In 2010, after a meeting of PEPFAR (the U.S. President's Emergency Plan for AIDS Relief, started by George W. Bush) in Washington, DC, I was confronted by one of our partners who wondered loudly why MTV wasn't doing more to promote abstinence. There are young people who do believe in abstinence and practice it, but most won't. They're young and they are not going to quit having sex. It isn't going to happen. I tried to be conciliatory, agreeing with her that maybe MTV should have more coverage of abstinence. When George Bush was in office PEPFAR spent a tremendous amount of its budget promoting abstinence, while I have always supported the UNAIDS response, the ABC program: abstinence, being faithful, and using condoms. MTV's campaign choose to focus on the most efficient way of protecting those young people who are sexually active, which is to educate them about the dangers and urge them to use condoms. But in some of our programming we also discuss abstinence, there is some mention of it in SHUGA, for example, and I am an advocate of doing more of it. Abstinence is absolutely an effective way of preventing the spread of AIDS and we should respect that point of view.

One issue I had to deal with was how much time I could spend on corporate social responsibility issues without it affecting our business. I tried to solve that problem by integrating it into everything I did. I can't remember a speech I've given in the last decade in which I didn't talk about AIDS. At every launch, every keynote speech, every external or internal speech I made, I attached our brand to the fight against AIDS. I took my role as a UNAIDS Ambassador very seriously, so I talked about it at every single opportunity—even in places where it made people uncomfortable.

Fortunately, my corporate responsibilities often took me to the same areas of the world in which we were doing the bulk of our public-service activities. For example, when I was in Nairobi for a music awards event I was able to spend some of my own time visiting AIDS hospitals or working with volunteers. The best question isn't how much time you allot, but rather how well you're able to intertwine it with your corporate efforts. If you're effective in doing that, you never have to be concerned about balance.

One thing I knew for sure was that there was a huge knowledge gap among our audience about AIDS. Our objective was 100 percent access to educating prevention, ultimately leading to an AIDS-free generation. This was a disease that could be prevented and the people who were being infected didn't have the information they needed. We had an obligation to educate them, to help them save their own lives. The problem was getting that information to them. We had to find a way of selling the message of safe sex. I knew we couldn't preach or lecture to them. So at every opportunity I made the point that living with HIV is not a death sentence; we now have the capability of treating it as a chronic disease.

But our major campaign was called "Staying Alive," which was launched in 1998. The theme of Staying Alive has always been "live life positively, with or without HIV." People with HIV or AIDS can live an almost-normal life, although treatment can have serious repercussions. But there is no reason or excuse to discriminate or stigmatize people living with HIV. The purpose of the Staying Alive campaign was to use our network, and eventually other broadcasters' networks, to teach young people how to protect themselves as well as to fight the stigma associated with being HIV positive.

■■■

Staying Alive began as a series of 15-to-90-second hard-hitting spots and documentaries that were broadcast around the world. We required each of our channels to devote a minimum of one minute every day to public-service announcements, although we strongly encouraged our channels in high-impact areas to devote a minimum of three primetime minutes a day to it. While that may not sound like a lot of time, for broadcasters who survive by selling time it is substantial. After a while we dropped the requirement because I began to understand that the carrot was much more powerful than the stick. By that time, fortunately, the campaign had become part of the DNA of most of our channels and they continued to run this programming.

Our first half-hour Staying Alive documentary, which ran on World AIDS Day and was hosted by George Michael, told the stories of six young people around the world who either were already infected by the virus or were concerned about getting it. In a very powerful way, they told their own stories in their own words. It opened in São Paulo, Brazil. Several teenage boys were in a van, cruising for girls. It was the kind of scene that in some version is repeated all over the world. In this scene, one of those boys looks directly into the camera and boasts, "I have sex in lots of places. I don't use condoms."

The next scene featured a young woman, sipping a cappuccino. "Some men have the false idea that they can't get the AIDS virus," she says, and then reveals that she is HIV-positive and was infected in her very first sexual experience.

The third scene takes place in Zambia, where a reggae band sings the happy chorus, "Use condoms—your mates will think you're smart." And then the lead singer reminds viewers that the disease "is like your shadow, wherever you go you have to think of AIDS."

While we rarely insisted that our local channels run our programming, we strongly urged them to do it. Consequently, this campaign was broadcast throughout the world. That first broadcast reached an estimated 275 million households. We encountered strong resistance in several countries that were still clinging to the fantasy that AIDS did not exist there. For example, China was really tough. They wouldn't allow us to run it there. In fact, China has been a very interesting story. Initially, the Chinese government was very much in denial about the existence of the epidemic. It took a long time, but the Chinese were finally convinced they had to confront the disease. At each channel we looked for an in-house activist to fight the epidemic. In China, that person was Marilyn Zhu, who helped put together a meeting between MTV and the local TV stations in the country. At that meeting the station owners agreed to support our AIDS initiative, which was a huge breakthrough. The government finally accepted the reality that this is a pandemic, capable of killing millions of people, and joined the fight to stop it from spreading. In fact, MTV and CCTV co-produced a beautiful commercial entitled the "Ninja Spot." Basically, it involved a condom flying majestically through the air. It is visually engaging—although the government wouldn't run it. Instead, they took an interesting approach to educating their citizens. Instead of focusing directly on people who had become ill or died because they'd had sex, they talked about the children who had been orphaned because their parents had died from this terrible disease. The Chinese refused to talk about gay sex or heterosexual sex; instead they discussed children who had lost their parents. All the visuals were about these AIDS orphans. Although it certainly was an obtuse way of getting to the point, I accepted it, knowing that *any* way we got there was okay.

Over time China has become a positive story. Things began changing there after the government received severe criticism for its slow response to an outbreak of SARS (severe acute respiratory syndrome) in 2003 that threatened to become a pandemic. In response, the government set up a nationwide disease warning system and created contingency plans to deal with a possible pandemic. I remember sitting with Bill Gates at the Live Eight concert in London in July, 2005, organized by Bob Geldof shortly after an outbreak of avian flu in Asia. The world was concerned about the possibility of a pandemic, but Gates was reassuring. "We can be less worried about the spread of disease in China," he told me. Then he pointed out that because of the nation's political structure, the central government had the ability to enforce steps that can't be easily taken in many other countries. For example, the Chinese government could effectively implement quarantine measures to prevent the disease from spreading.

Staying Alive and the subsequent spots MTV ran resonated so strongly with our audience that within two years Georgia was receiving phone calls from around the world asking what we were going to give them for 2000 World AIDS Day programming. What we gave them was our second Staying Alive documentary, which was hosted by Ricky Martin, and the following year it was hosted by P Diddy. To get the greatest possible distribution for our shows we did something that, as far as I know, no other broadcaster had ever done: We gave them away free to any broadcaster, anywhere in the world, who would run them. "Any broadcaster" meant exactly that, including channels in direct competition with us. We went even further; to increase distribution, we permitted anyone who chose to run our shows to take off our logo and broadcast them without acknowledging MTV in any way—completely free, no branding, no strings attached. In fact, when we produced these shows we cleared rights not just for MTV, but for all broadcasters, which increased our production costs. By giving the shows away, no channel could claim it didn't have the budget or lacked the resources to produce this type of vitally important programming. And as far as I know, this is the first time a TV channel has produced programming and given it away, often to its competitors, without any branding. Although most channels run this programming with our logo, they retain the option to remove it. In fact, I didn't simply offer it to other channels, I specifically challenged them to run it. "Here it is," I said. "This material is vitally important to your viewers; it's very high quality and it is absolutely free! I challenge you to run it!"

Among the channels that ran our second show was Thailand's national channel, the National Geographic Channel, and CCTV, which ran it across China. Our potential audience for that show was 743 million households—far more than a billion people. As a result, we built up an additional distribution network for our programming that more than doubled our own distribution. It has become almost automatic now that this makeshift network will run the AIDS programming we produce. By 2008, this network had enabled us to achieve 100 percent distribution in the top-50 AIDS-impacted countries.

Even before we ran the second show my involvement in the fight had extended into my personal life. A turning point for me was meeting the amazing Dr. Peter Piot in 1997. I often refer to Peter as my mentor, even though I'm older than he is. Peter is a microbiologist who in 1976 co-discovered the Ebola virus in Zaire and later was one of the original researchers who unraveled the mysteries of the AIDS virus. When we met at a UNICEF function in Brussels he was an assistant-secretary-general of the United Nations and the newly appointed executive director of the Joint United Nations Programme on HIV/AIDS (UNAIDS). We instantly bonded, discovering that we had similar interests ranging from global health to exotic restaurants. Several weeks later we had lunch in London, where he told me that I was the guy he'd been looking for. He was desperate to find a way of reaching young people, he explained, and needed someone with broad international experience. The lack of knowledge about this disease, especially in the third world, was abysmal and very dangerous, especially since as many as two-thirds of all new cases could be prevented by education. Throughout the world a sizeable number of young people believed AIDS could be transmitted by kissing, or holding hands, or mosquitoes. As he pointed out, I was the guy sitting on top of the largest global organization directed specifically toward the demographic most severely impacted. He asked what I wanted to do with that power.

Eventually he asked me to do a few simple things: Continue our highly visible campaign against AIDS on MTV, become a spokesman for the AIDS community, and mobilize the business community to fight the epidemic. And then he offered to make me a UN special ambassador. It was an offer, but Peter made it sound like a mission. And much like in the army, I saw it as a tremendous opportunity to make a difference.

Kenneth Cole once told me that he'd initially gotten involved in this fight "because it was good for the corporation, but very quickly it felt personal." For me, the disease became personal with the death of Nelson Benedico in 1999. Having made many friends in the Hollywood community when I was living in California, I had known people who had died from AIDS, but no one I was as close to as Nelson. Nelson Benedico was my business colleague, but he was also my close friend. He was a gay Cuban-American who had been in charge of marketing and communications when MTV Latin America was launched. I traveled with him throughout South America and he introduced me to the exuberance of the Latin culture. On those trips I bonded with him. If you knew Nelson, if you spent any time with him, it was hard not to. He was smart and warm and charismatic and brought joy to everyone around him. He lived in Miami, and because my mother lived there, Alex and I would visit often and we began socializing with Nelson and his partner, Danny. Some people close to Nelson had rejected him, which was difficult for him. The pain that caused him may have added to my determination to fight discrimination wherever I encountered it.

One day I noticed Nelson was losing weight and I began teasing him about it, as friends often do—until it became obvious he was ill. That was devastating. What made it even worse was that the stigma attached to it was still so strong that for a long time he had to hide it, even from his family and his closest friends. There wasn't anything Alex and I could do except encourage him. He struggled bravely. Watching him deteriorate and being helpless to do anything about it was heartbreaking. It just seemed like there had to be more we could do. There wasn't. We shared this mammoth reality, but we never spoke about it. I learned from him how to celebrate life rather than accepting death. As challenging as his life was near the end, the most important thing we did was keep his hope alive. Alex and I were with him as much as possible and on July 19, 1999, my friend Nelson died.

Peter Piot gave me a direction, Nelson gave me a personal reason, and MTV gave me the vehicle with which to try to make a difference.

By 2002, we were reaching 500 million homes in 166 countries, more than 60 percent of all the television households in the world, making our Staying Alive campaign by far the most successful media awareness and prevention effort in the world. Each year it grew bigger. In 2003, our hour-long special, *Meeting Mandela*, in which we brought together those four young people who had been through such hardships, was hosted by Beyoncé. This show was a little different from the others we've done as it was more about forgiveness than the virus, although we did include Henry Hudson, who had contracted the disease. I used to joke with him, "Henry Hudson? With a name like that I'll bet you'll go far in this world." (Please note that I never claimed I *good* joked with him.) In other years, stars like Justin Timberlake, Mary J. Blige, Kanye West, and Kelly Rowland hosted our specials.

Eventually, our Staying Alive programming seemed to lose some of its energy—*viewer fatigue* I called it—and it was obvious we had to find a new approach. So instead of the documentary-style programming we had been doing, we decided to create long-form scripted dramas—movies. That was a bold move. MTV had never produced a movie for television.

Our first movie, *Transit*, premiered in 2005. It followed four young people around the world as their lives—and fates—become entwined. But the program that has made the strongest impact was *Shuga* (Sugar Daddy), the story of a group of students in Nairobi, Kenya. This was a three-part series, closely supervised by Georgia, that dramatized the main messages we have been trying to communicate: the refusal by many men to use condoms, the reluctance to get tested, the stigma attached to the disease, the dangers of sleeping with multiple concurrent partners, and even the powerful—in this story a boss—taking advantage of the powerless, his young female employees. But we did it as a soap opera—it was

Gossip Girl meets Staying Alive. We promoted it as "the story of bright lives, entwining and colliding. It's the story of morning-afters and sweet departures—and the indelible marks we leave on each other." For Africa this was revolutionary programming. It was highly produced, featured charismatic Kenyans, and pushed the sexual envelope. While it wasn't especially provocative by western standards, this was the first time that intimate relationships were depicted on Kenyan TV. So kids watched it and were captivated by it.

Because many Kenyan families don't have television sets in their homes we also screened it for free in assembly halls. For the most conservative nations we produced a slightly censored version—which 85 of the more than 100 countries that ran the show decided to broadcast. In addition to Africa, we used the same script to make three-part TV movies for the Ukraine and Trinidad and Tobago. As Georgia said, "Our aim was to make a really good drama that people would watch. The messages were almost subliminal, but they were there."

Eventually, the lessons of our campaigns were absorbed by our corporate culture and have been interwoven in subtle ways into most of our long-form programming. What we've tried to show is that living with AIDS has become a part of all of our lives. If you're watching a reality show, for example, and two people are going to have sex, at some point a condom will be visible.

As we've learned, as most corporations have learned, it's difficult to accurately measure the impact of public-service programming. When we donate millions of dollars to Paul Farmer's Partners in Health to help build a hospital in Haiti, as we've done, we can pretty much determine how many patients will be treated annually, how many lives are going to be saved, and how many people will get medical care who previously would never have gotten it. But trying to accurately measure the value of public-service messages or documentary programming is almost impossible. We were contributing millions of dollars a year in airtime, production, distribution, and overhead in the belief that we were changing behavior and thereby saving lives. Fortunately, that was confirmed by a study conducted by researchers from Johns Hopkins University in Baltimore and the Bill and Melinda Gates Foundation. The results of this study were beyond our hopes. And our hopes were pretty high. While a movie we'd made for the Caribbean, *Tribes*, was seen by slightly less than

10 percent of our audience, *Shuga* was a huge hit. More than 60 percent of Kenyan youth had seen it—and more importantly, they "understood and remembered the main messages and could identify the lessons to be learned." The results were astonishing. About half of the viewers interviewed reported that after seeing the film they had discussed the messages with close friends and family members and an amazing 90 percent of Kenyans said they felt *Shuga* had made an impact on their thinking. Almost 80 percent of those people said *Shuga* had changed their attitude about getting tested, and because of the lessons they had learned it was their intention to have fewer sexual partners. A great majority believed they would think differently about people who were infected. While the study couldn't prove there had been an actual change in behaviors, I was assured by the researchers that an intention to change is considered a direct connection to the actual change in behavior. In 2011, producer Jaka Bizilj's Cinema for Peace honored *Shuga* with its annual award for fighting the disease.

My personal involvement in the battle against this disease outside the company had begun in Edinburgh, Scotland, in 1997, even before I'd met Dr. Piot, when Georgia and I helped found the Global Business Council (GBC) on AIDS. "Outside the company" is technically correct, as this was work I was doing on my own time without any corporate involvement. But as every executive knows, everything they do in their personal life reflects on their employer. It's important never to forget that; I knew that the only reason I had been invited to participate was because of my position at MTV Networks and the work we'd done. So unofficially, at least, everything I did was closely involved with MTV. In 1997, I was invited to meet with representatives of four major pharmaceutical companies. At that time the big drug companies were being bludgeoned by the media for the high prices they were charging for drugs that appeared to slow the progression of the disease, as well as their lack of progress in discovering new and more potent treatments. The objective of this meeting was to find a way to organize the greater business community against the disease. I was among the very few non-pharma people at this meeting, which is probably why I was named chairman.

In fact, I was well aware that the business community hadn't done very much to fight the disease. To me that was shortsighted. We all shared the same problems: Our customers were dying and our workforce was being depleted. And thus far the response from the wider business community had been inadequate. International corporations in particular have an infrastructure, distribution, sales, and marketing that no single government could match. But, unfortunately, few companies had chosen to become involved, and that included media companies. While corporations like Coca-Cola, Kaiser, ChevronTexaco, DaimlerChrysler, Anglo-American Mining, and M-A-C Cosmetics were committed to the fight, too many other companies doing business in those parts of the world severely impacted by the virus had not gotten involved. We hoped that for some companies, at least, the reason for that might have been something as simple as not knowing how and where to get started; we were going to provide the structure that allowed them to participate.

At that first meeting we exchanged best practices and designed a sample HR policy for dealing with HIV/AIDS. Our initial objective was to sign up as many companies as possible. The requirements for membership were simple. Companies were required to make a small financial contribution, initially $5,000, but more importantly they had to make a commitment to institute HR policies to treat, counsel, and test employees and create an educational program to reduce the stigma associated with the disease, and take the steps necessary to become a role model in the community. "Role model" did not mean "donate more money"; it was an intentionally vague term we used that required them to play to their strengths. It was more important than money, I explained; it meant simply using what resources they had in the best possible way. Coca-Cola, for example, the largest employer in Africa, had a vast marketing and distribution network, which theoretically they could use to help deliver antiviral drugs to distant villages. It meant doing what was possible, the best you could.

The goals of the Council differ from the work being done by MTV. There are two elements in this fight, prevention and treatment, and unfortunately at times they compete for resources. MTV almost entirely emphasized prevention. Some people argue that prevention has a better ROI (return on investment), because with very inexpensive methods we can stop the spread of the disease. As a TV channel we had limited capability to help on the treatment side. So at the GBC, and later as part of my work with the Global Media AIDS Initiative, I stressed that every person should have universal access to treatment. Let me repeat that because I believe it is so important: Every human being, no matter where he or she lives, no matter how rich or poor that person may be, has the right to treatment.

As founding members of the Council we spent a considerable amount of time searching for ways to convince companies it was to their benefit to join us in this fight. It was difficult at times. Inside every corporation there will be people who argue against this type of involvement. They claim it affects the bottom line by sucking up time, energy, and sometimes money, as well as blurring the focus, which should be strictly on their business.

In response, just as Kenneth Cole had learned, I argued that the business community can help save the lives of our customers, that involvement is also good for employee morale, and ultimately it benefited your brand.

Among the people I worked with who proved that argument were John Dempsey, CEO of M-A-C Cosmetics, who committed a percentage of his profits to the fight and told me flatly, "I know that our customers feel good about buying our products because they know where some of the proceeds are going," and the late founder of The Body Shop, Anita Roddick. Anita and I agreed to create co-branded products for her stores and donated much of the proceeds to fighting HIV/AIDS. We found that Dempsey was absolutely right, that customers tended to buy products whose sales benefited a cause with which they agreed. So as I often pointed out to corporations, there was a strong argument to be made that associating your brand with a cause like stopping AIDS made sense as a business proposition.

While our organizing efforts ultimately were successful and the Council continued to grow, I felt that if we intended to take it to the next level we needed a high-profile full-time person to run it. In January 2000, the American ambassador to the United Nations, Richard Holbrooke, convened the first Security Council meeting in history devoted strictly to a health issue. It was at that historic meeting that Vice-President Al Gore declared that AIDS was a security threat to the entire world. A year later, when Holbrooke announced plans to leave that job, I was told by Tim Wirth, the former Colorado governor running Ted Turner's UN Foundation, that Holbrooke might be interested in running our organization. It was a very exciting possibility, and I met with him several times. Richard Holbrooke, who died suddenly in December 2010, was a fascinating and complex man. He was forceful, direct, and the type of person who never wasted one second of his life. As a result he was remarkably effective. Upon leaving the UN he became president and CEO of the Global Business Council.

Holbrooke succeeded in taking the Council to the next level, and by 2007 the renamed Global Business Coalition on HIV/AIDS, Tuberculosis, and Malaria had become a vast international organization with 225 members. McDonald's, for example, gets criticized in the media for its products but deserves credit for its very strong pro-social agenda. In addition to M-A-C and The Body Shop, the Gap created its RED product line from which it donates 50 percent of profits to the Global Fund, and also began sourcing some products from severely affected countries. HBO produced two films that highlighted the plight of women facing this disease. And Nike (South Africa) began community outreach programs and provided HIV-related services to its employees. When Holbrooke left to join the Obama administration, John Tedstrom took over sole leadership and has continued to build on the strong foundation.

But even with the involvement of all these companies it had become obvious to me that there was even more we could do to get out the message. The harsh reality was that we had the capability of stopping the spread of this disease by educating people—and for whatever reasons, in many parts of the world we weren't getting it done.

Considering the number of people who had been affected and the economic consequences, AIDS remained the most underreported epidemic in history. In fact, when I was privileged to address the United Nations General Assembly Special Session on HIV/AIDS in 2001, I told them,

> During this high-level meeting more than 43,000 people globally have been infected, more than half of these new infections will be among young people 15 to 24, and more than half will be among women. If they had been infected by chickens with bird flu, it would dominate the media . . . but because HIV is still considered to be a disease of the marginalized it is treated differently. This must stop.

What had happened, I felt, was that rather than continuing to sound the alarms we had learned to live with the monster. We had accepted it, which I felt was unacceptable. There is a misconception in the United States that in the battle against AIDS we have blunted the attack and are on the offensive. That isn't true. One section in Washington, DC, for example, has an incidence rate as high as the most severely affected countries in Africa. We have made progress, but the harsh reality is that around the world the numbers remain staggering. To the surprise of many people, although the death rate has declined, the disease is still raging out of control. By the end of 2010 there were an estimated 33,000,000 people living with AIDS; 5,000,000 people around the world were in treatment—but for every person added to treatment there still are two new infections. And there are another 10,000,000 who should be in treatment but the funds are simply not available. While there is some statistical movement in the right direction, deaths and new infections have gone down, the disease is still ravaging nations.

People need to be reminded continuously that we haven't conquered this disease. And no industry is better suited to doing that than the media. In 2004, the Kaiser Family Foundation under the direction of the talented Drew Altman, and UNAIDS convened a meeting of executives from 20 of the leading media companies in 13 nations and we formed the Global Media AIDS Initiative. The objective was to simply use all the available resources of the media to spread as much information as widely as possible. In Russia, for example, 40 media companies brought together broadcasters, advertising agencies, and media sales companies to create TV public-service announcements and nationwide billboard advertising. I followed UN Secretary-General Kofi Annan as the chairman and eventually more than 140 companies in 70 nations agreed to follow MTV's example and create rights-free programming that would be made available to anyone willing to broadcast it. As I pointed out often and loudly in my role as chairman, "The UN says education can prevent two-thirds of all new infections. If every media company gave at least one minute of its daily primetime schedule to the AIDS message, the impact would be immeasurable."

Unlike many executives, I was incredibly fortunate that my professional and personal lives were so complementary, and that I had a management team that understood and encouraged my active participation in social issues. Sometimes, though, it was difficult to make the leap between those two aspects of my life. In the AIDS community there are people who are known as "peer counselors," typically young teenagers and young adults, who volunteer to fight the epidemic. At one time I spent several days in Zambia going from place to place with one of these peer counselors as he handed out educational materials that he carried in a paper bag. This brochure explained in simple language and illustrations the dangers of the disease and the way to prevent infection, as well as encouraging testing. This young man was in his early 20s and he had almost nothing of his own; he was quite smart and easily could have gotten a full-paying job, but instead he had dedicated his life to helping others. As I got ready to leave, I complimented him on his dedication and his personal sacrifice, and then asked, "What do you need? What can I do to help you?"

He thought about that for a moment and said, "You know what I really need? I need a good bag to carry my materials. I could carry so much more if I had a good bag." He didn't ask for money, he didn't ask for transportation, he didn't even ask for help. All he wanted was a bag. Just a bag. For him a bag made a significant difference. Obviously we provided it for him, as many bags as he needed, but it was a strong reminder that many little steps can make a major difference. This young man's unselfish dedication reinforced my belief that young Africans can teach the world how to fight the epidemic.

I flew from Zambia to New York to attend a major musical event at Lincoln Center. As I watched great artists walking the Red Carpet, several of them carrying expensive Louis Vuitton bags, my thoughts wandered back to Zambia. My travels often swung widely between the haves and have-nots, and it was impossible not to feel uneasy about it. I suspect most people who have worked for a multinational company for any length of time have crossed this same societal bridge, although rarely is it quite so dramatic. They have learned, as I have, that this is the world as it exists. And the best we can do to change it is to give our best efforts.

While filming the *Staying Alive* documentaries the producers met a number of extraordinary young people, among them a Ugandan who night after night was creating AIDS awareness materials by hand, then distributing it during the day. Because he had no electricity he was working by candlelight—literally by candlelight, until he was forced to stop because he no longer could afford candles. Obviously something had to be done to help him, and that peer counselor in Zambia, and the thousands of other people who had made it their life effort to fight this disease. So in 2004 MTV formed the Staying Alive Foundation, which was established to offer financial support to young people engaged in grassroots prevention efforts. I was the chairman, but eventually Georgia ran it on a day-to-day basis. Basically, we'd select a person or a small group of people and give them seed money to start or continue programs dealing with the prevention, treatment, or the stigma associated with the disease. By 2010 the Foundation had awarded 272 grants to 135 organizations in 58 countries, none of them for more than $48,000, or $12,000 for four years, and most of them for considerably less. The selection criteria have been intentionally broad: Recipients had to be between the ages of 12 and 24 who otherwise wouldn't receive grants. The funding is raised from a number of business and private sources; Foundation board member Chris Davis, Head of Global Campaigns for the Body Shop, has helped lead the fund-raising efforts. Among the recipients were an Algerian theater group that uses live performances to teach how the virus is transmitted and how young people can protect themselves; a Nigerian who provides information about the disease to the hearing impaired; a Kenyan radio station delivers messages specifically to truck drivers (who meet commercial sex workers teaching how to prevent infection and rejecting common misconceptions, like having sex with a virgin will cure the disease and mosquitoes carry the virus); a Chinese man who teaches life skills to middle school students in Beijing; a Ukrainian who has created an informational website for children and adolescents; a Vietnamese who established and runs the Youth Counseling Centre on Love, Marriage, and Family, which provides face-to-face or telephone counseling services to answer questions about sex; and even an American, Natalia Cales, whom I have mentored, although mostly by e-mail. After Natalia's mother died of AIDS in 2006, she used a grant from the Staying Alive Foundation to run the Carolina Empowerment Group in Charlotte, North Carolina. She regularly holds workshops where she teaches girls about sexual health, including how to use a condom, alcohol abuse, and lifestyle issues.

I've seen about 10 grant recipients at work. In Ethiopia we drove almost a full day along basically nonexistent roads to watch a theater group perform in a township. Unfortunately, I've seen a lot of poverty and suffering in my career. I've seen many children suffering from malnutrition; I've seen amputees sitting on a hospital floor. This particular township was a collection of huts covered with corrugated roofs and no electricity or plumbing. A dirt road ran through it; there were outdoor latrines and families of eight or more were living in one room. But suddenly this acting group of energetic, excited young people arrived, set up their props on the road, and started their show. They acted out several different scenarios that are familiar to the poor everywhere: male domination, as a boss or teacher threatening an female employee or a sugar daddy promising gifts. They showed the stigma attached to the disease and the fear of testing. There was no dialogue, but the message was quite clear. Gradually, the residents of the township drifted over to watch the performance, and soon the audience grew to more than 100 people. I've also sat in on training sessions, which are vitally important to educate the grant recipients.

Some of the Foundation grants have been very bold. In addition to funding grassroots AIDS programs, it also has awarded grants to young Egyptians engaged in the effort to stop female genital mutilation, as well as to people trying to bring attention to forced marriages.

I speak about the war against AIDS all the time. I'm sure there are some who wonder how that actually benefits my employer. I understand the question, but I have no doubt about those benefits. In every one of the hundreds of speeches I've made or events I've attended there has never been a moment when it was not well known that I was representing MTV. It didn't matter if I was there for an MTV-sponsored event or it was my personal time; I was always representing the brand. I've spoken at the United Nations four times, and each time my introduction always acknowledged MTV. And when I spoke at a Latin American AIDS conference in Havana, every person there knew I was the guy from MTV.

As I said when addressing the UN,

> It might seem strange to talk about an organization as noble as the UN in the same breath as MTV. We're not used to that kind of respect. But we understand the power of bringing people together for the greater good. In our case it's through working together on a daily basis with creative young people

> around the world who understand the unique power of music and culture [to be] an ultimate form of diplomacy.

In return, when I was recognized by the UN Correspondents' Association in 2009 as its Global Citizen of the Year for MTV's efforts in fighting the disease, Secretary-General Ban Ki-moon of Korea made a point of emphasizing, "The partnership between the United Nations and MTV is very valuable to us."

In response I said graciously and very seriously to him, "What an incredible honor to have you present this award to us. I hope to be able to do the same for you one day when you win a Video Music Award. Or a Kid's Choice Award."

From one channel with limited distribution we had built a vast network that enabled us to reach as many as 2 or 3 billion people. While AIDS always had been our primary public issue involvement, I also believed we had a responsibility to make our audience aware of at least some of the other social issues that might well affect their lives, which is why we chose to get involved with national politics, climate change, human trafficking, drug abuse, and disaster relief.

Ironically, there is far more debate about the existence of climate change, and, if it is a reality, how much human beings can really do about it, than about AIDS. No one doubts that AIDS is a major health crisis, while a significant number of people believe strongly that global warming and climate change is a political hoax. Because of its connection to the young audience MTV has always gotten requests from charities and issue-oriented groups asking for some type of involvement. Usually it's something like, "Would you please host a fund-raising concert for us? Just one." I wish it were possible, but MTV has focused on those causes that will affect its audience and its employees. As Ted Turner would say, MTV was involved in environmental issues before it was cool. Or in this issue, warm. The channel was doing energy awareness and green initiative spots as early as 1981. Al Gore's documentary, *An Inconvenient Truth*, was distributed by Paramount, a Viacom company, so when he came to London to promote it I was invited to meet him at a screening.

The battle to raise climate change awareness had been going on for a long time without drawing tremendous attention, but Al Gore changed that. When it became a major political issue we made the decision that

MTV would get actively involved in educating our audience because it is an issue that may directly affect their lives. I appreciate the fact that many people don't believe climate change is real, but my feeling is that if it *is* real, it is going to change the way our audience lives, and at worst, taking steps now to protect our environment can only be positive. Becoming more aware of our planet and taking steps to conserve natural resources are beneficial in all circumstances. I didn't think anyone could find fault with that objective.

We had learned from Staying Alive how to attract the attention of our audience. We knew we had to communicate our message creatively—and we also had to activate our audience. It isn't sufficient to tell them something terrible is happening to their world but there's nothing they can do about it. This was the genesis of our "Switch" campaign, which we launched in 2007. We began by broadcasting 40 colorful, creative, and very cutting-edge public-service videos created for free by six Los Angeles advertising agencies. One lush spot set to choral music showed normal men and women urinating in public, ending with the suggestion, "Save water—flush less."

Our overall message was a simple one, and it went all the way back to the lesson I had learned from J.C. Sparkman at TCI: A small number multiplied by a big number equals a big number, or in this case a big impact. That was the whole premise of our campaign, that there are small things each of us can do to slow down the acceleration of global climate change. "Climate change is a DIY issue," we told our viewers, and then directed them to a website that gave them various suggestions for doing it themselves. Among the simple energy-conserving tips were unplugging their mobile phone chargers when they weren't using them, turning down the thermostat in their homes by one degree, and shutting off their computers at night and on the weekends.

In addition to this message being broadcast on 55 channels in 162 nations, we created material for 44 websites and 16 different mobile phone services, all of it directing people to a multi-language website where we provided the necessary information. We also supported the campaign on our programs, doing an eco-friendly episode of *Pimp My Ride* in which we installed in a 1965 Chevy Impala an 800-horsepower diesel engine that ran on biofuel. There is no question that MTV, and many other organizations, has successfully raised environmental awareness. But as other issues having an impact on young people, such as the recession and natural disasters, have generated headlines, the debate over global warming has cooled. To reflect that, MTV's Switch campaign was taken off the channel and is now run online.

In 2008, a year after launching the Switch effort under the passionate leadership of Simon Goff, who originally had joined MTV as an intern working in the Staying Alive initiative, the company launched MTV EXIT (End Exploitation and Trafficking across Asia and the Pacific), a campaign to focus attention on the horrors of human trafficking. Again, this was an issue that directly impacted our audience. The campaign originally had begun on MTV Europe in 2004, this phase of it was aimed primarily at Eastern Europe and Asia, where the problem is especially severe. *Human trafficking* is a form of modern-day slavery; it's devastating but until recently, few people were even aware it existed. The UN estimated that at any one time there are 12.5 million people being held hostage in some way, being used for everything from labor to sex—and the majority of them are young women. But the harsh fact is that that number is just a best guess. It's probably a minimum and could be substantially higher than that. The selling and buying of human beings is a $10-billion-a-year industry, after drug trafficking the second largest criminal activity in the world. MTV's definition of human trafficking included arranged marriages, sex trafficking, migrant workers, and forced domestic servitude. While it takes place around the world, it is an extremely serious problem from the Philippines throughout the Middle East. There are both source and destination countries, and what made this campaign relevant to me was the fact that we have distribution in both source and destination countries, so we have an opportunity to make a difference.

As I explained when we announced this campaign,

> Victims [of human trafficking] are subject to horrendous abuses, including rape and torture, with young women and girls particularly affected. Education is the key to prevention. MTV EXIT is part of our commitment to help highlight issues affecting young people in Asia and across the world.

Obviously, these campaigns can be expensive and we look for partners to help fund them. In this case, the United Nations Agency for

International Development used the resources of MTV to help spread this message. We produced several videos; the first one, *Inhuman Traffic*, was hosted by Angelina Jolie and focused on sex trafficking. As we had done in our AIDS campaign, we let young people who had been exploited tell their dramatic stories. In 2009 MTV released its first animated public-service film. *Intersection* is high-quality anime, a type of stylized animation, and is the story of people caught up in Asian human trafficking and sexual exploitation. It had a soundtrack by Radiohead and Thievery Corporation, and it was made available to broadcasters in 14 languages. As EXIT's Executive Director, Simon Goff, explained, "The idea of fusing a social message into a creative format like a music video was something that we had wanted to experiment with for some time. By integrating the message into this format we could reach many more people than if we created a standard public service announcement." Groups including Radiohead, The Killers, R.E.M., and Muse worked with us on this campaign. A split-screen video produced by Radiohead, using a track from their latest album, showed the life of an average child in a safe and structured environment on one side, while the other side showed a child the same age working in a sweatshop. As in every other instance, all of our programming and supporting materials are rights-free and available at no cost to any broadcaster or organization.

Our objective was educating our audience so they can protect themselves from traffickers and take action if they become aware of human trafficking in their countries. MTV has produced training materials in 40 languages, including 22 languages in Asia, for everyone from its audience to border guards. In addition to programming, MTV produced concerts, mostly in those countries where trafficking is most prevalent. A five-concert series in Indonesia, including one in East Timor, attracted 160,000 people; four concerts in Nepal drew 60,000 people; and 65,000 people turned out for four Cambodian concerts, including the first concert ever presented at the temple at Angkor Wat. We held concerts in Sarajevo, on Albanian and Romanian beaches, and in Russia, the Ukraine, and Tokyo, among other places. Most of the bands were regional stars; in Thailand the Thai-American hip-hop group Thaitanium performed. The Vietnam tour included Korean superstars Super Junior, and the American pop band The Click Five. The concert in Kiev featured Ukraine's top acts, including S.K.A.Y. and Esthetic Education. The literature we handed out at every concert, as well as our programming, directed viewers and concertgoers to our MTV EXIT website, which featured all of our programming as well as information about how to protect yourself from becoming a victim and how to get involved in stopping human trafficking.

Finally, MTV both domestically and internationally has contributed its resources and been actively involved in disaster relief efforts. Two weeks before our 2004 *MTV Asia Awards* show was scheduled to be held in Bangkok, that region of the world was devastated by the tsunami. More than 200,000 people died. We immediately canceled the show. Instead, within a few days it had been transformed into *MTV Asia Aid*, a worldwide telethon to raise funds to help the survivors. In particular, because kids had suffered so disproportionately, the majority of the money we raised was to go to UNICEF for direct aid to children.

Thailand was a nation in shock. Alicia Keys hosted this telethon and many stars who couldn't get to Thailand made videos asking for assistance. Our goal, I said when announcing the program, was to reach "at least three-quarters of the world's TV households with this event." Maybe I was exaggerating again. But we were the only media company in the world capable of organizing an event of this size, and we were fortunate to have been preparing for our awards show in Bangkok.

Almost exactly four years later, we again mobilized for *Hope for Haiti Now: A Global Benefit for Earthquake Relief*. The Haitian earthquake had occurred on a Tuesday, and within days our plans for a benefit concert were already progressing when George Clooney called Judy McGrath in New York to suggest that MTV host a global telethon to raise the desperately needed funds. Judy didn't even hesitate, telling him, "Yes, everybody'll do it. Everybody's in." Judy played a huge role in this event, putting together a worldwide network that included both terrestrial networks and cable channels, to broadcast a superstar show. We had production centers in London, New York, and Los Angeles. The telethon raised almost $70 million from public donations alone, and including revenues from album sales the total was close to $100 million. The money went to a variety of charities, including the Red Cross, UNICEF, and Wyclef Jean's YELE Fund. From that we also contributed about $15 million to Dr. Paul Farmer's Partners in Health, a nongovernmental organization that used it to help build a desperately needed state-of-the-art solar powered 300-bed hospital in Haiti's

Central Plateau. The country's main hospital had been completely destroyed in the earthquake, with more than 200 nurses dying in the collapse of a single floor. In addition to serving Haiti, this is the largest hospital in the entire Caribbean. Dr. Farmer invited me in September 2010 to help lay its cornerstone. While the human tragedy continues in Port au Prince, in the Central Plateau I saw how effective Partners in Health has been.

The largest concert that MTV supported was Bob Geldof, Harvey Goldsmith, and Kevin Wall's Live 8, which was held in 2005 to put pressure on the most affluent nations to increase aid to the poorest nations. It included more than 1,000 musicians performing in 10 concerts, and drew an audience estimated at two billion people on 182 TV networks and 2,000 radio stations. Within days, the wealthy nations pledged to double 2004 aid levels to $50 billion within five years.

The value of these campaigns to a corporation is difficult to measure statistically. But I have no doubt about their importance.

I believe that there is such a thing as *corporate social responsibility*, and the payoff for it is not easily calculated. But with the massive number of young people MTV reaches, it has always had both an obligation and a desire to deal with the issues that affect their lives. When speaking at corporate events I almost always reminded my colleagues of the fact that MTV is trusted by more young people than any other brand in the world, provides a unique opportunity to make a global impact. And as I like to tell my colleagues throughout the media world,

> Never underestimate your power, and never miss an opportunity to speak for those with less voice, less influence and less opportunity than we have. This is your chance in life to make a positive contribution by bringing people closer together and creating an understanding among diverse cultures.

The bottom line is that for the bottom line, doing good in the world is good business.

Chapter Eight

Where Do We Go from Here?

We have the smartest, most talented, most creative people in the world in our communications industries—in radio, television, film, newspapers, magazines, advertising, publishing, public relations, marketing. These men and women want to help their country, and will volunteer eagerly to help get our message across. One of the first people we should enlist is a West Point graduate named Bill Roedy. His enterprise reaches one billion people in 18 languages in 164 countries. Eight out of ten MTV viewers live outside the United States. He can teach us a lot about how to tell our story.

—Newton Minow, *Winning the Information War*, 2002

One night I had a date with the Dallas Cowboys Cheerleaders—not *a* Cowboys cheerleader, *all* of them. At times, executives have to make sacrifices for their company. In the 1990s, the National Football League was considering launching a new league, the NFL Europe, and had approached MTV about forming a joint venture. MTV would have owned half the league. For several months I'd been having conversations about this with NFL Commissioner Paul Tagliabue, future Commissioner and then COO Roger Goodall, and the

American Ambassador to Germany, Bob Kimmitt, who had been a year ahead of me at West Point. The NFL had approached MTV Europe because of our success in bringing the continent together as a single business entity. To promote American football in Europe the league was staging an exhibition game in London's Wembley Stadium. I got a call on Friday afternoon telling me that an event that the entire Cowboys' cheerleading squad had been scheduled to attend had been canceled. Would I take care of them that night?

Would I take care of the Dallas Cowboys' cheerleading squad? Well, it was my professional duty. That night I took the entire squad to the hottest nightclub in London. As you might suspect, we didn't have to wait outside.

The fact that Neil Braun, Senior Vice-President in charge of Corporate Development at Viacom in New York, was trying to negotiate a deal with the NFL wasn't surprising. One truth about building a business is that you never stop building that business, especially when you're in the entrepreneurial stage, as we were at that time. There is always another step to be climbed, another deal to be made. The message is that you always have to keep growing. MTV was continuing to grow vertically across the world while at the same time expanding horizontally within each country. In many instances, once we'd managed to build a distribution network inside a country we aggressively tried to add MTV Networks' other brands, which included VH1, Comedy Central, and especially Nickelodeon.

Nickelodeon had grown to become as important a property as MTV. It had been launched in 1979, on the Qube network in Columbus, Ohio. Tom Freston was confident that just as music connected young people around the world, children could be connected by their love of animated characters and green slime dropping from the ceiling on someone's head. He was right; when the first guest was slimed in 1982, kids fell in love with it. The live quiz-game show *Double Dare* made its debut in 1986 and within four days Nick's ratings had quadrupled. Within a month *Double Dare* had become the highest-rated series in cable TV history.

Gerry Layborne, who built Nickelodeon into the most successful children's channel in the world, began international distribution of the channel by selling formats to broadcasters in Europe, allowing them to create local versions of Nick's most popular shows, especially *Double Dare*. MTV Networks launched the first international Nick channel,

Nick U.K., in 1993. That actually was Viacom's first country-specific channel in Europe. But while MTV and Nick had the same parent, those channels operated independently of each other. Efforts to expand Nick slowed down in 1996 when Gerry left Viacom to become president of Disney/ABC Cable networks, a position she left two years later to found the Oxygen Network, the first channel aimed specifically at young women. She was replaced as head of Nickelodeon by Herb Scannell, who launched *Dora* and continued the impressive domestic growth of the channel, while at about the same time I was given the responsibility to expand Nick around the world.

While domestically Nickelodeon eventually became the highest-rated cable channel in America, globally it trailed MTV in distribution. So in the early 2000s MTV Networks began an aggressive international expansion program for Nickelodeon. While Disney was focusing on the tween market, research pointed us toward the preschool-to-about-12-year-old audience. In addition to Nick, we aggressively distributed brand extensions like Nick Jr. and NickToons, which had proved to be popular with younger viewers. As a result MTV Networks captured that demographic around the world.

Ironically, considering Viacom is competing against Disney and Cartoon Network, both of which established their reputation with animation, it has been animated programming, such as *SpongeBob*, *Dora*, and *Rugrats,* that has made Nick successful. Animated programming travels more easily around the world than live action. And while Disney has done a brilliant job with its *High School Musical* series and Miley Cyrus's *Hannah Montana*, Nick continues to make inroads with the tweens. Cyma Zarghami, who replaced Herb Scannell in 2006, has focused on increasing Nick's popularity to that demo. Innovative shows that integrate music into the storyline, like *iCarly*, *Victorious*, and *Big Time Rush*, have all been successful outside the United States. Cyma also made the decision to develop the English-language version of the telenovela *House of Anubis*, the first series that originated internationally to be produced for the domestic market, which is targeted directly at tweens. It was filmed in England with a non-American cast and has become the first internationally produced show to be a hit in the United States.

In the international market, syndication can be an important revenue source, but the complexity has to be managed astutely. One night, for example, before MTV bought VIVA, I happened to be in Germany and turned on that channel. Obviously it's important to know what your competition is doing, especially when that competition is consistently beating you in the ratings. I wanted to know what they were doing that we weren't. As it turned out, what they were doing was running our programming. VIVA had purchased the German syndication rights to *South Park*, Comedy Central's highest rated and longest running program. Being faced with the irony of having Viacom's own programs competing with its own channels was a problem.

Obviously there was a sound business reason for this. A division of MTV Networks, Program Sales, essentially syndicates programming to other channels around the world. Syndication is an important way to monetize the large investment in programming. It's a very profitable, successful business. In addition to allowing MTV to spend more money on production, in certain situations it was also very good for the multi-billion-dollar consumer product business. In those markets where Nick wasn't on the air, syndicating our programming to other channels provided the exposure needed to sell SpongeBob lunchboxes, Dora-branded T-shirts, and thousands of other consumer products. For example, when Nick was off the air in Germany, we licensed *SpongeBob* to the channel Super RTL in order to keep the brand visible.

But in some situations MTV's production partner retained certain international rights, which led to my turning on German television and seeing our programming running on competing channels. Any large corporation is going to have divisions that are occasionally in conflict. What works best for Program Sales, for example, doesn't always work best for MTV Networks. It's a difficult corporate balancing act. While Viacom will never completely eliminate this kind of problem, mechanisms have been established that have greatly reduced situations in which it is competing with its own programming. International now has the first right of refusal to programming produced domestically, and while we try to avoid direct competition, on occasion the amount of money offered by third-party distributors for those rights is too substantial to refuse. And often, after establishing a presence in a market, we reclaimed our programs. When Nick began broadcasting in Germany, for example, after *SpongeBob's* contract with Super RTL expired, he came home.

Whereas Nickelodeon's audience was younger than MTV's demo, the music channel VH1 was aimed at 25-to-44-year-olds, a slightly older demographic than generally watched MTV. VH1's expansion was launched in the U.K. in 1994, applying the hard lessons learned distributing MTV. By this time we knew what worked in the European market. MTV Europe had been successful as a pan-regional channel while VIVA had proven there was also a viable market for local programming. We took the VH1 format that had been successful in the United States and produced it in London, creating a channel that appealed directly to British tastes.

VH1 was launched using MTV's infrastructure, which greatly reduced costs. This was an example of building vertically and VH1 was an instant success. Within six months it had total distribution throughout the U.K., the shortest time period any channel had ever accomplished that. This success encouraged us to expand into our most profitable territory, Germany, a year later. And there we learned an important lesson: VH1 couldn't just hitch a ride on MTV's channels. Although some Viacom brands are distributed internationally under different names, because a considerable amount of VH1 programming was produced with an onscreen logo it made sense to retain that name. We also saved money by using much of the same packaging, which gave it a consistent look throughout the world. But while in the U.K. VH1was accepted without difficulty, that name didn't work in Germany. Too many Germans associated it with the infamous World War II German rockets, the V-1s and V-2s. Also, English-speaking Germans pronounce *V* as "we," which meant they couldn't properly pronounce the name of the channel. It sounded something like *We-H-one*. When marketing a product, it helps when your consumer is able to pronounce its name. In 2001, we accepted the fact that the name VH1 wasn't going to work in Germany and renamed the channel "MTV-2 Pop."

Because there is considerable competition for VH1's older demographic, it proved more difficult to attract a large audience than it was with MTV. So, rather than expanding by individual countries we targeted larger regional targets, eventually resulting in generic brand extensions that are distributed throughout the world. While VH1 has had only moderate success in Europe, for example, it has been very successful in Latin America. On a 2011 trip to Argentina, Brazil, and Uruguay, I saw

VH1 MegaHits being played in the same clubs and hotels where MTV had previously been popular.

Comedy Central has been a very different and in many ways more challenging story. There are few things more local than a sense of humor. Two guys walking into a bar in New York will not be as funny walking into a bar in Tokyo. It isn't just the language, the sensibility about what is funny differs tremendously among nations. If music is the international language, comedy is a regional dialect. But for MTV Networks, comedy has become a serious business. Advertisers spend considerably more money trying to reach the adult demographic than any other potential audience. But unlike VH1, which faces enormous competition from other music and lifestyle channels, there is less competition in this genre. MTV Networks increasingly has been successful in reaching those people through Comedy Central. MTV Entertainment Network Group head Doug Herzog, who championed both the iconic Jon Stewart and Stephen Colbert shows, is responsible for establishing Comedy Central domestically. In 2005 we jointly committed to rolling out Comedy internationally.

In 2005, when Tom Freston became Viacom's CEO, he turned over our comedy channels to me. My initial decisions were to rebrand, expand, and extend distribution. We launched the first Comedy Central–branded channel in 2006, when Comedy Central Poland went on the air—although it actually was our fourth channel in that country. Most of Comedy Central's programming consists of American sitcoms. Among the most popular shows on Comedy Central Poland, for example, are *Hożу Doktorzy, Posterunek w Reno, Seks w Wielkim Mieście*, and of course, *Jak Obrabować Micka Jaggera*, which translates to mean *Scrubs, Reno 911, Sex and the City*, and *Knights of Prosperity*.

Before launching Comedy Central in Europe, MTV experimented to determine the most popular format for American sitcoms. An episode of a popular show was broadcast with subtitles, then the same episode was dubbed into the local language. The result was overwhelming: The ratings for dubbed shows were as much as four times higher than for those shows with subtitles. People are more comfortable with the sound of their own language. Unfortunately, high-quality dubbing is considerably more expensive than adding subtitles, especially for smaller markets.

In the States, as both Comedy Central and HBO have proved, stand-up comedy is an inexpensive and very popular form of programming.

The problem is that English-language stand-up comedy doesn't translate into other languages. So rather than running American programming, Comedy Central has used local comedians, much like we've always tried to give exposure to local bands. When Comedy Central Spain started, for example, it relied primarily on local stand-ups.

Jon Stewart's *Daily Show* and Steven Colbert's *Colbert Report* are among the most popular Comedy Central programs in the United States, and I'm often asked how well they work overseas. The answer is not very well. What is brilliantly funny in America often results in confused stares in the rest of the world. The humor of Stewart and Colbert is based on a familiarity with American events, as seen from an American point of view. So while their material may not work internationally, the format can be successful and Comedy Central has launched versions of the *Daily Show* with local hosts in both Holland and Germany, although thus far neither show has had the same impact. It's often surprising to me to see which shows work in the various markets. I thought Stewart and Colbert would be successful in the U.K., for example, but they never found a large audience. I also believe those shows can work in Israel, and in 2011 Comedy Central Israel began broadcasting both shows with Hebrew subtitles.

Doing research about humor is like looking at photographs of a sumptuous meal. No matter how long you do it, you're just not going to get the full flavor. But Comedy Central has done a lot of research, trying to find the right formula. What seems to work best around the world is a stew of American and British comedy shows mixed with live local programming. Sitcoms tend to travel well. In many countries sitcoms are the most popular genre and American sitcoms are the most popular. Comedy Central syndicates a substantial amount of American programming. *Scrubs* and *Two and a Half Men* have been among its most successful shows. Surprisingly, often programs that were only moderately successful in the United States can become substantially more popular in other countries. In Holland, for example, *Californication* has been very successful and Ted Danson's *Becker* has been a hit in Italy. While distributing comedy has been complicated, the response actually has been good. MTV Networks' highest growth in advertising dollars has come from this genre, or as it might accurately be stated, the revenue MTV Networks has begun generating from Comedy Central is nothing to laugh at! In terms of advertising sales it is Viacom's fastest growing brand outside the United States, and moving forward there are plans to continue expansion.

When MTV Europe was launched in 1987 the goal was to attract as many eyeballs as possible, believing that the only way to succeed was by generating advertising revenue. In the beginning we traded cable subscription fees for increased distribution in order to sell advertising. After being successful we encrypted the channel wherever possible to add subscription revenue to those advertising fees. Then we went local, building more regional audiences. But with more than 175 local audiences production costs in each country sometimes became prohibitive. It was almost as if we were inventing 175 wheels. So we shifted once again, taking advantage of our global scale in which many channels contributed to the cost of producing programming with a broad appeal. But at the same time, we also pursued new technologies to find new applications for the content we were creating.

The accepted wisdom in the media has long been "content is king," and there is considerable truth to that, but when you're building an international business, technology and distribution reign. In the international media environment, *distribution* is at least the crown prince—relentless, aggressive, creative distribution. When I began working in the cable industry the technology revolution had just begun. Giant satellite reception dishes were the state-of-the-art, while the smaller dishes that would enable individual homeowners to receive programming were still years away from becoming reality. I've lived in and worked through—and made all the necessary course corrections—at least two, and probably three, media revolutions. I was a foot soldier when the upstart cable TV industry dared challenge the kingdom of the three networks. It's difficult to remember that an industry that now generates $150 billion annually was considered the underdog in the 1970s, when the television world went from three channels to 500. But I remember it; I remember walking into apartments in Manhattan to hook up HBO and watching J. C. Sparkman roll up his sleeves at a head-in in Laramie, Wyoming, and fix an electrical problem seconds before a new cable system was scheduled to go on the air. I remember being at HBO when it bought the satellite transponders that made direct-to-home broadcasting possible in Europe, and I certainly will never forget standing in the Russian cold in the Moscow suburbs as an apartment door was opened by a cable operator dressed in red thong underwear.

But as the cable-TV industry was disruptive to broadcast television, the digital revolution is changing the media landscape profoundly and permanently. At the beginning of the digital revolution I was running a major media organization that depended on increasing distribution to grow. In the 1990s that new digital technology resulted in substantially increased opportunities for distribution; basically it provided more shelf space, which resulted in more capacity for content, product innovation, and cheaper satellite transmission. More channels with lowered distribution costs allowed us to deliver content to a niche audience, which for MTV meant small homogenous groups. For example, for the first time Indians living in England could receive MTV India or in the United States subscribe to Colors, Koreans in America could subscribe to MTV Korea, Russian expats in Israel will be able watch MTV Russia, and the Portuguese will receive MTV Brasil. The cost of content was basically zero, and the cable operator could charge a substantial fee; a Korean Dish or Direct TV subscriber living in California might pay $30 for basic cable service—and happily pay an additional $10 to receive MTV Korea. Indian viewers in the U.K. pay as much to receive the Bollywood programming as they do for the entire basic cable spectrum of programs.

The availability of niche channels also has allowed us to return to our roots. I often hear people claim that MTV no longer plays music. That couldn't be more inaccurate; digital capabilities allow MTV to play more music than ever before, not less, and just not *on your television set.* In fact, MTV has become mostly regularly scheduled programming—think *Jersey Shore* (but don't think about it too much). Ironically, MTV's only TV channel in the U.K. and Ireland that rarely plays music is named "Music Television." But in those countries, MTV offers 10 cable music channels to satisfy all tastes: MTV Hits, MTV Rocks, MTV Dance, MTV Base, MTV+1, MTV Classic, MTVHD, MTV Shows, VH1, and VIVA. That's the good news.

Digital technology has also made it possible to transmit content to computers, mobile devices, e-readers, and tablets. In the 1980s, MTV was like a bible for young people; it was the theme music for two generations, but for a time it lost that cachet. Unlike previous generations, the Net Generation is connected to mobile devices as much as or even more than television. Surprisingly, researchers have found that TV usage is as high as it has always been; the difference is that now viewers are multitasking.

While watching TV they are also on their laptops or texting or doing some other task. In my house, when my kids are in front of the TV their laptops are right next to them. That means broadcasters face more competition for the attention of the audience as their choices proliferate. That's a primary reason why MTV's Internet properties have become so important.

We moved early and aggressively into the multiplatform world. As Tom Freston explained, "We will live or die in this next phase. We go from being TV-centric to brand-centric. Viacom's brands have to prosper on every platform that's out there—TV, digital TV, online, wireless, video on demand, and so forth. We've got to prosper or else." Van Toffler, president of MTV Music Networks and the man responsible for keeping MTV U.S. hot, is leading the company's efforts to extend our brands to all available distribution platforms and new media. By 2010, MTV International had successfully morphed into multiplatform distribution and was operating more than 400 digital platforms throughout the world. With more than 53 million unique visitors per month, MTV was the popular music site on the Web, and the approximately 25 million unique visitors per month to its gaming sites made it the most popular destination for online games. In fact, by early 2011, all Viacom-branded sites had become among the top three aggregate destinations on the Web, attracting more than 100 million unique visitors monthly.

Like most other media companies it took some time to get it right. When the dot-com boom began, MTV created a parallel organization to create and manage Internet properties. There was a separate management team, a separate sales and marketing organization, located in a separate building. The strategy was to create an online business, MTVi, as a separate company, do an IPO, and walk away with a mountain of operating capital. It went against all business models, there was no strategy for generating revenue, but every other media company had similar strategies. I remember visiting those high-tech offices and meeting several Internet gurus and hearing them paint this incredible picture of a business model that didn't generate sufficient income but somehow was still going to become extremely valuable. The attitude in the entire industry was that if we built it, revenue would come.

When the dot-com bubble burst in 2000, media companies took a hit. After that a lot of people questioned the wisdom of getting back into the Internet business, but MTV had no option. Young people embraced it, so

MTV had to have a strong presence. And from out of the rubble a viable business structure was created, but this time it was integrated into the core business. MTV's online presence has become attractive to advertisers, who have difficulty reaching young people through other mediums. Eventually MTV even created dedicated broadband channels. In 2001, MTV's first completely interactive broadband channel, MTV Live, was launched in the Nordic regions and France. It allowed viewers to vote for the videos they most wanted to see or to respond to an instant poll. Interactive TV, which allows viewers to respond to onscreen content, is potentially a next step, although initially in the U.K. it has had mixed results. And in Israel, where until 2011 government regulations made it impossible for MTV to get cable or terrestrial television distribution, MTV Israel existed only as a broadband channel that was streamed live to the entire country.

The Internet has fundamentally changed the world, but as a standalone business the Internet has been a challenging environment. With few exceptions advertising revenue doesn't support the site, but for MTV, as with companies in every industry, it has become a fully integrated business. By adding MTV's online presence to its other platforms it can offer advertisers a comprehensive package, a *360-degree buy*. MTV's advertisers can choose a geographic region and a specific demographic, and then some combination of analog, digital, and mobile platforms.

The mobile phone is also an essential platform in that 360-degree buy, and eventually it may be the mobile phone that becomes the dominant entertainment device. Since the introduction of the World Wide Web by computer programmer Tim Berners-Lee in 1991 we've depended on computers to provide access, but that is becoming as old-fashioned as big band music. Mobile devices now allow us to carry that access with us. The phone used to have one function—it enabled us to speak to another person. It has become an information and entertainment platform that can be used for almost any media function. It can be a computer, a TV monitor, and a game console. And sometimes a telephone. The first "app" was introduced for Apple's iPhone in 2008 and by the end of 2010 the word had become part of the vernacular; more than a million different apps were available, with more being added daily. It took the cable industry longer than a decade to wire most of the United States, while a huge industry creating and selling apps became part of our culture in less than two years.

Perhaps because other countries were not already wired as extensively as the United States, the mobile phone business has grown much faster throughout the world than in the United States. More than 8 out of 10 mobile phone users live outside the United States. Emerging nations, especially in Africa, are going to bypass hard-wire connections and go directly to mobile. In 2008, while I was having dinner with the Korean Minister of Communications at the World Economic Forum in Davis, he told me that if a consumer reports he or she can't get a signal in a certain spot, the government will erect a transmitter to fill that void. In 2011 announced a tenfold increase in the speed of its Internet connection. In Italy there are 1.2 phones for every person; in the UAE it's two phones per person. Kenya has more mobile phones than indoor latrines. In 2006, while the United States was just beginning to adapt to 3G technology, Kuwait was already developing a 4G system. By 2008, mobile entertainment services, meaning music, games, and video access, generated worldwide revenues of $24 billion. And by 2010 MTV had struck deals with mobile providers around the world giving it access to more than a billion people. The numbers are staggering. In Africa there are 300 million potential customers; in China there are 800 million mobile phone users. Every media company has to be in this business.

More than three decades ago I remember Ed Horowitz at HBO telling me that there is an insatiable appetite for the electronic delivery of information and entertainment—and that has never been more accurate. Whether it's apps or downloads or content on demand, throughout the world the amount of money people will spend for mobile content continues to rise steadily. It takes time and experimentation to develop pricing models but thus far no one has found the ceiling.

So far at least, rather than cannibalizing the TV audience, these options have increased the viewing audience by making it possible to watch on-demand video anytime and anyplace. A 2011 BBC study confirmed that the peak usage of these devices occurs during non-primetime television hours. But considering how rapidly the media environment is evolving, it would be very dangerous for a company to look at this and draw any firm conclusions. Rather, while it is important to be aware of this, it is much more important to be adaptable to whatever comes next.

No one can predict the impact that mobile is going to have on the television industry. Digital devices are killing the CD, but it's extremely unlikely it will have that type of profound effect on the television industry. To most people music sounds the same on a CD or an iPod, but the small screen of a mobile device can't replace or reproduce the visual effect of a large screen. Mobile television is a convenience but it never will duplicate the quality or effect of the big screen.

While MTV has adapted as much of its TV content as possible for mobile, including content in the local language, it also has focused on developing original content. Mobile TV can be live or a loop that has been created especially for mobile phones. Much of that programming is in short 3-to-5-minute blocks, fortunately about the length of a music video. (MTV has been described as the "creators of the short attention span." In my speeches I often promise, "We have been accused of inventing the short attention span, and in keeping with that I'm going to make this speech brief.") MTV has also begun experimenting with methods of using the phone to complement existing programming. At our EMAs, for example, while watching the show the audience in the theater could also watch what was going on backstage on their phone. At other events MTV has offered mobile-only interviews, alternative camera shots, and brief artist bios—material especially created for the mobile device. It took industries like retailing, publishing, and advertising a substantial period of time to finally figure out how to use the Internet; the learning curve for the mobile phone will be shorter. The question is how those other industries are going to adapt the capabilities of mobile for their own business purpose.

The value of the MTV brand in establishing a presence in each new platform can't be overestimated. It's the difference between a friend and a stranger walking into a room. Brands carry with them an emotional and psychological content; that's why protecting the brand has always been so important. I took nude wrestling off MTV Taiwan because it wasn't consistent with our brand image. Young people expect cutting-edge entertainment from MTV; they trust MTV to respect them, to understand their tastes, and be ahead of the trends. Kids feel the same way about Nickelodeon. So when MTV Networks takes the MTV or Nickelodeon brands onto a new platform the instant recognition is invaluable. The audience is at least willing to take a look at the product.

This brand identification can also be important to Viacom's gaming strategy. Online and console games are a natural fit for the demographic, gaming is among the top leisure time activities for that audience. Any company that wants access to young people has to be in the gaming business, especially outside the United States. One of the last strategic moves Tom Freston made before leaving Viacom in 2006 was to make a major investment in gaming, purchasing several companies, including the online gaming site Addicting Games.

There are two different gaming platforms: console gaming, for which you buy both the hardware and the games, and online gaming, which is accessible through the computer and mobile phones. Both are exploding, although Internet gaming is growing more rapidly. My children have grown up with these games, while for me they are a learned experience. "Native versus immigrant," is the way I refer to it—and I'm always going to be the immigrant who doesn't quite speak the language.

While MTV has almost always grown organically, starting its own channels, gaming is an area built through acquisitions. In 2006 MTV Networks acquired a company called Harmonix, which created the popular console games Rock Band and Rock Band II. This was an attempt to diversify into a new area. MTV is very good at many different things, but this was a new market. It required setting up a retail distribution system to stock boxes on shelves. After buying the hardware, players could purchase the music they wanted to use online. Thousands of songs were available, including the Beatles catalogue. For a time the download business was relatively strong, but a combination of factors, including the recession, increased competition and inexperience in this area led to failure. In 2011, Viacom sold Harmonix.

Addicting Games offers the entire spectrum of online gaming experiences, from one-player shooting games to sophisticated virtual social games in which the player creates his or her own avatar and can interact with the cast of MTV programs, going as far as spending real money to purchase online objects.

For 30 years I have been actively involved in all aspects of the television industry, from the creation of cutting-edge content to the distribution of programming to the largest cities and smallest villages. As I once dreamed growing up, television has been my life. I've spent more days and hours than it is possible to count learning about technology and distribution and programming and talking to leaders of the industry and performers and viewers to ensure that I was always aware of what was happening then and what was coming next. Like any experienced executive, I've sat through literally thousands of meetings discussing and debating strategy. The one constant is the absolute understanding that we couldn't be left behind. Wherever our audience wanted to go, it was essential that we were there with them. And, if possible, be there to greet them with our content when they arrived.

After all that experience I may be better prepared than most other people to answer the questions, "What's next?"; "What's the future of television?"; "How is the structure of television programming going to change?"; "Will people be watching TV rather than Internet TV?"; "How will TV on demand affect the industry?" In the past I've always been able to give a reasonable answer. But recently, when I have been asked those questions I've always responded the same way: I don't know. More accurately, I warn them that if anyone tells you they know, don't believe them. Nobody knows for sure. The architecture of the business is changing and every media company is grappling with it. This kind of earthquake can destroy great companies but it also provides tremendous opportunities. There are huge shifts in the wind and the goal is to catch that wind and go with it.

However, there are certain trends developing. For example, we are moving toward the ability to get any content you want, anytime, anywhere, through the delivery system of your choice. Growing up, I had to be in front of our television set at a specific time on a specific night if I wanted to watch *Have Gun—Will Travel*. If I missed an episode I might be able to see it during the summer when it was rerun. Now, I can go to Netflix and see that episode I missed 50 years ago almost instantly. We are moving rapidly toward the point where almost all content will be available anytime and anywhere.

■■■

The media world is growing and evolving, changing and transforming every day. To even begin describing the shape of that world in the future would require a very thick book—and that book would have to be rewritten almost monthly. A company or concept that doesn't exist as you read this may possibly become a dominant player in the industry within a few years. Google was founded in 1998 and is valued at more than $190 billion. Facebook was founded in 2004 and by 2011 was worth at least $70 billion. Twitter was founded in 2006 and it's impossible to estimate its multibillion-dollar value.

The basic concept behind all of the media world hasn't changed since I was sitting in my living room in Miami: the ability to send pictures and sound through the air so countless people can see and hear them at precisely the same time. That's the miracle that has changed the world, that has enabled us to watch history being made, and in some cases enabled people to make it happen. What has changed, and is continuing to change, are the delivery systems, the way content is distributed and the ability of a viewer to choose what and when they want to see.

Judy McGrath, the chairperson and CEO of MTV Networks, describes the changing media landscape as "the socialization of all media." As she explains:

> Everybody who is making TV content now is thinking about Twitter, Facebook, and some sort of social media connection. For MTV Networks, that basically means we'll consider all of these platforms a mobile phone—but we want to be the conversation.
>
> The biggest question is: what kind of content will be successful on the widest variety of platforms? What I believe is happening is that the big things are getting bigger, the small things need to be cool and influential, and the middle, the average programming, that's over.
>
> Very big things like the Super Bowl, MTV Music Video Awards, SpongeBob, those things that everyone wants to see are getting bigger. They're being socialized and a lot of people show up for them. The smaller things are tastemakers; they have a smaller but loyal and social-media-active audience. The stuff in the middle isn't working at all. It's either aim for the stars or aim for the cool, influential fringe.

Going forward the buzzword is *mobile*. The industry used to brag that we could bring the world into your living room, which by itself was quite extraordinary, but now it can put it in your pocket. It can deliver it to a

BlackBerry, iPod, iPad, and eventually every mobile device. Throughout the entire media industry the theme going forward has become television anywhere, anytime.

That means that in addition to traditional television viewers, MTV will deliver its content to the entire range of mobile devices and smart TV. Smart TV is essentially a television capable of accessing the Internet. In the past TVs were sold as *cable-ready*, but in 2010 21 percent of the TVs sold to consumers were *Internet-enabled*. The technology is evolving and there are still difficulties to be resolved like ease of navigation and eliminating the keyboard, but in the past technology has been able to overcome every hurdle. I believe that gradually all TVs will evolve into a combination of television and computer. That's going to happen. So Internet services and websites like Twitter, Netflix, Google TV, Apple TV, and Amazon's streaming service are all going to be available on the living room television, as well as on smartphones and tablets.

Distribution has always been the challenge facing content providers. For content providers like MTV, the business model has been relatively straightforward: Provide content for the cable system operator and the direct-to-home operator. Suddenly there are more distribution platforms than ever before and that business model has become much more complicated. The only thing that all distribution platforms have in common is an insatiable need for content, and fortunately Viacom is one of the leading providers of content in the world. Only a few years ago many people were writing off content, believing that the ability of people to upload material to the Internet would result in a world of *user-generated content*. That was the original appeal of YouTube. User-generated content is available now and some of it is very good. If you'd like to find someone who sings like a young Beyoncé or a newer Beyoncé, there are sites that will lead you to her. But the fact is that the vast majority of the audience wants Beyoncé—not a younger or newer version, but the real thing. Professionally produced storytelling remains by far the most popular programming across the entire spectrum of platforms, from cable TV to mobile phones. The most-often viewed videos on YouTube, for example, are highly produced materials that either are pirated or licensed, a trend that I believe will continue.

The most serious challenge facing content providers is figuring out which distribution services in what form produce the best revenue stream. No one knows those answers, which has made it impossible to determine what the business model going forward will be. The equation is what screens among all the possible distribution methods to license with how much content, and under what terms and conditions. On top of all that, you have to determine what kind of viewing windows will allow you to best protect the basic product, the channel. How does a channel like MTV keep sufficient viewers to hold on to advertising and cable subscription fees while at the same time maximizing revenue from the exploitation of its content online? It's an extraordinarily complicated problem and it's only going to become more complicated. In 2011 Viacom completed a large deal with Hulu, a website that runs TV content for free to viewers after it has aired and profits from advertising, and Hulu Plus, which offers a greater variety of programming and charges subscription fees. A key point in that deal was a 21-day window. Unique in that agreement was the provision that Hulu Plus would wait 21 days after Viacom's most popular shows, *Jersey Shore* for example, are initially broadcast before making them available online. Nobody yet knows if 21 days is the correct model, but it's just another step in this evolutionary process. The whole objective is to find the balance between the industry's $150 billion business model and the future. As Hulu CEO Jason Kilar wrote in announcing the deal with Viacom, "Content owners will license their best content in the best windows to those distributors that pay the most on a per-user per-month basis . . . (but) customers will ultimately make the decisions here."

There are a lot of unknowns, and media companies are experimenting with various solutions. Mistakes have been made by moving forward too quickly or by waiting too long. For example, Starz, a collection of pay TV channels, licensed its programming to Netflix in 2008 for three years for a total of $25 million, essentially giving it away. In contrast, in 2010 the Viacom-led partnership with MGM and Lionsgate, Epix, licensed its 3,000-plus movie titles to Netflix for five years for almost a billion dollars.

The availability of these alternative delivery systems could threaten the cable TV industry. It is unbelievable for those of us who were there at the beginning of the cable TV revolution and became part of its huge success to see that threat, but for the first time cable TV has to respond to the possibility of a declining subscriber base. *Cord cutting* means the consumer cancels their cable subscription to receive content through the Internet, content that can be viewed just like television on a smart TV. There are many possible factors for this, among them convenience and cost. It's not unusual for an American to be paying as much as $150 a month to their cable company for the media triple play, cable TV, a broadband connection, and a phone service. But by subscribing to Netflix for less than $10 monthly, paying separately for broadband for less than $50, and using an Internet phone operator, that same consumer can cut his or her costs by about half. That's a challenge to the cable operators. In 2010 it was estimated that about 14 percent of televisions were connected to the Internet, a figure estimated to rise to 38 percent by 2014; in the second quarter of 2010 the cable industry lost 216,000 subscribers. They just went away. In the third quarter an additional 120,000 left. Obviously there could be many reasons for this, including the economic recession, and while too early to be considered a trend, two consecutive quarters of declining subscriptions is a warning flag. The general consensus in the industry is that cord cutting won't be a serious problem for the short term—and conditions are changing so rapidly it's not possible to make even an educated guess about whether or not it will be a problem for the long term. For example, Netflix' $25 million deal with Starz expires in 2012—and renewing it will be very expensive, so Netflix' cost of content is going to raise rapidly, costs it will have to pass along to its customers. It's possible that Netflix one day will be as expensive as cable TV, eliminating their price advantage. But certainly, with advertising and subscription revenues of $150 billion the cable TV industry will do everything possible to protect its revenue stream. The industry has continued to upgrade its capabilities, which now include HD, TVR, wireless, VoD, and eventually 3D. In addition, cable operators are increasingly broadband connection providers; by the beginning of 2011 54 percent of Internet connections were provided by those companies.

Mike Fries, the president and CEO of John Malone's Liberty Global, the largest cable company outside the United States (which is creating the cable box of the future, Horizon), pointed out, "Something like 99 percent of all television is still viewed on the living room TV set. The cable industry has reinvented itself many times over the past 50 years. Half our revenue today comes from IP services that didn't exist a decade ago. But the pace of innovation needs to find a new gear. We'll always be the best in broadband, but to keep our video customers from cutting the cord we have to do three things now: Connect our content to other devices, including PCs, tablets, and smartphones; bring third-party online content and apps to the TV; and revolutionize the user interface and experience."

In terms of delivering content, Time Warner Chairman and CEO Jeff Bewkes has proposed an innovative model called "TV Everywhere," which essentially is a one-stop market for programmers. It means that the content provider will give all rights to a single distributor, the cable operator, or the satellite operator, who will take it everywhere—to the Internet, the mobile phone, everywhere—in return for premium licensing fees.

The challenge to MTV, to all media companies, is how to protect the core business, advertising, and subscription-supported television channels, while successfully integrating the new technology. Those companies that deal with it directly and intelligently can prosper; other companies will miss the opportunity and have a difficult time surviving. The movie business first started dealing with new distribution opportunities in the early 1970s when HBO went on the air, and since then it has gone through a seemingly endless evolution, including licensing content to other cable channels and Internet providers, selling or renting tapes and DVDs in stores like Blockbuster, and delivering them to computers through Netflix, while still trying to build and maintain a movie theater business.

The music industry, with all of its licensing agencies, failed to protect its product and has been devastated. It watched helplessly as file sharing got out of control and decimated its business. Ironically, there is more use of music content than ever before in history, but those companies that controlled the music industry failed to capitalize on it. A few people, like Warner Music head Edgar Bronfman, have had some success adjusting to the digital world.

The newspaper and magazine publishing industries simply gave away their products but are now trying to regain control by finding that elusive balance. In 2011 Time Inc.'s *Sports Illustrated* became the first magazine to abandon the traditional subscription model and offer only a combined print magazine and online content subscription package, or simply an online subscription.

The TV industry—and I give credit for this mostly to the cable operators and programmers—has not given away its content. In fact, it has aggressively protected it. For example, when YouTube began running segments of MTV's programming, especially clips from Jon Stewart and Colbert, which were very popular, MTV litigated to protect its copyright. In 2007, Viacom sued Google and YouTube for more than $1 billion. After three years of legal battling, in 2010 the court ruled that as long as YouTube removed copyrighted material as soon as it was notified of its existence it was not guilty of copyright infringement. Viacom has appealed that ruling and there has been no decision. This is a lawsuit that affects all content owners. For the creative community there is nothing more important than aggressively protecting copyright protection globally.

It used to be that it was possible for the international market to look at trends in the United States and predict with some accuracy their own future. The advantage I had when I arrived in the U.K. was that I had seen the future. I knew what was coming to Europe and I was prepared for it. In some instances that is still true. For example, MTV Brazil's partner is a major magazine publisher who is well aware of the wave coming towards him, having seen it happen in the United States, and has the opportunity to react to it. But in most instances that is no longer true.

One of the most important lessons I learned is that it is a global business world and it's no longer possible for an American corporation to do business in only one market, even if that market is the United States. The world has grown too small for that. In fact, the reality is that in the future the United States may no longer be the world's dominant market, so to grow, a business has to be global. In some instances that change has already begun. The United States is still the world's only military superpower, but economically that is no longer true. People no longer have to go through the U.S. banking system; people looking for investment go to China now. In fact, in 2011 the International Monetary Fund suggested the possibility of dropping the dollar as the world's reserve currency, which would have been unheard of only years earlier. And the chief economist for Citibank predicted that within two decades China will overtake the United States as the world's largest economy. The most significant change I have seen in the international market is that the United States no longer dominates the world economic environment.

Part of my desire to be everywhere was the recognition that geographic diversity, programming diversity, and product diversity made MTV Networks less vulnerable to the vagaries of any one market. It allowed MTV to hedge its bets. When one territory was struggling, for example, another might be flourishing. When programming revenues were static, consumer products might be growing. That worldwide footprint gave MTV Networks the opportunity to keep its business in balance.

When I sit through a presentation and see the entire spectrum of our activity, it can be overwhelming—particularly when I remember that we started with one channel in a small office on Mandela Street with fewer than 20 people. It's almost impossible to accurately express how complex our international business has become. I've never been able to do it to my satisfaction to my domestic headquarters. For a long time no one there understood how completely different it is from the U.S. environment. While many Americans think of the international market as one entity, in fact it is actually 200 different and unique countries. Unless you experience it, there is no way of grasping the level of complexity.

Most American corporations divide up the international world into Europe, Latin America, and Asia. Obviously, that's oversimplified, but to make MTV Networks' properties more manageable MTV International President Bob Bakish and CEO Pier Luigi organized the world into six international clusters. The makeup of those clusters has changed several times, but generally they consist of the South, headed by Antonio Campo Dall'Orto, which consists of the southern European countries including Italy, Spain, Portugal, France, and Greece; the North, headed by Dan Ligtvoet, which includes Germany, the Nordic countries, and Holland and Belgium; the U.K. and Australia, headed by David Lynn; Latin America, run by Sofia Ioannou; the Emerging Markets, which is run by Bhavneet Singh and consists of Russia, India, the Middle East, Eastern and Central Europe, and Africa; and Asia, which consists of China, Japan, Korea, and Southeast Asia, and is headed by Indra Suharjono. There are sensible exceptions to this structure. For example, Tr3s, MTV Networks' domestic Hispanic channel, is run by the Latin American cluster. The Miami-based Latin American division has the necessary skills to make this work. Moving forward, as America's Hispanic population becomes an increasingly important economic force, Tr3s may well become a significant part of the business.

It's a diverse organizational chart, and the key to its success is giving individuals clearly defined responsibilities, the support they need to do their job, recognition for their achievements, and the freedom to be creative.

When I started building MTV Networks in 1989, I set out three objectives: First, build a successful global business with great people that reached every country in the world. I wanted our products in every household in the world. Second, do that by respecting and reflecting the world's amazing diversity—I wanted to bring the world to each country and the culture of each country to the world in a sustainable way. And finally, I wanted to use this global footprint and local connections to make this world a better place. I don't look back very often, mostly because I don't want to miss anything up ahead, but when I do I'm excited by what we've done. In fact, my objectives have been fulfilled.

Chapter Nine

The Beginning Is the End Is the Beginning

It's a beautiful day
Don't let it get away

U2, "It's a Beautiful Day"

Sitting in the audience at the 2009 EMAs in Berlin, it was impossible for me not to look around and feel a sense of completion. Precisely 20 years earlier, just a few months after I'd arrived in London to begin building MTV Europe, I'd been at meetings in the eastern sector of that great city when the Berlin Wall suddenly and unexpectedly came down. Five years later, in 1994, after we had successfully established the company and had started to expand throughout the world, we had returned there to present our first EMAs, an extraordinary celebration of the unity that I believed was symbolic of our dreams. And now we were back as the world celebrated the 20th anniversary of freedom.

This was the first time the EMAs had returned to the same city. In those two decades we'd built MTV Networks into the largest international media company in the world. In creating that business, I had visited as many as 150 countries, and met more than 30 heads of state, from Chinese President Jiang Zemin to U.S. President Barack Obama;

nine Nobel Peace Prize winners, including the Dalai Lama and Nelson Mandela; and just about every major recording artist of our time, from Paul McCartney to Beyoncé—as well as less known international stars like the Russian group t.A.T.u. and my personal favorite, the Mongolian rapping family Jixiang San Bao.

Two nights after the EMAs, I presented MTV Networks' special Free Your Mind Award, given to those people who have made a significant contribution to human rights, to former Russian President Mikhail Gorbachev. I had come full circle, I realized, from commanding nuclear missiles created to destroy the Soviet Union's forces to handing an award to the man who had brought freedom to that country. "Missile man," Gorbachev called me, and pointed out, as I have often done, that music can have more power to shape the world than missiles.

I'm not sure if it was at that moment or soon after that I began wondering if that time in Berlin wasn't symbolic of something else. The expression often used to describe leaving is to "pack your bags." In my case that is inaccurate. I'd spent most of my adult life traveling, possibly more than any executive in the world. In my case, maybe it was time to *un*pack my bags.

■■■

Change is absolutely essential both for an individual and for a company. Change is renewal—it's exciting and energizing. Change carries with it a spirit, an enthusiasm, and an optimism about the future. The situation had begun changing for me in 2007, when I appointed Bob Bakish president of MTV International Networks. For more than a decade we had been expanding aggressively, relentlessly, and creatively, but that period of rapid expansion had ended. We were less entrepreneurial; from those early days on Mandela Street we had become a global media organization that was no longer manageable as I'd been doing it. The job had changed; it was much more day-to-day problem solving, planning, and restructuring for the global properties we owned or were operating than charging up the hill into new territories. And something inside me missed the excitement of charging up those hills.

I have always been detail oriented; I wanted to know about everything from cable system negotiations to artist appearance schedules to the delivery dates of shows to the profit and loss (P&L) for 175 separate channels. I wanted to know who was going to be starring in our *World Stage* show in Kuala Lumpur, Malaysia. I wanted to know what programs were going to be on Comedy Central Israel. I wanted to know when we would confirm the cast for the second Staying Alive movie, *Shuga II* Kenya, and where in Prague the European sales staff was going to stay for its meeting; and I wanted to know how we would get our partners in Thailand to pay the license fees on time. It was labor intensive, and although I didn't realize it, the complexity of the business had made it difficult for me to focus on both the everyday details and long-term strategy. For two decades I'd been a field commander, but I found myself spending more and more time dealing with process.

More than two decades earlier at HBO, Stan Thomas had asked me, "Would you rather do 10 things half-well or five things *really* well?" Well, my responsibilities had multiplied so many times it was more like would I rather do 100 things half-well or 10 really well.

Viacom was changing, too. In 2004, a colleague in New York I'd worked with for decades, Judy McGrath, was named chairperson and CEO of MTV Networks, which made her, according to *Fortune*, the 10th most powerful female executive in America, as well as my boss. Several months later she promoted both Herb Scannell, who had built Nickelodeon into the most successful children's channel in the world, and me to vice-chairmen of the entire company. It was a great honor. In September 2006, Tom Freston was replaced by Philippe Dauman, who was named president and CEO of Viacom. Philippe had been Viacom's deputy chairman and a long time board member and confidant of Sumner Redstone.

I finally recognized the fact that I was stretched too thin. It was time for me to give up some of my responsibilities. I needed another General. I began recruiting someone who either could run Europe or possibly could run Europe and take on a larger role. I interviewed eight people from around the world, some of them corporate heavyweights. I was working my way through that list when I found Bob Bakish, who had spent the previous decade working in a number of areas at Viacom, including corporate strategy, digital development, and ad sales. He knew Viacom's business, and had risen to become an executive vice president.

He was the perfect fit for the job. And in 2007 I named him president of MTV Networks.

Letting go of my responsibilities was considerably harder than I had anticipated. I knew how to build a business, I knew how to make important decisions and get on an airplane late at night and fly to China to solve problems, and I knew how to talk to world leaders and sing with Bono; what I did not know was how to take my foot off the pedal. I'd never slowed down before; I'd never let anyone else drive. The final thing I had to learn about running a company was how to smoothly relinquish responsibility.

While I was still deeply involved in management, gradually Bob began making the day-to-day decisions that had been my responsibility for 20 years. My initial response to that should have been expected: *Hey, you can't do that!* But soon it became: *Wow! This is pretty good*. After 20 years, somebody else was getting that phone call in the middle of the night about a problem in Indonesia. Somebody else had to resolve the daily crisis. What surprised me was how quickly I stopped missing it. As I discovered, once I gave up control, Bob and I agreed on everything! By 2009 the company that I built and loved had solid management. With Pier Luigi and the six cluster heads in place, its performance was extraordinary. I didn't have to worry about the future. Instead, I was able to spend more time thinking strategically, mentoring my team, and taking MTV's social responsibility initiatives to the next level.

In 2008, when I signed my seventh three-year contract with Viacom, essentially I knew I was writing myself out of a job. I was still having a good time but I realized I probably had stayed too long. Even the best jobs have a natural expiration. In early 2011, that time had come.

It's estimated that an individual entering the workforce today will have more than 10 different jobs in his or her career. Counting the military, I've had three. For all those reasons it was time to leave—maybe it was past time. But when you have such a good gig it's difficult to give it up, especially when your life is wrapped around it.

In September 2010, Philippe Dauman announced, "As chairman and CEO of MTV Networks International and vice-chairman of MTV Networks, Bill has crisscrossed the planet, planting our flag on nearly every continent and spreading the gospel of quality, audience-first programming from Beijing to Bangalore to Buenos Aires and everywhere in between. . . . He has established the most well-respected and most popular stable of international television channels in the universe. . . . Today, I am writing you about a new chapter in Bill's extraordinary career. After 22 years, Bill has decided to step down from the nonstop globetrotting and audience building and leave Viacom at the end of 2010."

Step down, not retire. I don't see a lot of golf or fishing in my immediate future. There's too much to be done. I have been fortunate that Viacom allowed me to create the perfect job: traveling the globe to build an international business, fulfilling my passions for world affairs, while using our brand to try to make the world a better place. That is something for which I will be eternally grateful. There is no greater gift that MTV could have given to me—except my wife, Alex, of course. So when Philippe Dauman announced I was leaving the company, it was not surprising that my BlackBerry began ringing. I haven't decided what my next venture will be, but there are several organizations to which I have been committed and intend to continue and perhaps even step up my involvement, and there are others in which I will now become an active participant. In addition to my work as a special ambassador to Michel Sidibés' UNAIDS, I will continue my involvement with the Staying Alive Foundation, the Global Business Coalition, amfAR, the Global Alliance for Vaccinations and Immunizations, and Health Right.

I'm going to remain as chairman of the Staying Alive Foundation, which has funded 272 small entities in 60 countries. This is a person-to-person organization that makes it possible for heroic young people to tackle the AIDS epidemic at the grassroots level in brave, bold, inspirational, and creative ways. It reaches people at the ground level and is saving lives every day through peer education (http://foundation.staying-alive.org/en).

I also have joined the board of directors of amfAR. Since 1985, under the leadership of Mathilde Krim and Kenneth Cole, amfAR's fund-raising efforts have helped support AIDS-related research, prevention, treatment, and education, while influencing public policy throughout the world. It is impossible to even estimate how many lives have been saved or changed for the better because of amfAR's ongoing efforts (www.amfar.org/).

I have been invited by John Tedstrom, president and CEO of the Global Business Coalition on HIV/AIDS, Tuberculosis and Malaria to become chairman of the Advisory Board. The GBC is an organization of major and smaller businesses using their corporate strengths to fight these three devastating diseases (www.gbcimpact.org/).

Mary Robinson, former president of Ireland and chair of the board of the Global Alliance for Vaccinations and Immunizations (GAVI), asked me to become that foundation's first envoy/ambassador to help raise its profile. Launched in 2000, primarily with $750 million donated by the Bill & Melinda Gates Foundation, GAVI focuses on saving the lives of children by getting them the vaccines they need, which have included everything from measles to polio. In the decade since its founding, 233 million children in 72 countries have been inoculated, saving an estimated 5 million lives. The two largest killers of children are pneumococcus, which is basically pneumonia, and the rotavirus, which results in a loss of fluids due to diarrhea. Vaccines are now available against both of these killers, but there isn't enough money available to inoculate every child who should receive these vaccines. At this point only 5 percent of global health funding goes to this effort, and my job as envoy will be to duplicate some of the strategies we used to bring attention to AIDS in order to raise the profile and the funding. With sufficient funding it's estimated we can save the lives of 4 million kids under the age of five in the next three years (www.gavialliance.org/).

I will also continue working with Health Right (previously known as Doctors of the World, an offshoot of Doctors Without Borders), which delivers health services to communities in 30 countries, but also provides the training and equipment that will allow members of the local community to continue providing basic health care. Health Right representatives often can be found in some of the most dangerous places in the world because the organization focuses on health and social issues made worse by human rights violations (www.healthright.org/).

And finally, I intend to continue serving on the board of my kids' school, the American School of London, which continues to provide a unique education that produces future global citizens, and the board of Fitsmi, the only social entertainment destination designed to support teen girls struggling with weight issues (www.fitsmi.com). Alex and I have decided to stay in London, which in the more than two decades I've lived there has been transformed from the capital of Great Britain to a truly global city.

In my life, I've made several significant transitions—from Miami to West Point, from Vietnam to nuclear missiles to Harvard, from the world of academics to business, from domestic U.S. cable to worldwide television. This, however, may be my biggest transition of all. Using the knowledge and experiences I've acquired in 30 years of working in global media, I will continue to speak for those with less voice and less opportunity.

What has been most amazing to me is how much we accomplished by never accepting "NO" for an answer, by taking risks and accepting the inevitable mistakes, by emphasizing and appreciating creativity, and, as David Ben Gurion often said, making miracles part of the planning, and finally, by charging up the hill.

I have been able to do what I love, and I've loved what I've done.

Acknowledgments

What makes business rock? A big part of the answer is that rockin' *people* make business rock. So many people have played important roles throughout my career and I am grateful to every one of them. If I tried to describe the contribution each one of them has made it would take several books, so let me offer my deep appreciation to the following people, who have worked with me, shared with me, and inspired me over the years: George Abrams, Rafael Akopov, Farah and Hassan Alaghband, Jumana Al-Ali, Faisal-Al-Ayyar, Linda Alexander, Ghazanfar Ali, Drew Altman, Roger and Martine Ames, Mark and Lynn Angelson, Mike Armstrong, Georgia Arnold, Peter Aspden, Janice Aull, Manoj Badale, Dee and Bob Bakish, Kristiane Bakker, Michiel Bakker, Laura and Peter Barton, Rebecca Batties, Carol Malanowsky and Bob Batty, Jean Paul Baudecroux, Dick Beahrs, Bob Becker, Peggy and Bart Behar, Lauren Behar, Barbara Bellafiore, Nelson Benedico, Monique Benitez, Ray Bennet, Lisa Bennett, Steven Berger, Seth Berkley, Jay and Rita Berman, The Wonderful Bernadette, Jeff Bewkes, Beyoncé, Lydia Biddle, Jon Billock, Frank and Carol Biondi, Jaka Bizilj, Aunt Blanche, Susan and Matt Blank, Annie Bloom, David Bloom, Ju Lan and Kenny Bloom, Jon Bon Jovi, Ali Hewson and Bono,

Lauren and Mark Booth, Sophie Bramly, Harriet Brand, Rich Bressler, Julian and Lois Brodsky, Clarissa and Edgar Bronfman, Susan and David Brown, Kerri and Frank Brown, David Bryan, Peter Buck, Kate Buckley, Ossi and Paul Burger, Naomi Campbell, Antonio Campo Dall'Orto, Annette Capizzi, Baron Capizzi, Nancy Capizzi, Larry and Joanne Carleton, Graydon Carter, Nathalie Casthely, Elaine Chao, Sam Chisholm, Giancarlo Civita, Roberto Civita, Rob Clarfeld, Adam Clayton, Fred Cohen, Peter Cohen, Ray Cokes, Kenneth Cole, Marc Conneely, Tony and Heidi Cox, Rosemarie Cresswell, Andrew and Louise Cripps, Steve Crisman, John Cucci, Donna Cuiffo, Debbie and Philippe Dauman, Wade Davis, John Defterios, Brian Diamond, Cherry and Rob Dickins, Larry Divney, Dizee Rascal, Barbara and Tom Dooley, Amir Dossal, Katherine and Bertis Downs, John Draper, Barbara Dugan, Cathy Dunkley, John Dunton-Downer, Tom Dyer, The Edge, Peter and Debbie Einstein, Barry Elson, John Ettman, Neville Farmer, Mary Beth Feeney, Paul Fegan, Alex and Lisa Ferrari, Lori Fields, Gigi Figueroa, David Flack, Bill Flanagan, Kim Luck and Karen Flischel, Carl Folta, Barney and Jane Forsythe, Peter Frame, Linda Frankenbach, Joe Franklin, Bill Freston, Kathy and Tom Freston, Elizabeth Murdoch and Matthew Freud, Bobby Friedman, Stuart and Dolly Friedman, Mike Fries, Mike Fricklas, Orly Fromer, Michael Fuchs, John Fyfe, Harvey Ganot, Les Garland, Tony Garland, Pier Gazzolo, Bob and Mariejeanne Geldof, Dee Sterling and David Giampaolo, Bruce Gillmer, Richard Godfrey, Diana and Harvey Goldsmith, Mikhail and Irina Gorbachev, Christine Gorham, Dieter Gorny, Annie and Donald Gould, Mark Greenberg, Brad Grey, JoAnne Griffith, Michael Grindon, Drew Guff, Elizabeth Guider, Simon Guild, Marc Gunther, Maxine Guthrie, Jules Haimovitz, Dave Hale, Hamish Hamilton, Doug Hanks, Pip Dann and Brent Hansen, Alan Hassenfeld, Moritz Herpich, Rob and Kate Hersov, Doug Herzog, Coreen Hester, Jack Heyes, Jason Hirschhorn, Anita Hohengasser, Richard Holbrooke, Bill Hooks, Ed Horowitz, Collette Horrell, Zhao HuaYong, Harry Hui, Susan Hunter, Tom Hunter, James Hyman, Sofia Ioannou, Ali Jaber, Jack Jacobs, Peter and Jane Jamieson, Wyclef Jean, Doug Jeffrey, Garland and Claire Jeffreys, Danny Jimenez, Spencer Kaitz, Sandra and Michael Kamen, Jonas Karlsson, Mike Kaufman, Pamela Kaufman, David Keefe, Sean and Jaqueline Kelly, John and Caroline Kennedy,

Gery Keszler, Riz Khan, Bob and Holly Kimmitt, James Kiss, Lindsay and Adam Klein, Dennis Kneale, Matthew Knowles, Carl Koerner, Jimmy Kolker, Jeff Kravitz, Lenny Kravitz, Bob and Sherri Kreek, Ynon Kreiz, George Krieger, Dr. Matilde Krim, Jeff Krolick, Ivan Kronenfeld, Alex Kuruvilla, Beatrice von Silva-Tarouca and Jorgen Larsen, Jeremy Lascelles, Sandra LaValle, Mallory Lawson, Jerry Layborne, Dede Lea, George Leclere, Debra Lee, Bob Leighton, Ken Lerer, Leslie Leventman, Gerald Levin, Lauren Levine, Yifei Li, Dan Ligtvoet, Vinnie Longobardo, Lem Lopez, Freed and Victoria Lowrey, Jeff Lucas, Dave Lynn, Tony Lynn, Alison Mack, John Malone, Nelson Mandela, Marialina Marcucci, Mark the Biker, Melissa Corken and John Martinotti, Lee Masters, Paul Maxwell, Kevin Mazur, Davina McCall, Scott McCune, Patty and Charles McGee, Michael Corbett and Judy McGrath, Paul and Kathy McGuiness, Yan Mei, Lebo Methosa, Albert Millar, Mike Mills, Udi and Racheli Miron, Saad Mohseni, Sean Moran, Cornelia Much, Bill and Mimi Mules, Larry Mullen, Trish Mulvany, David Munns, James Murdoch, Joe Nagy, Masahiko Nakagawa, Victoria Nathan, Nick Nicholas, Eric Nicoli, Claude Nobs, Jobeth Nova, Derek Offer, Ned O'Hanlon, Alex Okosi, Tom Oliver, BS and Christina Ong, Tony Orsten, Susan and Bill Packard, Glenna Patton, Mom Peg, Bruce and Tracy Peltier, Jim Perry, Brian Phillips, Peter Piot, Darcy and Jeff Pollack, Heidi and Klaus Rabe, Jason Ray, Les Read, Phyllis Redstone, Shari Redstone, Sumner Redstone, John Reid, Jessica Reif-Cohen, Greg and Nancy Ricca, Paul and Tina Richards, Nigel Robbins, Brian Roberts, Ralph Roberts, Carol Robinson, Victor Roccki, Anita Roddick, William H. Roedy Sr., Mark Rosenthal, Mila Rosenthal, Kelly Rowland, Xavier and Sophie Roy, Julie and Bill Ryan, Mo and Susan Sacirbey, Lorena and Pino Sagliocco, Richie Sambora, Laura Santini, Herb Scannell, Steve and Lenore Scheffer, Mark and Candace Schneider, Jane and Frank Seaman, Vicki Sharp, Ron Shindel, Bobby and Malissa Shriver, Dave Sibley, Anant and Vanasharee Singh, Bhavneet Singh, Bill Sloan, Harry and Florence Sloan, Robin and James Sloan, Nell and Jim Sloan, Marva Smalls, Howard Smith, Hy and Suki Smith, Ray Snoddy, Cristina Falcone and Martin Sorrell, Michael Soussan, J.C. and Dolores Sparkman, Bruce Spear, Seymour Stein, Ashley and Bruce Steinberg, Lelia Pissaro and David Stern, Michael Stipe, Hannah Strickland, Rob Stringer,

Stuart Sucherman, Indra Suharjono, Coach Sullivan, John Sykes, Manisha Tank, Hannah Tawlby, Dame Elizabeth Taylor, Terri and Bill Taylor, John Tedstrom, Minister Thian, Stan Thomas, Susan and Jon Thompson, Nancy and Wade Thompson, Ean Thorley, Sonia Thornton, Jonathan Tisch, Van and Cheryl Toffler, Tico Torres, Jacques Tortoroli, Joe Trapodi, Mimi Turner, Ted Turner, Terry Collins and Eric Tveter, Bobby and Lynn Urband, Connie Valente, Johnny and Sarah Van Haeflen, Mishal Varma, Roberto and Soledad Vivo, Alina Vogtner, Kevin Wall, Susan Ward, John Wells, Graeme Weston, Tom Wilkerson, Peter Williams, Tim Wirth, Klaus Wowereit, Janice and Chris Wright, Jim Wyatt, Cyma Zarghami, Paul Zilk, Min Zin, Boris Zosimov, Dinorah and Alex Zubillaga.

I would also like to offer my appreciation to all of the other people I've worked with and known at MTV, a unique and wonderful place. You made every minute worth it and *you* made MTV into the global phenomenon it has been and will continue to be in the future.

This book could not have been written without the immeasurable help and support of so many people. Special thanks to David Fisher for his quick work and writing acumen. This book would not be what it is without your expertise. I'd also like to thank my agent, Frank Weimann, and the people at John Wiley & Sons, my book publisher, who guided this book through what was for me uncharted territory. Thanks to Joan O'Neil, Pamela van Giessen, Bill Falloon, Meg Freeborn, Todd Tedesco, and Tiffany Charbonier.

Finally, I would like to thank the people I love the most, my wife Alex and our four children: Noa, Liam, Rocky, and Tiger.

■■■

David Fisher would also like to offer his appreciation to those people at John Wiley & Sons without whose incredibly hard work and invariable good nature it would have been impossible to complete this book. It is tremendously reassuring to know that the people on the other end of the phone care as deeply as I do. I would also like to note how much I have enjoyed meeting and working with the many people from all over the world who helped Bill and me with the details. Of course I appreciate the efforts of our agent in New York, Frank 'Frankie Books' Weimann, his assistant Elyse Tanzillo, as well as the inimitable Ivan Kronenfeld.

The greatest pleasure in working on this book has been getting to know Bill and Alex Roedy, people who literally try every day to make the world around them a better place. I appreciate all of your kindnesses directed at me, and I appreciate the two of you.

And nothing in my life could ever be done without the continued support of my wife, Laura Stevens, and our sons, Taylor Jesse and Beau, and our arrogant dog, Belle.

Index